The
Beat

Go-Go Music
from Washington, D.C.

Kip Lornell and Charles C. Stephenson, Jr.

UNIVERSITY PRESS OF MISSISSIPPI
Jackson

American Made Music Series
Advisory Board

www.upress.state.ms.us

The University Press of Mississippi is a member of the Association
of American University Presses.

Library of Congress Cataloging-in-Publication Data
Lornell, Kip 1953–
The beat! : go-go music from Washington, D.C. / Kip Lornell and Charles C.
Stephenson, Jr. — Updated and revised new ed.
p. cm. — (American made music series)
Includes bibliographical references and index.
ISBN 978-1-60473-241-2 (pbk. : alk. paper) 1. Go-go (Music)—Washington
(D.C.)—History and criticism. 2. African Americans—Washington (D.C.)—Social life
and customs—20th century. 3. African Americans—Washington (D.C.)—Social life
and customs—21st century. I. Stephenson, Charles C. II. Title.
ML3527.84.L67 2009
781.64089'960730753—dc22   2009011967

British Library Cataloging-in-Publication Data available

Contents

Acknowledgments

Initially we wanted to (at least) speak with everyone involved with D.C.'s go-go scene, but this quickly proved to be an impossible task. Then we realized that the admirable goal of formally interviewing dozens of the go-go community's members was equally insurmountable. The community is simply too large and diverse to mention every crew, every band, or even every venue that's been associated with go-go since the mid-1970s. Eventually we settled for interviewing a sampling of musicians, promoters, managers, and others who make go-go happen in our nation's capital.

Many people helped us in putting together this study. First, we'd like to thank Michael Licht for getting us together early in the process. Bob Nirkind, our editor at Billboard Books, lent his enthusiastic support for the project from the beginning. Tom Goldfogle helped in many ways—not the least of which was in his capacity as the CEO of Liaison Records and Distribution. Cathy Dixon at the Martin Luther King Branch of the District of Columbia Public Library embraced the ideas of a conference on go-go and of the library as the repository of the primary material that went into writing this book. And to the Humanities Council of the District of Columbia, which funded the April 15, 2000, conference ("Gimme That Beat: 25 Years of Go Go on the Streets of Washington, D.C.") that was co-sponsored by the Africana Studies Program at The George Washington University. Janice Carroll, Soldierette, and Michael Cotgrove contributed very personal short essays about their own involvement in the go-go community. They write from the heart and their first-hand accounts offer perspectives that are simply beyond our experiences. Ignatius Mason offered us advice, lent images, and proved to be helpful in many ways. Ron Dellums, Charles's boss and mentor, gave him the vision and time to pursue this dream. We can't forget Stride999 (aka Il Brown) for his help in hooking us up with a few folks—especially with his connections in England. Kato assisted in many facets, from his advice to his help in publicizing the go-go conference in April 2000.

It's also important to acknowledge the following, who have been, or are, players in go-go: Daniel "Breeze" Clayton of Deno's Night Club; Bobby Bennett (the Mighty Burner); Darryll Brooks, Carol Kirkendall, and Gerald Scott of CD Enterprises for believing in go-go and going the distance to prove it; Bill Washington of Dimension Unlimited for respecting the music; Reo Edwards for being patient with the go-go musicians for 25 years and for being responsible for the music in many ways; former mayor Marion S. Barry for recognizing and respecting the power of go-go musicians; Kemry Hughes and Norm Nixon of the Mayor's Youth Leadership Institute for believing in D.C.'s youth and in go-go, in particular; the D.C. Commission on the Arts and Humanities for ensuring that go-go will always be recognized as an indigenous music genre; the Malcolm X Cultural Education Center for insisting that go-go always be a part of the annual tribute to Malcolm X, and Kay Shaw and Malik Edwards for their support of Charles; Carl "C.J." Jones; Maurice Shorter; Donnell Floyd; Ken Moore; Ms. Mack; Charlie and Leora Fenwick; James Funk; and André "Whiteboy" Johnson for believing in the project from the beginning.

Our thanks are also extended to the folks who helped to transcribe the interviews that form the core of quotes that punctuate the book. The list includes Laura Schulz, Chris Flores, Anna Teideck, and Sara Bryan. Transcribing interviews is tedious, but necessary, work and they all did a great job.

We would also like to thank Sarah Fass (crack Associate Editor at Billboard Books), who guided this book through copyediting and the galleys with good humor and moxie.

Finally, we have to acknowledge the ladies in our lives. Charles thanks God and his wife Judith (editor, inspiration, and drill sergeant); his daughter Zora for allowing him to find the time to write; his son Brandon for being understanding; and his parents, Mr. and Mrs. Charles C. Stephenson, for his birth. Kip lives peacefully and lovingly with Kim and their two little babes (aka the half monkey and the full monkey)—Cady and Katherine (aka MaxC). This book could not have been written without the many indulgences of our families. Thank you, ladies!

The unfortunate truth is that in a project of this magnitude we will undoubtedly miss the contributions of some essential people without whom this book would not be possible. If we missed you, we apologize. And if your favorite band doesn't receive the attention that you believe it deserves or you wonder why we did not interview anyone in your crew, we apologize again!

Kip Lornell and Charles Stephenson

January 5, 2001

Preface

"Go-go is Washington's unique personality; kind of the African American community's musical way of saying 'This is something that is intrinsically ours, we have created it!'"

Jill Nelson, from the documentary *Straight-Up Go-Go*

"My grandmother called it pot-and-pan music."

Big Al, bouncer and bodyguard

"A regional subculture rooted in 70's funk music."

Richard O'Connor, "Go-Go Music Go" *Streetbuzz*

"It ain't no party like the RE party like the RE party, 'cause the RE party don't stop!"

Rare Essence

"We learn to appreciate go-go because we were born and raised in it."

**Big Youngin, member of Junk Yard Band, from "Getting Ready for JY2K,"
TMOTTGoGo Magazine, #6, p. 4**

"A vernacular dance music unique to Washington, D.C.: a non-stop, live party music in which a pulsing bass drum beat blends with African rhythms and the sounds of timbales, cowbells, and conga drums as trumpets, trombones, saxophones, and synthesizers belt out licks from jazz, funk, and soul, punctuated by rapped dialogue between the dance floor and the band."

***D.C. Go Go: what's the time?,* a brochure published by Folk Arts Program,
D.C. Commission on the Arts and Humanities, 1991**

"Heavy One loves to eat and he sure knows how to keep that beat!"

Almost any performance of "Sardines" by Junk Yard Band

"No matter what you've read, no matter where you've read it—the bottom line (the essence of go-go) is—you've got to put that hamburger down, Archie, and dance!"

Tom Terrell, "Go-Go Music," *Rock America Magazine*, June 1985, p. 13

"Go-go? Do you mean those girls wearing white boots and dancing in cages?"

Almost any white person from outside of Washington, D.C.

Attending a go-go in Washington, D.C., is much like going to an African American Pentecostal church service. The participants (musicians and patrons alike) know one another, they are passionate about the music, and they usually attend their "services" on a regular basis. Two other parallels to consider: both are highly improvisatory and last for an extended period of time (often three or four hours) with few—if any—breaks. Go-go may not be "church" in the conventional sense, but it clearly serves some of the same functions.

Go-go is more than just music. Since its arrival on the scene in the mid-1970s, it has reflected the experiences of black Americans living in Washington, D.C. For the District's black citizens under the age of 50, go-go is often a source of pride. When Trouble Funk opens a show by asking "Who we gonna put on display tonight?," Rare Essence inquires "Where my troopers at?," or Backyard wants to know "Who's in the house?," *everyone* wants to be recognized. Much like enthusiastic elementary school children who know the answer to a question and are begging to be called on, the crowd's response transcends mere enthusiasm and enters the realm of the ecstatic. This ardent "testimony" draws the audience into the show, personalizes the experience, and promotes racial and neighborhood pride.

Perhaps even more importantly, go-go provides a voice for members of D.C.'s often overlooked, much maligned, and truly disenfranchised African American community. Its younger members identify with go-go musicians in much the same way that blues artists once provided a voice for the black community and rappers do today. The identification is perhaps even stronger with go-go artists than with rappers because go-go originated in D.C., while rap is an international phenomenon. In D.C. you are at least as likely to hear Trouble Funk, Junk Yard, or Chuck Brown as D'Angelo or the Nastygang streaming from the speakers of automobiles driven by younger African Americans.

For those readers who have never heard go-go music, here are its 10 basic characteristics:

1. African American
2. Washington, D.C.–based
3. Contemporary and popular among its audience
4. Rooted in funk and hip-hop
5. Male-dominated
6. Highly syncopated
7. Driven by a variety of percussion instruments

8. Thrives in live performances

9. Utilizes call and response

10. Features extended performances, sometimes grouped in "suites."

Some of these are go-go-specific traits, but most are found in other genres of black American music. In the final analysis, it is "the beat" that stands out as the compelling attribute that both propels go-go and makes it distinctive. "The beat" is a rhythmic pattern created by the interaction of the drums, congas, and rototoms. Both a musical and cultural phenomenon, it is difficult to describe in words, but that is one of this book's purposes.

Wherever black folk live in or around our nation's capital, you will hear groups with names like Junk Yard Band, Northeast Groovers (NEG), Chuck Brown and the Soul Searchers, Backyard Band, Rare Essence, and Trouble Funk streaming out of cars as they drive by, from open windows, and—if the headphone-wearer has it cranked way up—on the Metro. The sound of go-go music can be heard throughout Washington, D.C., and Prince George's County, Maryland, where the population is predominately African American. Go-go's funky and very black sounds filter out to near-by Charles County, into Baltimore, and sometimes even to Richmond, Virginia. But except for the brothers and sisters and a few other enlightened people who have lived in Chocolate City and had first-hand experience with go-go, the power of this music doesn't extend much further.

However, even if you do not live in or near the District of Columbia you can still easily find go-go right in your own 'hood...so to speak. All you have to do is turn on your computer, click on the modem, and point your Web browser towards one of the unpretentious, rather down-home go-go sites on the Internet. In the new millennium, some 25 years after the birth of go-go and in the infancy of the World Wide Web, go-go exists in cyberspace just as it does in the ears and minds of listeners in Southeast and Northeast D.C. Kevin Hammond's (aka Kato) Take Me Out To The Go-Go site (www.tmottgogo.com) towers above the rest. The sites maintained by the P.A. Palace (www.papalace.com) and Funkmaster J's Go-Go Links page (http://funkmasterj.tripod.com/gogo.htm#Gogo) are also worth visiting, and by the time you read this, there will doubtless be others.

In many ways Take Me Out To The Go-Go reflects the milieu in which go-go thrives. Of course it has all of the requisite features of a contempo-rary Web site: links, an e-mail contact address, Real Audio/MP3 clips, photographs, and streaming video. But it is the content, not the form, that is so reminiscent of the musical culture it salutes, celebrates, and promotes.

The site is very local and Afrocentric in its focus: the most prominently displayed links include the home pages for D.C. high schools, a site that reviews African American literature, and a Community Forum Board.

And, inescapably, there is plenty of information about the music. You can go to "Scenario" for an up-to-date list of local show dates, and links to other go-go sites. The Article Archives includes short profiles and articles about Junkyard Band, Chuck Brown, as well as links to other go-go sites.

Go-go, you can see, is so intimately connected with Washington, D.C., and its black citizens that you can not separate the two. And Washington, D.C., itself is a singular place. Can you think of another city that issues its own driver's licenses? Are there any other citizens of the United States of America who pay federal income tax, but are not represented in the House and Senate? What other city has such a high percentage of black Americans, while also hosting one of the largest contingents of Salvadorians outside of El Salvador?

It is the overwhelming presence of the federal government, exemplified by the White House, the Smithsonian Institution, and the various presidential and war monuments, that epitomizes Washington, D.C., for most Americans, but the District of Columbia is home to a half-million people, most of whom do not work for the government. They are teachers, laborers, lawyers, non-profit executives, law enforcement officers, or small-business owners. These folks are all but invisible to the millions of people who reside outside of the Beltway and only hear about the crime, the scandals, and the deal-making that goes on there. And yet, they raise families, play field hockey, watch television, and work in more creative endeavors, just like everyone else.

The city itself is divided into four sections: Northeast, Northwest, Southeast, and Southwest. Northwest encompasses most of downtown, the White House, and Georgetown, and has the highest per capita income. In contrast, Southeast has the highest percentage of black Americans, the highest rate of violent crime, and the lowest income per capita. This is especially true across the river in Anacostia, in far Southeast, where the population is nearly 100 percent black, where there are some lovely rolling hills, and where the main street is Martin Luther King Boulevard. This section of Washington, D.C., is a true stronghold for go-go; the music emanating from automobiles there is as likely to be the Backyard Band as it is Whitney Houston. Southeast has been a black stronghold for decades. Relatively few whites from D.C. or any of the nearby suburbs have even been "east of the river" (as they say locally) and even fewer live there.

Make no mistake about it, our nation's capital is a city divided. Washington is largely a city for tourists and includes the Mall, the White House, the Library of Congress, and all of the other sites that attract hundreds of thousands of annual visitors from around the world. The District of Columbia, on the other hand, encompasses neighborhoods like Shaw, Mount Pleasant, and Brookland. It's a vibrant community where babies are born, lawns are mowed, and television is watched in living rooms. And it is largely a world of black Americans.

The black presence in Washington, D.C., is both pronounced and profound. Before the 1968 riots following the assassination of Martin Luther King, Jr., the city had several important business corridors—most notably along H Street Northeast (NE) and U Street Northwest (NW). These sections of the District, gutted by the violence and mayhem of the riots, have never fully recovered, though many of the small businesses have been limping along for over three decades. U Street has undergone exciting changes since the early 1990s, due to the re-opening of the Lincoln Theater, the addition of a Metro stop on the green line, and the establishment of many small, ethnic restaurants. H Street has not fared as well, though near the corner of 7th and H is a small business, Planet Chocolate City, that exemplifies the minor renaissance of small businesses in the city (some of which have grown due to African American and local pride) and the emergence of hip-hop culture in the early 1980s.

Planet Chocolate City, a small homegrown business opened in 1996 as a clothing and accessory emporium. Its two owners, Shawn Henderson and Derrick Price, would like to think of their business as the black Gap, supplying people in the neighborhood with clothing suited to their contemporary urban black lifestyles. Their plans include expansion into other sections of the city, the Chocolate City Diva Line (for women), and a Go-Go Wear line. Nowhere but the District of Columbia would anyone even dream of naming a clothing line after this music. In fact, the confluence of the store's Chocolate City moniker and its intention to launch a go-go clothing line is emblematic of the cultural development and evolution of the musical form.

Step back to the mid-1970s. George Clinton, leading the Parliament-Funkadelic crew, had just released an album entitled *Chocolate City,* which asked the question that was on all of the city's streets: "What's happenin', CC?" The riot had happened eight years ago and the Afrocentric core of Washington, D.C., was just beginning to flower. Kenneth Carroll evoked this time with humor and great insight in a *Washington Post Magazine* article dated February 1, 1998:

Walk up to any black person who was in D.C. in the '70s
and ask if they remember Chocolate City. If they stare at
you blankly or mention Hershey, Pa., you know you are
dealing with a mutant strain of squareness or, God for-
bid, a 'bama—an individual rank and unrepentant in his
or her backwardness. But the reaction is likely to be a
smile and shared memories of Parliament-Funkadelic, the
struggle for home rule...[or] talk about old hairdos,
blowout kits, the Flagg Bros. shoe store on 10th and F,
Chuck Taylor sneakers, quarter parties, waist parties,
graduations at Constitution Hall, the back of the bus on
the X lines and picnics at Hains Point.

The fact is that the rise of go-go corresponds with the post-riot rise in
black consciousness and connects that era with the more contemporary
hip-hop nation. And the phenomenon of go-go also underscores the segregated nature of Washington, D.C. Like the aforementioned blowout kits
(for hair grooming), go-go is a product of black America that is understood
and accepted in many of the District's Southeast neighborhoods but far
less in Northwest, where the average home costs about 400,000 dollars and
where many of the world's embassies sit at the foot of the hill on
Massachusetts Avenue. So, it's an expression of one's financial situation as
well as race. In Washington, D.C. (and elsewhere), the two almost always
go hand in hand, and these factors help to create the starkly contrasting
worlds inhabited by most Washingtonians and the official Washington,
D.C., seen on CNN Headline News, which features late-breaking news
brought to you by reporters standing near the Supreme Court, in the
reporters' "swamp" on the southeast side of the Capitol building, or by the
gate in front of the White House.

This book is not only about music, although music forms its core. No,
the book is equal parts black life, youth culture, local politics, the mass
media, hip-hop culture, urban aesthetics, entrepreneurship, and the struggles of everyday life. It is about Washington, D.C.'s singular statement
about self, local, neighborhood, and city-wide pride. But perhaps most
importantly, the book describes a unique expression of blackness, a celebration and reflection of life in the 'hoods of Washington, D.C., and
Prince George's County, Maryland.

Preface to 2009 Edition

Kip Lornell and Charles C. Stephenson, Jr.
November 10, 2008

Much has changed in Washington, D.C., since Billboard Books published *The Beat! Go-Go's Fusion of Funk and Hip-Hop* in the summer of 2001. Nationally, the reelection of President George Bush in 2004, the Iraq War, the tandem mortgage and credit crises, and Barack Obama's election as president of the United States clearly top the list. Locally, "Chocolate City" is less so. While Washington, D.C., remains majority African American, the immigration of various people to D.C. has resulted in greater diversity. In 2006 the city elected a new youthful mayor—Adrian Fenty—who is firmly rooted in Washington, D.C., and understands the go-go culture.

Washington, D.C., sports a new National League baseball team, and in April 2008 Nationals Stadium "second-to-none" home opened along the waterfront, providing the Nats with a venue that sits next to the Anacostia River at the foot of Capitol Hill. Downtown is vibrant and at times resembles neighborhoods in New York City, with snarling traffic, trendy restaurants, and crowds of people flocking to and from basketball games or cultural events. Parts of Southeast Washington, particularly along Southern Avenue, have the feel of the bedroom communities in the surrounding counties of Prince George, Montgomery, and Fairfax, and have attracted young families. There is an increasing sense that Washington, D.C., has become the preferred home for young professionals of varied hues and religions, who are committed to raising families in the city. D.C., in short, has evolved mightily over the past eight years.

Despite all of these changes go-go remains the dominant local musical form in a city that, despite its demographic evolution, remains predominately African American. As go-go enters its fourth decade, it is noteworthy that the music's popularity has not waned and much has happened within the go-go community. The passage of time and these important changes necessitate this new edition of *The Beat!*

Although the acknowledgments are dated January 5, 2001, we finished writing *The Beat!* late in the fall of 2000. *The Beat! Go-Go Music from Washington, D.C.* reprints the original manuscript published by Billboard Books in 2001. The cover, however, is totally redesigned, and the new title helps to identify go-go's epicenter. We have also added many new photographs and a lengthy Epilogue that brings the music and culture into the twenty-first century.

For this new edition we'd like to thank Thomas Sayers Ellis (aka TSE), in particular, for his generosity in providing several dozen new images for this book as well as his pungent observations about the current scene. Likewise we need to extend our appreciation to Malachi, Kato, Tom Goldfogle, John Mercer, Emily Abt, Dene Mitchell, Maurice Shorter, and Lindsay Christian, among others, for helping us to bring *The Beat!* up to date. We also appreciate American Made Music series editor David Evans's belief that a new version of the book deserves to remain in print as well as the hard work of Craig Gill and the staff of the University Press of Mississippi. We send a shout out to Brandon Stephenson, who shares his father's go-go past and passion for its history. Finally, we need to acknowledge the love and support of our spouses (Kim Gandy and Judith Burrell) as well as our teenage daughters—Cady, Max, and Zora, who were too young to understand go-go when the first edition was published in 2001. Now they know.

Photographer's Preface

You Never Saw a Pocket Like This I Swear,
We Ain't Going Nowhere

The day hustler and lead talker Kenny Magee asked me to join Petworth Band, I was across the street from Paul Laurence Dunbar High School with Itchy, Vic, and Moose, standing around a yellow and chrome Deuce and a Quarter (Electric 225) and listening to a Rare Essence tape. The moment Itchy told Kenny that I owned a set of rototoms like the ones David Green played in Essence, I was in. By neighborhood standards, our tape was clear enough to share with anyone who walked by, especially the honeys; and I know because I spent three hours holding my boom box above the Howard Theater crowd. I'd done everything right, pressed Play and Record then Pause. The red light came on. I'd even caught the beginning of the show by releasing Pause a few moments before Tricky Rick, the D.J., asked, "Who's the trickiest guy in town?" Catching the beginning of the show was a big deal, especially to those of us who would eventually graduate from listening to playing. A good show was one when the band both cranked and grooved, your name was called, you met a girl, and you (and your whole damn crew) were photographed by Mr. G., the smoothest Picture-Man in the history of Go-Go. How many times did we jump, last minute, into

The Original Petworth Band (featuring Thomas Sayers Ellis), Mr. G., 1981.

Shredded go-go poster.

one of his flicks, or just stand there (three of us, one in a wicker chair), kneeling and pointing and looking away, in a pair of school boy frames, a Members Only jacket and a pair of Jordache jeans? Looking back it's amazing how much posing went on and how it influenced what many of the bands played. Our all-time favorite song to pose to was Herman Kelly and Life's "Dance to the Drummer's Beat" and posing was so popular that when Experience Unlimited performed "E.U. Freeze," Sugar Bear chanted "Aw pose y'all" and "Take the Picture." We loved the stop and go, and a spotlight was our camera as we danced like sharp, human shutters. I left Petworth and joined Heavy Connection because they were opening shows for Trouble (later Trouble Funk) and because they got their name and logo on the Globe Day-Glo posters that mysteriously appeared on trees and abandoned storefronts while we slept. At Dunbar, I was a member of the Creative Writing club, an editor of our school paper, and a Humanities

Little Benny Harley.

Student, and although I played in a band, I secretly wanted to be a writer. I left Heavy Connection and returned to Petworth my senior year of high school and wrote many of the words to our grooves. Our band's name on a poster was like being published for the first time.

My first 35 mm camera cost $40 and it was "hot," slang for stolen. I purchased it from a trombonist who had played in several bands. He popped his trunk on Georgia Avenue and there it was. I just happened to be home from school for the weekend and just happened to run into him and just happened to have access to a dark room in the house I lived in, in Cambridge, Massachusetts. One of my housemates taught me how to develop photographs, and I took my first serious pictures at James Baldwin's funeral in 1987. My first Go-Go related photos were of the show posters. Often they would stay up for weeks, stapled one on top of the other, creating collages that were brilliant, textual documents. When Me'Shell Johnson (later Ndegéocello) joined Little Benny and the Masters, the focus of my photography shifted to the inside of the Go-Go where my instincts as a percussionist allowed me to think of the camera as just another instrument in the band, a participant in the performance and one that could actually photograph the music as well as the musicians. Two years earlier, I had played cowbell at Breeze's with Rare Essence during the John Cabalou era when I auditioned for the rototom-timbale spot, so I did not see myself as separate from the band. I've also been lucky. I was at the original 9:30 Club for the cast party for *She's Gotta Have It* when Spike Lee first heard E.U. I went with William "JuJu," House, friend and former Heavy Connection drummer. In Boston, I co-founded The Dark Room Collective, a forum for emerging and established African American writers and before earning a M.F.A from Brown University in 1995, I worked as a projectionist at the Harvard Film Archive where I was Spike Lee's teaching assistant for two years. I was photographed by Bruce Weber for *Interview* magazine under the caption "Literary Activist" and although I stopped taking photographs in 1993 to write poetry full-time, I never stopped listening to Go-Go or writing about it. In 2005, after the publication of *The Maverick Room* (my first collection of poems), I decided to begin work on *The Go-Go Book: People in the Pocket in Washington, D.C.* For this, I purchased a Leica SLR, a Hasselblad 500 c/m, moved to D.C. for the summer, and submerged myself in the Go-Go community via TSE's Pick of the Week at www.tmottgogo.com. The moment a camera is raised someone poses, and the moment you accept posing, you've lost the possibility of improvisation, the visual groove. I often position myself between the conversation between the drums and congas, or the lead talker and audience, etc. I like pretending that what the pocket is saying has to travel through my lens, first, becoming photograph at the same time it becomes Go-Go. In manual or automatic, the D.C. beat has helped me to keep going.

Thomas Sayers Ellis
2008

My Introduction

by Kip Lornell

The horrific nature and senseless brutality of the crime leapt off the page of the *Washington Post*, riveting me to every word. My close attention to the newspaper almost caused me to miss the sight of actor Kevin Costner strolling down the sidewalk about 15 feet from where I sat. Costner was in Washington, D.C., filming *13 Days,* a movie about the Cuban missile crisis. I was down at the end of the Mall on a sunny, 75-degree day — October 30, 1999 — playing volleyball on the courts next to the Potomac River — only about a quarter of a mile from The George Washington University, where I teach courses in American music. The film crew had closed off a quarter-mile stretch of Rock Creek Parkway, filled the parking spots with automobiles (all built prior to 1963), changed the light fixtures to reflect the era, and were filming a scene with Costner and a small group of extras. The crew set up at noon and remained until about 4:00 P.M., when almost everyone, including me and my two daughters (MaxC, age four, and Cady, age six), left to go home, up on Capitol Hill, near Union Station.

Even after I returned home, the newspaper article remained etched in my brain. The headline, "'KDY': Gang Symbol or Block Pride? — Mark Carved on Slain Toddler Focuses Unwanted Attention on Kennedy Street NW," reminded me that the mean streets of Washington, D.C., are not too far from the world that I usually inhabit. Kennedy Street NW is less than one mile from one of the oldest and most prestigious Historically Black Universities and Colleges (HBUC), Howard University, and only about three miles from the Kennedy Center, outdoor volleyball, the White House, the Smithsonian Institution and the numerous memorials that annually attract millions of tourists to Washington, D.C. The Anacostia section of the District — a large neighborhood full of rolling hills and lovely detached single family homes, as well as some of the city's most dangerous (and most heavily African American) neighborhoods — lies a few miles down and across the Potomac River from where played that Saturday afternoon.

The newspaper article, a follow-up piece about the recent murder of two-year-old Julio Guy Thomas, who had been found beaten to death in his own home with "4KDY" carved on his back, got me thinking about D.C. and go-go. That mark refers to the intersection of Kennedy Street and Fourth Street in Northwest Washington, D.C., and appears scrawled on walls throughout the immediate neighborhood. The legitimate and frightening question is whether these letters symbolize a gang or a crew. A gang holds clear negative connotations and is often associated with criminal activity, while a crew is a looser group of kids (many in their teens) who hang out together and "represent" their neighborhood.

As their members age, some of these crews have evolved into gangs that have been closely allied with violence and illegal activity. The First and Kennedy Crew, for example, was associated with 10 murders in the early 1990s and was decimated in 1995 when federal racketeering charges brought down about a dozen of its key members. The controversy that always arises in the local press is whether all of these groups are gangs or merely crews that reflect neighborhood pride and hold similar tastes in clothing, language, and go-go music. Youths at D.C. clubs often identify with their block or neighborhood, holding up signs or wearing T-shirts bearing their names. On its 1997 live compact disc, *Skillet,* the local go-go band Backyard's performance of "Life, Money, Struggle, Crime" announces "I'd like to thank the KDY." In another song, "It's the Bomb," the band hollers out, "Ninth, Seventh, First, KDY." Terrance "Coop" Cooper, the band's manager, was quoted in the *Post* article as saying that the songs don't recognize gangs but rather neighborhoods. By mentioning Ninth, Seventh, and First, he said, the band spans the entirety of Kennedy Street NW. "People come to the show. They have signs [of neighborhoods]. We call them out," he added. Chris Burch, a promoter for the Icebox, was quoted as saying: "It's not seen as any type of gang thing. I think more than anything, it's more pride."

This newspaper piece once more reminded me why Charles and I were writing this book. When most people think of Washington, D.C., they think of two distinct places. There is "Washington," home to the White House, the Smithsonian Institution, and the grand Mall that stretches out in front of the Capitol. Then there is "D.C."—the perceived dysfunctional urban wasteland, replete with too many black folks, plenty of violence, and a wealth of drugs and crime. Unless you are intimately familiar with the District of Columbia, you would never think of its unique contribution to the American performing arts—go-go music. Although it is true that go-go is the only artistic expression that originated in our nation's capital, it's often overlooked because go-go reflects popular, contemporary, African American culture. Go-go is further marginalized because it's not part of mainstream hip-hop. And even in the District of Columbia, go-go music is often associated with all of the city's negative stereotypes...if you know about it at all.

I learned about go-go after I moved to Washington, D.C., in 1988 from Ferrum College, a small liberal arts institution located just south of Roanoke, Virginia. Between 1988 and 1990 I was a post-doctoral fellow at the Smithsonian Institution. My project—to explore the Smithsonian Folkways Archive under the direction of its curator, Tony Seeger—culminated in a textbook, *Introducing American Folk Music,* and a biography of Huddie Ledbetter, *The Life and Legend of Leadbelly* (co-authored with Charles Wolfe). As an ethnomusicologist with a special interest in black American music, I was pleasantly surprised to discover go-go, a musical genre previously unknown to me. First I noticed the posters on telephone poles near my home on Capitol Hill, then I found P.A. tapes being sold at the tri-weekly farmer's and flea market in the RFK Stadium parking lot. I gradually learned more about the music and began to present papers on it at scholarly meetings and to include go-go in my courses at The George Washington University. By 1997 I had completed two more books, my wife's travel schedule had grown more hectic, and the children demanded more time. It was clear that I would no longer be able to travel as I once had, taking long fieldwork trips and extended visits to far-away archives.

I cast about for my next book project and go-go provided the perfect topic. It was a singular musical community about which no one had seriously written, it was based practically in my own backyard, and I liked the music. I started talking with people around town, musing about the project. Susan Levitas (producer of *District Music,* an excellent documentary about indigenous black music in Washington, D.C.) suggested that I speak with Charles Stephenson—Congressman Ron Dellums's top aide, former manager of Experience Unlimited, and a very helpful advisor on the go-go portion of her film. Her suggestion was seconded by Michael Licht, the former D.C. City Folklorist who knew Charles from his work with the D.C. Commission on the Arts and Humanities documenting the local vernacular music scene.

I called Charles and he was eager to talk. We met several times at the House cafeteria and talked at length over lunch. We were very much on the same wavelength in terms of our thoughts about the music and how it should be presented to a general audience in book form. Before long, we agreed that collaborating on the book made sense, so we wrote a proposal that my book agent—Gabriella Pantucci—shopped around, and late in 1997 we signed a contract with Billboard Books. *The Beat* has been about four years in the making. Unless I am mistaken, it is the only published study focused on an American vernacular music genre that is unique to a single city.

These years have not been entirely focused on research and writing, of course. Both Charles and I have families and other work obligations, but have chipped away at the interviews and writing until we finished. Although books always evolve when you actually sit down to write, *The Beat* is largely as we originally envisioned it. The source material for the book comes from a score of taped interviews that we conducted as well as shorter journal and newspaper stories that appeared in the *Washington Post,* the *Washington City Paper,* and other local publications.

I am pleased that this book gives both voice and recognition to a musical culture that is too often overlooked in its own 'hood. It also documents a highly evolved system of entrepreneurs—ranging from the musicians themselves to street peddlers in downtown D.C. hawking the most recent P.A. tapes of Rare Essence. They represent a do-it-yourself spirit that is integral to the evolution and spread of African American culture, not just in our nation's capital but across the United States. Finally, *The Beat* discusses some of the common elements of African American music (among them are poly-rhythms and call and response) that have been recast into an artistic expression that resembles funk, soul, and hip-hop but is, in fact, singular. Like reggae, ska, or any other postmodern musical product of the African diaspora, once you hear and understand go-go, you'll never mistake it for anything else.

My Introduction

by Charles C. Stephenson. Jr.

At times things seem to come together for a reason. In July 2000, I sat in a Durban, South Africa, hotel room while I attended the VIII International Conference on HIV/AIDS. This is probably the most important conference I have ever attended, because the problem of global HIV/AIDS threatens the entire world and it is imperative that we all focus and do what we can to combat this horrible disease.

Prior to leaving Washington, D.C., I told Kip that I would use the opportunity created by travel (idle moments in my hotel room) to start writing my introduction to this book. For nearly two years I have thought and thought about what to write and more importantly how to begin my writing. Yesterday, my wife Judith and I were on our way back from meeting Shembe, a well-respected religious leader in the KwaMarsch region near Durban. Looking out the window of the van in which we were riding, I noticed a sign for a convenience store that said Gogo Convenience Market. In surprise, I said to the driver that the sign was interesting and he responded with a smile that *gogo* means grandmother in Zulu.

At that moment I knew that I had an opening for my introduction for the book. We all know that the grandmother in the black family is very important. The grandmother is the link to the past and has an enduring spirit that keeps the family centered and together. I knew at that moment that go-go was without a doubt linked to our roots in Africa. In a strange way, this explains the almost spiritual nature of go-go and its cosmic hold on me for nearly three decades in Washington, D.C. This moment also added to the lessons of Melvin Deal, the premier African dance instructor in Washington, who educates his students about the links between go-go music and African culture.

The Zulus are indeed a strong people who fought and withstood the challenges of great armies from England and elsewhere. Despite being outgunned, the Zulus fought on and on. Much like them, go-go has remained strong and vibrant despite the constant challenges presented by the government and others. In many ways, it is the Zulu tribe of the music industry. It has survived against the odds and continues to thrive in spite of countless obstacles.

I believe strongly that the real story about the development and continued popularity of go-go must be told. I very much wanted to be part of this project because I believed for years that the go-go community was misunderstood and dismissed as a fringe element. This book discusses why this is, and also why it should not be. In it, Kip and I explore the many musicians and bands that have contributed to go-go's success. We will also share with you the frustrations and the many battles fought by go-go musicians to just play the music.

For you to really understand the plight of the go-go community in Washington, it is important to recognize the political disenfranchisement of the city. Washington's 525,000 citizens (this number is based on the 2000 census) have very little political say in the running of the city. The United States Congress must approve virtually all legislation pertaining to the government of the city. In fact, the residents of Washington, D.C., are not fully participating citizens of the United States. Residents are taxed, yet they do not have the right to elect representatives who have the authority to fully represent their views and wishes in the House and Senate. This fact contributes greatly to political apathy and the feeling of disempowerment that is widespread among the citizenry.

I believe this connection is very important because it helps to explain why the go-go community in Washington feels the need to "go it alone." Go-go music has been all but ignored by the national music business. Radio stations throughout the country ignore the music, major record companies have denied record deals to popular go-go groups, and the hip-hop community completely dismisses go-go music as an entity.

Despite being ostracized by the music industry, go-go music (much like the citizens of Washington, D.C.) has continued its quest for success and acknowledgment. Much like the city of Washington, go-go musicians have developed a survival mechanism that sometimes pits their interests against all others. Very few in the nation really care that Washingtonians do not have full voting rights; likewise, few outside of Washington seem to care that go-go music exists. The goal for the city is full voting rights, and for go-go it is national and international recognition and respect.

Local respect is less of an issue because thousands and thousands of fans continue to patronize go-go concerts weekly, throughout the Washington metropolitan area. Groups such as Rare Essence, Junkyard Band, Northeast Groovers, Backyard Band, and of course Chuck Brown and the Soul Searchers enjoy popularity that is unmatched by other local entertainment groups anywhere else in the country. But why does the go-go phenomenon continue? Why do thousands of loyal, dedicated go-go enthusiasts continue to flock to go-go shows daily? And why does the so-called legitimate music industry continue to ignore the existence of go-go music? These are fundamental questions that we will pursue and discuss.

I moved to Washington, D.C., from New York City in July of 1970. While employed as the director of a clerical skills program in Southeast, I would overhear my staff discussing that they were going to a "go-go" after work or during the weekend. At first I did not think anything about what they were saying, but finally I asked them, "What is a go-go?" They told me that it was a dance where they went to party and enjoy themselves with their friends, and that a live band provided the entertainment. Coming from New York, I was curious about the popularity of the go-go. It seemed to me that the young people were always excited about them and I would notice them talking about various bands that honestly had no meaning to me.

Simultaneously, in the apartment building where I then lived, I would overhear the music of young men practicing across the hall. I enjoyed what they were doing because it was positive activity. During the early 1970s I was a social activist—very active in trying to end the war in Vietnam and involved in work to improve the quality of life for black people in Washington and the rest of the nation. So the fact that young black men were organized and engaged in something meaningful appealed to me.

One evening, my best friend, Morris G. Johnson, Jr., and I decided to knock on the door in an effort to meet the guys and hear what they were doing. We were very impressed and we immediately began to give the guys advice and feedback. Before we left the apartment, the guys asked us if we were interested in managing the band. At the time, neither one of us had any experience in management of an entertainment group. However, I felt it was important to work with these guys because they were involved in something affirming and I had a responsibility to assist.

I agreed to manage the band, which decided to call itself Experience Unlimited and later was referred to as "E.U." After agreeing to manage E.U., my antenna went up and I began to notice how important music was to young people in Washington, D.C. Of course, music is an integral part of most youngsters' lives; however, in D.C. it was different. Growing up in New York, the central activity for young black males was sports, with basketball at the top of the list. In New York you would witness guys walking down the street with their caps on backwards, bouncing a basketball. In D.C. it was a little different. You could still see the brothers with a basketball; however, you would also see a crew of guys carrying guitar cases or horn cases, and many of them were into go-go.

It soon became evident to me that the "go-go" referred to the actual physical location of the dance. Instead of calling the happening a dance, in Washington, it was called a "go-go." Virtually every community in the nation parties during the weekend, but I would wager that not many enjoy live bands like the folks in Washington, D.C. Not only do the bands make the people jump and sweat weekly or daily, they are local celebrities without equal. Washington, D.C., places good go-go musicians on a pedestal for their musical excellence. As a result, bands have been able to make a living performing for their fans.

By 1973, I recognized how important go-go was as a part of Washington culture. I began to notice the dress styles and the general attitude that permeated the community. Go-go's mass influence was evident. Young people looked forward to attending go-gos because it was the center of the their world, and it was the "hip" thing that represented their age group's culture and lifestyle.

It is important to place in perspective that during this time the struggle for social justice was raging throughout America. In some communities, rebellions were taking place and America was focusing on the war in Vietnam. Discussions about the role of the artists in the movement for freedom were swirling. James Brown, Sly and the Family Stone, War, and Earth, Wind & Fire were all popular bands that used the stage as a means of delivering a message to black people.

Go-go bands, at times, would recognize the "movement" by covering the songs of the popular groups. Also, the go-go became a place where people would just party and not worry about the harsh realities of life. Unemployment and the other social ills were real and people needed a relief that the go-go provided. Unofficially the role of go-go was to occupy the time and attention of thousands of inner-city young people each week, while a city too busy to care went about its business. Although most groups were covering popular songs, each go-go group was also striving for its own niche—struggling to find its own identity. For example, the Soul Searchers came to be known among black Washingtonians as the best party music band in D.C. During the early '70s the Soul Searchers were famous for playing Top 40 hits and keeping the dance floor full. Other groups played funkier music. The Young Senators were noted for their outlandish attire and professional showmanship. I can recall the first time I heard the Young Senators; I could not believe they were playing live!

They were playing a Sly and the Family Stone tune that rocked the dance hall in a way that kept me mesmerized for the entire evening.

Eventually—once the city needed a target to blame for its societal ills—go-go evolved from being a fringe element to taking center stage in the local music scene. A movement of sorts developed to protect the business of go-go and also to join with responsible citizens to combat the ills facing the city. I joined and led efforts by go-go groups that eventually produced anti-drug records and music videos that brought positive messages to the audience. The go-go groups were forced to occupy a more mature place in society; that of responsible citizens. Like proponents of its distant cousin, rap, go-go musicians and artists joined with social activists in a movement to transcend the problems of drugs and violence. A new day was born and go-go proved to some that it was a part of the solution and not the problem.

Again, despite the negative efforts of the media and local politicians, go-go continued to play into the twenty-first century. The *Washington City Paper* once said that go-go's popularity would not go beyond the Beltway, and this may or may not be true. However, for over three decades, go-go culture has remained part of the Washington, D.C., community. Chuck Brown, Sugar Bear of E.U., and members of Rare Essence can say without being challenged that they have played a role in raising two generations of Washingtonians.

This book will examine why go-go has survived as an integral music genre in D.C. *The Beat* documents go-go's history, players, bands, and trends over nearly three decades. Despite all the obstacles, trials and tribulations, go-go has survived. Like the Zulus, it has kept going against all odds. Ultimately, Kip and I seek to explain why, for 30 years, the people of Washington, D.C., have been continually asking their bands to give them "the beat."

1 • The Roots and Emergence of Go-Go

"Trouble Funk wasn't the first go-go band (Chuck Brown and the Soul Searchers were), but they were the foremost ambassadors of Washington, D.C.'s great contribution to popular music. Over a polyrhythmic base using timbales and other Latin percussion and funky bass, go-go uses chanted vocals and little splashes of horns, keyboards, chunky rhythm or scorching lead guitar. It's an extraordinarily supple, extensible form—you can play anything from an MOR ballad to a car commercial over a go-go beat and make it danceable."[1]

Wilson & Alroy's Record Reviews

THE BASIC INGREDIENTS

If you go back far enough, go-go's fundamental musical roots can ultimately be traced back to West Africa. First and most profoundly, it is the beat that characterizes and distinguishes go-go's utterly distinctive rhythmic drive, the essential element that keeps the troopers on the dance floor. The complex syncopated beat underpinning go-go represents a trait brought to Western culture in general and to America in particular by way of the interlocking percussion ensembles of the savanna.

The sounds of drums spice nearly all of the music heard in the villages and small towns that fleck the hot, often dry and dusty savannas of present-day Ivory Coast, Ghana, and Senegal. In West Africa, drums of different shapes and pitches form the core of most musical experiences and their complex, interlocking polyrhythms are essential. The percussion instruments so well known to fans of go-go—differently pitched drums, timbales, and various cymbals—have their counterparts in west-central African rattles, gongs, and xylophones, in addition to drums. The non-stop percussive core of traditional African music encourages movement and the interaction between the drummers and the dancers. In many

African communities it is difficult to separate these components because they are so intertwined they cannot be unraveled without changing the very nature of the event.

But it is the way that these instruments work together that is critical and establishes the exceptional level of cooperation necessary to produce "the beat." In go-go, the pitched percussion instruments work together in syncopation; instead of producing a single meter, the drummers work a feeling of two (duple meter) against three (triple meter) to create a poly-meter. This might sound complicated, but anyone familiar with twentieth-century American music forms like rock, hip-hop, jazz, or gospel instant-ly recognizes polyrhythms such as those produced by the two drummers in the Grateful Dead, the complex drumming of Tony Williams backing Miles Davis in the mid-1960s, or Jabo Starks and Clyde Stubblefield's titanic contributions to the carefully crafted and meticulously drilled — but oh so funky — sound that James Brown has demanded of his back-up band (the JB's) over the years. In the 1990s, the go-go beat has been best driven by Junk Yard's Heavy One, E.U.'s Ju Ju, and the Soul Searchers' Ricky Wellman.

Go-go's essential beat is characterized by a syncopated, dotted rhythm that consists of a series of quarter and eighth notes (quarter, eighth, quarter, (space/held briefly), quarter, eighth, quarter) that sounds like "boomb, bah, boomb, boomb-bah-boomb," which is under-scored most dramatically by the bass drum and snare drum, and the hi-hat. This basic rhythmic unit is ornamented by the other percussion instruments, especially the conga drums, timbale, and hand-held cow-bells. It's quite reminiscent of a combination of the clave beat heard so often in Afro-Latin music and the Afro-Cuban mambo rhythm, both of which infiltrated this country by way of the Caribbean and South America. A variant of this beat is central to calypso and soca (Trinidad) and samba (Brazil).

This background for the go-go beat became part of American popu-lar music by the late 1940s by way of Afro-Cuban jazz when Dizzy Gillespie and other musicians added percussionists like Machito to their ensembles. It was reinforced in the 1950s and 1960s through the popu-larity of salsa and by way of the New York–based bands lead by Tito Puente, Ray Barretto, and Mongo Santamaria. In D.C., Carl Hawkins, Julio Miranda, and Stacy Edwards are some of the percussionists whose work contributed to the multi-layering of rhythms that is so critical to go-go. These artists' use of "exotic" instruments like Ghanaian hand drums and cowbells (which came from Africa via South America) helped to create a music that is very African in its construction.

Go-go's beat is usually performed at a comfortable tempo, somewhere between 80 and 94 beats per minute. This tempo sets up a groove similar to that of many funk bands, but is slower than many disco tunes. Disco was often marketed using the term "bpm" (beats per minute), and standards like the Village People's "Macho Man" (138 bpm) and "The Hustle" by the Van McCoy (116 bpm) carefully and clearly announced the speed of the tempo on the record sleeves. This underscores the primacy of the beat to dance music in general. Once you get it in your gut, (internalize it, so to speak) you'll always feel and immediately recognize it. Go-go's beat provides it with its distinctive sound—its musical trademark—aligning it with funk but at the same time setting it apart.

Another of the most bedrock elements of go-go—the talking and gesturing between the audience and the musicians—is also integral to West African pop and traditional music. This form of communication, antiphony—more commonly known as "call and response"—informs nearly all forms of African American music. Call and response simply refers to the (mostly verbal) interaction between a song leader and his/her group. The leader sings, chants, or speaks and the group reacts by echoing or responding to the leader in a time-honored fashion that is well understood by all of its participants. Call and response, a format that has been heard for decades in the black church (especially Baptist and Pentecostal), work songs, and even in the interplay between a down-home blues singer and his guitar, heightens the intense, emotional communication between the musicians and the audience. When go-go singers inquire "Is Alabama Avenue in the house?" the brothers and sisters know what to say . . . "Hell, yeah!"

Third, the griots of Africa—whose lineage can be traced back to at least the seventeenth century—have a kindred spirit in the "talkers" who front contemporary go-go bands. Griots serve a variety of functions in Africa's complex musical culture. Some are keepers of oral history; others perform while workers are in the fields; in northern Nigeria, a small band of griots is employed specifically to praise local butchers! In a more generic way, griots are often viewed as a vox pop—a voice for the people. It's a role most widely associated in the United States today with earlier black musicians as disparate as Charlie Patton (on his heartfelt "High Water Everywhere," about the destructive Mississippi River floods of 1927) and native Washingtonian Marvin Gaye (whose contemplative 1970s songs about about black urban life include "What's Going On?"), but embraced by contemporary rappers and go-go bands as well. This role is part of African American music's conversational nature, which invites the audience to interact with the band. The vocalists lead the way to the music... to the party ("This is the way we rock in Southeast!"), but the talkers—for example, Buggs of Junk Yard Band—provide the commentary about black life in the District of Columbia and events with more national significance. Perhaps most importantly, talkers also instill the audience with a sense of pride and a renewed appreciation of being African American and living in our nation's capital.

The go-go audience's response—adoration and expressions of understanding and respect for the musicians—is similar to the responses of music audiences in places as far flung as eighteenth-century Nigeria and the Mississippi River Delta in the present day. At a go-go, audience members communicate directly with the band. They dance with both hands in the air and their feet on the floor, signal to the band by way of a complicated series of hand gestures, and wave their bodies in unfettered (almost ecstatic) homage to the band. In this respect, a go-go is similar to a fife and drum band picnic in the hill country of present-day Mississippi or a contemporary New Orleans funeral parade. The appreciation is based largely on shared experiences and the prominent role played by go-go bands in local culture. For many young black Washingtonians and citizens of Prince George's County, go-go bands are the most visible and public manifestation of black (youth) culture. Go-go bands empower them to shout out and express themselves in a public forum; it is an emotional release. To paraphrase a song by Junk Yard Band, it allows them to "let the beat ride in the jungle."

But no matter what some people in Iowa or Italy might think, Washington, D.C., is not located on some dark and dangerous continent, and go-go's African roots have been filtered through the decades following Emancipation. And as anyone living in the greater Washington, D.C., area knows, most blacks look towards southeastern Virginia and North Carolina—not Africa—when they think of going "back home." From there, the parents and grandparents of Chuck Brown, Big Tony, "Whiteboy," Funky Ned, and others moved north, carrying their musical culture with them, transforming it into something new.

Like so many expressions of African American music and culture, go-go is all but invisible to white people, even in its own hometown. That has been the nature of black culture in Washington, D.C., for many years; it is a colony that in the early twenty-first century remains largely occupied by black Americans who remain—literally—disenfranchised. Known in the vernacular as "Chocolate City" (aka C.C.), D.C. is still the initial destination for many immigrants from eastern Virginia and North Carolina.

But go-go is more than music; it's a complex expression of cultural values masquerading in the guise of party music in our nation's capital. Like their counterparts in Ghana who play ju ju music (which is discussed in greater detail in chapter 2), go-go musicians unite people within the black community, providing the otherwise voiceless a forum in which to speak. Go-go reflects the concerns of black citizens living in D.C. in very public ways; over the years it has been used by political leaders at rallies, served as the principal draw at numerous community celebrations and block parties, and has been the sole entertainment at huge outdoor concerts. Whether it is a youthful Junk Yard finding and making their own instruments while growing up in the Barry Farms projects or Sugar Bear from E.U. singing about the use of guns on the streets, go-go musicians call upon their everyday experiences to create this music. In this way, they are not unlike the visual artists who construct their work from found materials, a process sometimes called "bricolage." Go-go "represents" for D.C. on many different artistic and creative levels.

THE R&B SCENE

Along with the earlier "Great Migrations," World War II brought many rural immigrants into the nation's capital, the majority of them arriving from nearby southeastern states. By the mid-1950s Washington, D.C., grew to be nearly 40 percent black. Some of the immigrants were attracted to the jobs created by the expansion of the federal government during the war; for example, R&B vocalist and trumpeter Frank Motley found a job as a messenger at the Department of Agriculture in 1946 and stayed on for many years. Others arrived because it was a natural stop on the trail to prosperity that eventually led many people north to Baltimore, Philadelphia, New York City, Boston, and other smaller cities. The same migration pattern by whites accounts for the prominence of bluegrass in Washington, D.C., and Baltimore.

In the years following the end of the war, Washington, D.C., like other places around the United States, became a town where vocal groups and rhythm and blues bands held forth. Both D.C. and nearby Baltimore (some 40 miles away) maintained very strong community and popular support for the four- and five-man groups that specialized in four-part harmony singing; many of these vocal groups enjoyed their strongest support in the small neighborhood clubs that dotted the city, especially in Southeast D.C. in the Anacostia section and the U Street Corridor. These local clubs, which also supported a thriving jazz scene, did not pay that well, but exposure—simply getting better known by their friends and peers—was the musicians' principal motivation. Of the many local groups, such as the Marylanders, Rainbows, and Jets, that enjoyed local renown, only two groups, the Clovers and the Orioles, gained national prominence.

One of the important though lesser-known local secular vocal groups, the Cap-Tans, had roots in a sacred group founded in 1932 known as the Progressive Four. They were managed by Lillian Claiborne, whose name continuously surfaces in D.C. as an entrepreneur from the mid-1940s through the early '70s. In many respects, Claiborne's career reflects the trials of the entrepreneurs who struggled to record and disseminate go-go some 30 years later. Around 1950, Claiborne lured Progressive Four member Harmon Bethea away from the sacred realm to join a Mills Brothers and Ink Spots–inspired group, the Buddies, to form the Cap-Tans. Bethea remained in the midst of the local vocal group and rhythm and blues scene over the next 30 years. He eventually led groups including the Octaves, the L'Cap-Tans, and in the late 1960s, the soul-inspired Maskman and the Agents, which was one of go-go's immediate predecessors.

Despite the fact that Ahmet and Nesuhi Ertegun both lived in Washington (they were the sons of a Turkish diplomat stationed there), they moved to New York City in order to start highly influential Atlantic Records (one of the first "national" labels to feature R&B music). There were, however, a number of small local labels and they had a small impact. Lillian Claiborne's DC Records, which released its first record in the summer of 1947, is at the top of this very short list. DC Records was the capital's first significant record company. The name refers not only to the city but also to the partnership between Claiborne and music publisher Haskell Davis. Claiborne was quite a colorful character; Jay Bruder describes her as "a middle-aged white woman, married to a successful businessman, with a fair amount of cash and an interest in all kinds of music. Between the end of World War II and 1950 Lillian assembled a virtual monopoly on recording talent in Washington . . . Her roster included White Pop, Black Pop, Hillbilly, Country and Western,

Gospel, and R&B."[2] Unlike many of the other independent record company owners across the United States, Claiborne not only worked hard to promote her artists locally, but also helped to move her artists to larger labels. The Cap-Tans, for one, released material on both Gotham (a label based in Philadelphia) and Randy Wood's Dot label in 1950. More importantly, in the fall of 1951, Claiborne was able to place both the Heartbreakers—another local vocal group—and Frank Motley under contract to RCA.

Throughout the 1950s, Claiborne struggled to record local talent, pushed songs that she thought would be a popular success, and tussled with the demands of keeping a small record company afloat. Despite all of these problems, she persevered, operating DC Records from a number of locations across the city (though she really ran the company from her home in suburban Rockville, Maryland) until ill health forced her to all but give up the company in the early 1970s. Less than a decade later, Max Kidd and other local entrepreneurs recording go-go bands would find themselves in a similar position, struggling to create a viable business.

With the exception of the work of the artists under the aegis of Ms. Claiborne, most of the black vernacular music (ranging from jazz to R&B to gospel) of 1945–1975 was recorded by companies based outside of the city. Like Bobby Robinson in New York City or Ivin Ballin in Philadelphia, many of the entrepreneurs were based in cities that were not far away from Washington, D.C., and had population bases that had followed a similar migration pattern. These label-owners struggled through many of the same problems (such as under-capitalization and spotty distribution) faced by Claiborne. The records issued by most groups from the Washington, D.C., metropolitan area gained regional popularity because they could be found in the neighborhood "mom and pop" record stores, but were all but unknown outside of the mid-Atlantic region. The lack of national exposure for D.C.'s black music talent remains a nagging problem into the twenty-first century.

SOUL AND D.C.'S PUBLIC SCHOOLS

Berry Gordy's Motown label was so successful at this that throughout the mid- to late 1960s, Motown and other soul artists were fully integrated into the playlists of Top 40 radio stations across the United States and their LPs sold more copies to the white audience than they did to black

Americans! The records sold well to youngsters in the slightly integrated suburbs of Vienna, Virginia, and Bowie, Maryland, as well as in tony Potomac. In D.C., of course, the records sold in the local shops like Maxie Waxie's, where people who wanted to get the latest Motown, Stax, or Atlantic soul single laid down their dollar (and got some change) in order to walk off with the latest 45 rpm platter.

Some people also suggest that this is the era in Washington, D.C., when go-go emerged. By this time "Going To A Go Go" by Smokey Robinson and the Miracles, which first hit the charts in 1963, was an established part of the black musical vernacular. But don't forget that in these heady days of the civil rights movement and the beginnings of chants of "Black Power," the District's majority black population continued to suffer the constraints of segregation. In the shadow of Abraham Lincoln's statue, not all of the city's venues were open to all of Washington, D.C.'s residents. Former go-go promoter Darryll Brooks observed:

> Clubs weren't letting black folks in. We would go to Northeast Gardens up off of North Capitol Street, and you could get a cabaret there. The place held about 400 people. Sororities and social groups would hire bands, and that was a way of employment. The Chuck Browns, the Scacy & the Sound Servers, Black Heat, and the Young Senators—those were the bands that they were using. And whichever band could keep people on the dance floor the longest was the hottest band.[3]

Many black Washingtonians who were born in the mid- to late 1940s and came of age in the early 1960s associate "Going To A Go Go," the Knights of Columbus Hall at 10th Street and K Street NW, and this time period with the type of music that became go-go. The K. of C. remains important to many people because it was *the* place for well-dressed and well-mannered black youths to show up, especially on Thursday night, when a relaxed and mellow club-like atmosphere prevailed and the music lasted into the hours past midnight. One of the bands that often played the Knights of Columbus Hall was the D.C.-based soul band, the Young Senators. Ironically, the hall was located within shouting distance of the White House, while residents of the District of Columbia were then—as now—unrepresented in the House and Senate. Young Senators, indeed!

The Young Senators were not the only band in town, of course. The ranks of soul- and Motown-inspired bands included the Matadors, Chilly Bopper and the Third World, the Dynamic Superiors, the El Corals, and Aggression. When major bands from outside of D.C. came to town, they would play at the Lincoln Theater or the Howard Theater, because in those days the U Street Corridor was happening. In addition to opening for national acts, the local bands would play at smaller clubs around the city. Dimensions Unlimited, a booking agency, opened the Panorama Room in Southeast in the late 1960s, providing another venue for D.C. talent, most of which favored the percussion-driven soul sound.

Percussion, not only the conventional drum and traps set but congas and timbales, remains one of go-go's core elements. Here is where the educational system in the District of Columbia helped to further the cause. In the 1960s the rivalry between the city's high schools really heated up, particularly on the athletic field. In the District of Columbia, marching bands are as much a part of the football field as the team itself. As Darryll Brooks observed, "There used to be a lot of competition between uptown bands and Southeast, like Springarn and Eastern bands. We were very educated, musically."[4] Go-go benefited from this phenomenon because so many of the students were involved with marching bands, which employed many, many drummers performing on a variety of percussion instruments. This background provided many future go-go percussionists, such as Junk Yard's Heavy One or T-Bone from Trouble Funk, with a solid foundation and prepared them for a career that their high school band director almost certainly had not anticipated.

The role of the D.C. public schools did not cease with the involvement of young men (and they were mostly males) with percussion. The junior and senior high school marching bands at Taft, Woodson, Coolidge, Cardoza, Dunbar, McKinley, and others included horn and reed players, of course, and many of the first generation of go-go bands utilized saxophones and trumpet players (part of the soul and funk legacy). The high school band experience helped the aspiring musicians in a number of ways. First, it taught them how to read standard musical notation. Secondly, they were placed in a context where they made music in large ensembles that required a great deal of cooperation. Finally, it reinforced the (essentially African American) concept that motion and music are highly compatible.

The public schools' musical instruction received strong reinforcement from the D.C. Department of Recreation, which also played a vital role in educating D.C.'s aspiring musicians. The Department of Recreation also provided music lessons, especially for horn players, and assisted in sending a "Showmobile" with musical groups into the city's neighborhoods. This travelling stage show often spotlighted a group called The Ambassadors, which played Top 40 popular music that attracted the youthful audience that constituted the Department's target audience.

FUNK ARRIVES

Funk is the most immediate predecessor of go-go and its closest musical and emotional cousin. Funk is also difficult to define. In his colorful book on the subject, *Funk: The Music, the People, and the Rhythm of the One,* Rickey Vincent struggles with this dilemma: "Funk is impossible to completely describe in words, yet we know the funk vibe when we see [hear] it. Funk is that low-down dirty dog feeling that pops up . . . and you get off your ass and jam . . . it's the earthy essence, the bass elements."[5] Funk is like pornography and go-go: you know it when you feel it and once you feel it you never forget it.

More specifically and tangibly, funk is African American and postmodern, and it projects the sound of a bass-heavy polymetered band playing in a cold sweat. Its most immediate musical references are to contemporary pop culture (movies like *Superfly*, peach-colored suits, big afro hairstyles), but funk pays homage to its secular and sacred forebears: gospel, soul, blues, jazz, and Afro-Cuban music. A wide range of bands come under this musical umbrella, from Kool & the Gang to Cameo to Con Funk Shun. In D.C., Parliament-Funkadelic was arguably the local favorite national band to play funk, but there is no doubt that James Brown is the godfather of funk.

James Brown, along with Duke Ellington and Louis Jordan, is one of the most important and influential black musicians of the twentieth century and his impact has carried into the twenty-first century, too. Born in Augusta, Georgia, in 1933, Brown has been on the scene since the mid-1950s. He was first labeled as an R&B singer (a generic term applied to any performer of black popular music) and then he became a "soul singer" when that term came into vogue in the mid-1960s. But Brown had funk in his heart from the beginning.

The earliest roots of postmodern funk can be heard in James Brown's recordings from the late 1950s, when Universal Attractions (his booking agency) established the J.B.'s—a tight, highly efficient band that Brown ruled with all of the grace of a harsh and unyielding dictator. In this regard he was as notorious as the jazz bassist and bandleader Charlie Mingus, who, during the same period, managed a top-notch band that thrived under his erratic leadership. It was the type of band that you loved (and hated) to play with and were eventually glad to leave when the leadership became insufferable.

By the mid-1960s Brown's musical vision was becoming evident and by 1964 he had gained complete control of the band. That same year, Brown (along with Brian Wilson of the Beach Boys) negotiated the right to supervise his own recording sessions without the presence of an A&R (artists and repertoire) man to help select tunes and run the sessions. This revolutionary act allowed each of the men to quickly establish their own distinctive stamp in the studio and on stage, creating a sound that is immediately identifiable. Wilson emerged as a pop-music icon and visionary in the studio, while Brown became known as the hardest working man in show business and as a taskmaster with few, if any, peers.

Brown's studio and live sound at this time can be described as proto-funk. In recordings such as "Cold Sweat," Brown broke away from the on-stage conventions that had held him—the constraints of time and of the popular song form. He moved towards a musical form that emphasized movement. He downplayed melody in favor of rhythmic figures propelled and defined by highly repetitive electric bass patterns (an ostinato or a minor variation from ostinatos) that were ornamented by sturdy, polymetered drumming. The music provided by Brown's horn section was usually led and arranged by alto sax player Maceo Parker and trombonist Fred Wesley. Their work punctuated the typical bass and drum combination (Brown sometimes employed as many as three drummers!) with strategically placed jabs and was accented by an electric guitar player who sounded like one of his counterparts in a South African highlife band. The music was harmonically simple—often based on one or perhaps two chord changes—but the combination was wickedly effective, and on recordings like "Out Of Sight" (1964) and "Papa's Got A Brand New Bag" (1965), Brown all but defined the sound that by the early 1970s was called funk.

While these recordings are milestones, it's a pity that virtually none of Brown's live performances were preserved and released to the general public. Get James Brown on a stage in front of an appreciative live audience and he would get as sweaty and funky as a preacher at 1:00 PM in a Church of God in Christ temple in south Georgia in August! The singing and playing were important, but Brown's presence and his choreography—

the term dancing seems too limiting—was equally important and influential. Brown's leaping, splitting, skating, acrobatic style clearly laid the groundwork for breakdancing, which moved the hip-hop nation some 20 years later. Esteemed dancer and rapper (M.C.) Hammer has nothing on Mr. Brown and, in fact, everyone in the hip-hop nation owes him a great deal.

Other musicians and bands soon followed the lead supplied by James Brown and the J.B.'s. Groups like The Meters (from New Orleans) and the Phoenix-based Dyke and the Blazers worked the soul circuit, recording and performing for a multiracial audience. Funk even returned to its oldest geographical roots as African musicians, most notably Manu Dibango, got into the act. And, of course, it was kicked along by the drummers, especially in New Orleans, where Earl Palmer (the unparalleled session drummer), "Honey Boy" Otis, and "Smokey" Johnson kicked out the beat influencing not only other local drummers but informing black music across the country.

In Washington, D.C., local R&B acts were beginning to feel the funk. One band (or is it two or three?)—Parliament-Funkadelic—had a strong impact on the region's black popular music. The brainchild of one-time barber George Clinton, this eclectic musical organization melded together the influences of blues-rock guitar wizard Jimi Hendrix, the proto-funk of James Brown, and the spaceship shtick and colorful costuming of Sun Ra and his Arkestra into a unique experience. Like James Brown's shows, the live, long, and kaleidoscopic performances by Clinton's organization were memorable, mesmerizing audiences for hours; these events set the stage for go-go to emerge. James Funk of Rare Essence especially appreciated the work of Clinton in the early 1970s: "I like the way how he always got into a groove, and just stayed there . . . just in the groove for however long that he wanted. That's what turned me on."[6] Their recordings from between 1971 and 1974—most notably "Maggot Brain," "One Nation Under A Groove," "Up For The Downstroke," and "Cosmic Slop"—echoed through the streets of Washington, D.C. In the spring and summer of 1975, the socially aware and highly politically charged "Chocolate City" ("When they come to march on ya, tell 'em to make sure they got their James Brown pass!") became a local anthem that persevered into the next year. Nineteen seventy-six was also the year that go-go really emerged in Washington, D.C.

GO-GO ARRIVES

Chuck Brown is the founder of this music, in the same way that Bill Monroe established bluegrass on our musical map in the mid-1940s.

Known locally as the "Godfather of Go-Go," Brown recalls "I put together the Soul Searchers in '66. Back in '71, I cut a record called 'We The People.' I had an idea for go-go at that time, but it wasn't time for it to catch on yet. Back then, you had to sound like a radio . . . in order to survive."[7] Brown's sentiments regarding the nature of black music in D.C. in the early 1970s resonate with some of the other pioneering bands in go-go. Percussionist Timothy "T-Bone" David recalls that "Trouble Funk was originally Trouble Band back in the '60s, and we were basically like a Top 40 Band."[8] The patrons wanted the familiar, and, of course, the band kept the customers satisfied. But the winds of change were blowing towards D.C.; Chuck Brown was ready to flow with them and then to actually effect a change himself.

The leader of the Soul Searchers since 1966, Chuck Brown's 1974 and 1975 live shows mark the clearest beginning of go-go. His experiment with a new performance style and music had its roots in two related factors that were affecting D.C.'s music scene. The first factor relates to the role played by DJs at local clubs. Brown observed that "Disco DJs started taking our shows. They were cheaper and, because of mixing, could keep the dance floor packed. People no longer liked the pause in between songs."[9] Brown replied in kind, performing non-stop with the percussion section keeping the beat, playing the funk, until the band grooved into the next selection.

The second factor is related to the extended performances that had become more common in black music (and rock, too) during the later 1960s. James Brown certainly liked to "perform long," but so did a jazz performer such as John Coltrane, whose 1963–65 live renditions of "My Favorite Things" or "Niama" might go on for a half hour or more. Certainly the George Clinton–led groups liked to play for protracted periods, often vamping for 10 to 15 minutes on a single chord while the percussionists, vocalists, and reed and brass instrumentalists put out some of the thickest, most richly textured music on the planet. Rock artists — ranging from the Grateful Dead to Santana to the Moody Blues to Frank Zappa — began following similar paths. The Dead, for instance, are noted for their extended and highly improvisational "jams," while others looked towards long, connected pieces of music called "suites" (check out Zappa's *Lumpy Gravy* for a good example of this). The time was ripe for experimentation and change, and Chuck Brown was there at the beginning of go-go.

But Chuck Brown was not the only one around when go-go was being launched. André "Whiteboy" Johnson recalls Rare Essence's beginnings in the mid-'70s, and his comments encapsulate the history of many go-go bands:

> When Rare Essence first started, the music wasn't even called go-go. I don't know what you call it, but it wasn't even go-go music.... Rare Essence came together when we were in elementary school. A couple of us were in the same class, and we knew that each of us played instruments. Everybody played baseball or football, but between seasons we were looking for something to do, so we got together to try and make some noise. And after a while, the noise started to make some sense. [10]

The lineup at this time included André Parker on guitar and Footz (Quentin Davidson) on drums and vocals. They first played in public at the Linda Pollin Recreation Center in Southeast D.C. Before long they were playing at a "kiddie cabaret" for the grand sum of 10 dollars, which was enough money to keep small boys of 10–12 years old interested enough to keep playing. Soon the band was playing in venues where they were too young to even enter as patrons.

Johnson's observations about the beginnings of Rare Essence are augmented by the recollections of Little Benny Harley:

> Rare Essence was the Young Dynamos back then. They were practicing in Whiteboy's living room. I was like 10 at the time. I came from [school] band practice one day and I heard them playing. I said "Lemme go ahead and knock on their door and play some Kool & the Gang, and blow their minds!" So I played for 'em, and they said "Oh, man we could use you." This was...'76. Footz changed the name from Young Dynamos to Rare Essence. He got that name from this perfume, Essence Rare. We were playing Top 40—a lot of Brick, the Ohio Players.... [11]

By the early 1970s the number of venues for these nascent go-go bands had also expanded. The Club Lebaron in Palmer Parker, Maryland, offered up groups like the Soul Searchers to an eager audience. Likewise, the squad room of the Kentland Volunteer Fire Department in Prince George's County provided space for bands like Al Mumphrey and the Embraceables Band. And the Wilson Boat Lines frequently booked these proto-go-go groups on their daily excursions along the Potomac. The Trouble Band and Show (later known as Trouble Funk) sometimes played at Anacostia Park and learned some of their earliest stage presentations from Chuck Brown and the Soul Searchers. By the late 1970s Trouble Funk had emerged as a band to rival Chuck and his group in the quickly developing go-go field.[12]

Even though go-go was in its developmental stages in the early to mid-1970s, Chuck Brown's music was heading there quickly. This is more easily understood in hindsight, of course, as Chuck added conga drums to many of his performances and the numbers themselves grew in length. No one could have predicted the impact of disco on popular music and culture nor how jazz fusion (whether with rock or with funk) would influence black music in the District of Columbia. But he was listening and absorbing, adding the ingredients that made sense to him. On a 1974 album, *Salt of the Earth,* on the tune "Blow Your Whistle," Chuck recalled that he had go-go on his mind and that the song was about his audience: "The idea came to me to make some go-go music, but I couldn't put it together until I heard a tune on the radio by Grover Washington [Jr.] called 'Mr. Magic.' [Kudo Records, 1974] . . . I noticed that the beat was an old beat that we used to use in the church that I used to belong to. It was a bomp-bom-bom-boomboom-bombom-boomboom. It was fast, and I said 'Wait a minute, that might be what I've been looking for.'"[13]

Drawing upon his vast storehouse of musical knowledge and professional experience, Chuck next looked to a rather unexpected source—Latin music—for inspiration. He had once enjoyed a stint as the guitar player with Los Latinos, a local band that employed a battery of percussion instruments. Recalling the impact of various percussion instruments (especially conga drums) on the texture of the band's music, Chuck decided to augment the Soul Searchers with "extra" percussion players. He wanted to add a bit of *picante* to the music and to its underlying rhythms, a mixture that brought it closer to what soon emerged as go-go. Chuck commented on this aspect of his development of go-go:

> After we got through a song, I would break the song
> down and let the percussion keep playing . . . So then we

got into the go-go groove. At that time, all the disco beats was like 120 beats per minute...so we said "We're going to chop that in half, 60 bpm, and slow that beat down and syncopate that beat so people can understand what's going on there."...I fired two drummers to get the beat the way I wanted it. I told my band that, after a while, everybody in town was going to be playing this beat.[14]

By 1976 all of the basic elements of go-go—the slow and deliberate groove, the added percussion (including cowbells and tambourines), the distinctive rhythmic pattern, the easy interaction between the band and the audience, the expanded performances—were all in place. Most of this occurred courtesy of Chuck Brown, and he must be given credit for go-go's genesis. But before long, others in town were catching on to this evolving revolution.

With their strong ties to funk and soul, the early go-go bands almost always featured a saxophone player or two. Carl Jones (C.J.), the sax player from Experience Unlimited, noted that percussion might be the heart of go-go, but the sax provided its soul. This may be less true in the twenty-first century, but in the late 1970s most go-go bands featured at least one reed player. C.J. observed:

Just like James Brown had Maceo, like Rick James has Daddy, go-go bands have their saxophonists who add so much. Chuck Brown has Leroy, Redds has C.J., E.U. has C.J. The saxophone is one of the lead instruments in go-go. It is important especially in go-go because when the lead rapper like E.U.'s Sugar Bear would get tired after forty-five minutes of straight singing, he would yell out "C.J., blow your horn, baby." And while he would take a break and get a drink, I would keep the show going.[15]

James Funk of Rare Essence caught on to the power of go-go early, extolling the virtues of this new music to his peers, most of whom were then in their teens and early twenties. They caught Chuck whenever they could—especially at clubs (when they could get in) and outdoor venues like Anacostia Park. "T-Bone" David recalls that his band Trouble Funk "open[ed] up for him in '77 at the Club Lebaron. We'd go from 12 o'clock to 6 A.M. The first time I heard Chuck, I was amazed! There was so much discipline in the sound. It was unbelievable standing right in front of him and hearing the sound that was coming off that stage. When we started playing at the Club Lebaron, we converted from Top 40 to go-go."[16] In 1977 and 1978 Trouble Funk sometimes played at the Barry Farms Recreation Center in Southeast. It was there that some of the younger bands from Southeast—most notably Junk Yard—heard go-go and became inspired to play this music.

"BUSTIN' LOOSE"

But it wasn't until 1979, when Chuck Brown recorded and released "Bustin' Loose," that go-go really hit the public consciousness in a big way. Disco was the queen of popular music in the late 1970s: glitter, bpm, and flashing lights were all the rage. The interest in rock-oriented groups had temporarily ebbed and funk had been around for nearly a decade. Rap was still decidedly undergrown but was slowly gaining favor in small— often Hispanic—clubs in the Bronx.

Chuck was playing small and large clubs around the District of Columbia and in Prince George's County. The Maverick Room emerged as one of his steady gigs in 1977–78 and "Bustin' Loose" became one of his most requested tunes. Chuck went through a number of drummers during this period and remarked that "I changed damn near the whole band to get that tune like I wanted it!"[17] "Bustin' Loose" was very popular with local audiences and a staple of his repertoire for over two years before he finally recorded it. The perfectionist side of Chuck made him too hesitant to record the song; he finally agreed to do it when his producer convinced him that someone would soon steal his thunder if he didn't. Chuck believed in the song—"I just had a feeling that if it was pushed right, it was going to be fairly big."[18]

Chuck's intuition soon proved accurate. He recorded this favorite song in the fall of 1978 as part of an album that was produced by James Purdie. "Bustin' Loose" was issued in January 1979, and *Billboard* reviewed it on January 27, 1979, as a highly recommended soul release. The brief review states that "the title cut allows the group to display its versatility—it comes out jamming. This project is energetic and spirited. Brown, who is a vocal stylist, much like Jerry Butler, offers some interesting phrasing."[19] The sales of the album started off briskly and picked up over the spring. "Bustin' Loose" sold like crazy in metro Washington, D.C., and very well across the rest of the United States—by year's end it was the hottest local soul record and was one of the top-selling soul albums across the country.

Other D.C. bands eagerly fell in behind Chuck Brown's successful lead. The Trouble Band and Show was now simply called Trouble Funk and they'd fallen under the go-go spell. Not long after "Bustin' Loose" hit the scene, T. Funk came out with "E Flat Boogie" followed in the next few years by "Pump Me Up" and "Drop The Bomb," (one of Big Tony's best vocals). These commercially and artistically triumphant releases helped to fuel the success of Trouble Funk, but "Drop The Bomb" emerged as the band's signature song: "People really knew 'Drop The Bomb' because it was the last song we played during the '80s. At the end of the show, we would always have a big explosion. We would say 'Drop the bomb!' three times, and each time it would get louder. And people would say when we came, 'Trouble Funk is coming. They dropping the bomb.'"[20]

Rap was also just beginning to appear in our musical landscape. Fueled by a thirst for the new and driven by small independent record companies, it was beginning to reach out to touch a larger audience. Part of the record companies' plan was to expand their roster of artists to reach the widest possible assembly of interesting folk and this meant looking at other expressions of hip-hop in addition to rap. Executives from New York–based Sugar Hill Records, which initially prospered with the Sugar Hill Gang, heard Trouble Funk and were impressed by the band's strong local following, their energy, and their unique repertoire. This meant that instead of shuffling to produce and distribute their own recordings, Funk waxed their two most popular records as well as "Hey Fellas," for Sugar Hill. The records sold very well locally but did very little outside of D.C. The brisk sales of "Bustin' Loose" were atypical; Trouble Funk's experience with Sugar Hill Records, on the other hand, seems to have begun a disappointing pattern that persists to this day.

"E.U. Freeze" by Experience Unlimited became another of go-go's anthems in the early 1980s, as Preston Blue experienced firsthand: "The summer of my eighth-grade [sic], I had gone out to California to stay with my aunt and uncle. When I came back, everybody was talking about 'EU Freeze.' I didn't know what they were talking about . . . And when we got out of school that year [1980], everybody would run home because at the same time every day they played 'EU Freeze' on WHUR."[21] For the next four years, Blue lived and breathed go-go 24/7, listening to P.A. tapes, going to hear the bands that he could see as an underage youth, and learning more about the bands. It's an interest that has not diminished—Blue is now a photographer for the Take Me Out To The Go-Go magazine and Web site.

Despite the fact that in the early days of go-go, the music remained almost exclusively the property of black Americans in Washington, D.C., a handful of local non-black residents were catching on to what was happening in the 'hood. The well-known punk guitarist Henry Rollins (a protégé of Dischord Records and Fugazi founder Ian MacKaye) grew up in the area. When Infinite Zero Records issued *Trouble Funk Live,* Rollins wrote a heartfelt account about "discovering" Trouble Funk:

> Ian MacKaye and I were driving in his car on Wisconsin Avenue in Washington, D.C. in 1980. We were going through the channels on the radio when we came across WOL-AM. They were playing what we found later was a song called "Pump Me Up." It was so good that we parked the car and just listened. It was nothing we had ever heard before...I saw the band play once....We were the only white kids there. Ian, myself and a few other friends went into the place and almost every head turned and looked at us like we were crazy...All I know is that I wanted to see Trouble Funk. They hit the stage in jeans and T-shirts. Big Tony, the bass player called out "E.T.! Phone home y'all!" The sound of the extra terrestial's code came through the PA via one of the keyboards and the entire band stepped on one so hard that I thought that I was going to fall over. They played a non-stop two-hour set and their energy and musicianship was beyond words.[22]

Although go-go is clearly African American, male dominated, and D.C.-based, go-go culture shares several important traits with the local hardcore punk scene that flowered at about the same time. Fugazi is the best known of the D.C. hardcore bands and the de facto leaders of a scene that is almost 100 percent white. There have been a handful of black punk bands (most notably Bad Brains) but local punk bands and their devoted fans are virtually all white. Fugazi and the other bands that recorded on Dischord Records were certainly aware of go-go, but the two groups of musicians rarely met; the crack epidemic and the racially divided nature of Washington, D.C., did not engender a strong musical dialogue between the two groups.

A few integrated shows were held in the halcyon days of the early 1980s. Chuck Brown and Trouble Funk, for instance, appeared on a handful of double bills with punk bands. David Rubin—a Washington-based concert promoter—organized highly successful "Go-Go/Thrash" concerts at several venues, including the Lansburgh Building in downtown D.C. These events brought together similarly aged black and white citizens, exposing them to live performances of music that they would probably have otherwise overlooked. It was an interesting and semi-successful experiment that—at least briefly—united the fans of Trouble Funk and Minor Threat.[23]

Race aside, the two musical movements shared some important commonalities. They both originated at about the same time—at the tail end of funk, the beginnings of disco, and the early days of hip-hop. Punk and go-go began as the music of disaffected youth, young men and women in their teens and early twenties. Both genres were marginalized by television and largely eschewed by radio stations in and around Washington, D.C. Despite this lack of recognition, D.C. punk and go-go developed a devoted following, with many fans who have been immersed in the music since the mid-1970s.

Perhaps most significantly, both genres have been self-reliant. There is a very strong "do it yourself" mentality that has propelled the music through its toughest times. This attitude has led to the formation of many small, locally-based record companies, a network of live music venues and clubs that are devoted to the music(s), and a small cadre of (mostly) men who have made a living by way of go-go and punk. Chuck Brown and the Ian McKaye–led Fugazi have been the most successful Washington, D.C., bands to emerge from these movements. For every successful local go-go band—such as E.U.—there is a punk band like Jawbox. True to the division between Washington and D.C., however, these forms have mostly evolved in parallel. Despite some striking similarities, the direct interaction and interchange between go-go and punk has been minimal. Richard Harrington, a longtime pop music writer for The *Washington Post* promoted go-go at every turn. But Harrington—who is white—was an anomaly as far as the go-go community was concerned. The clubs were owned and patronized by local black residents, the bands were nearly 100 percent African American (Chuck Brown's unit being the sole notable exception), and the general interest in go-go remained Afrocentric.

In the early 1980s, go-go really caught fire among black

Washingtonians. The number of local bands playing go-go increased and such long-defunct but memorable bands as the Petworth Boys cropped up around town. These bands played at a bewildering variety of venues, such as schools, recreation centers, old movie theaters, and small clubs, in the District as well as Prince George's County. The list includes places that no longer exist or have changed so radically that in the twenty-first century you would never guess they once hosted a go-go event: Potomac High School, Atlas Disco, Paragon II, Washington Coliseum, Oakcrest Recreation Center, Maverick Room, Oxon Hill High School, Evan's Grill, and the All Around Race Club. Many of the bands are all but forgotten today—Ayre Rayde, Class Band, Peacemakers, and Pumpblenders, among them—except by the patriarchs of go-go who lived through the day.

In Chocolate City, go-go had emerged as *the* dominant form of popular music in the African American community. Its following rivaled any of its "urban" (a code word in the commercial music industry for African American) musical forms. E.U., Trouble Funk, Rare Essence, and Chuck Brown and the Soul Searchers had little trouble getting local gigs and were working regularly. Go-go was beginning to be heard on a few more radio stations—like WOL, WHUR, and WPGC—though it had no block programming of its own. Out-of-town promoters almost always booked go-go bands as opening acts when any of the national soul/urban/funk acts came to town to play at the Cap Centre, the Howard Theater, or any of the other larger venues in town. Its success also opened the door to the national audience for groups like E.U., who toured with Earth, Wind & Fire and Grover Washington, Jr., in 1983.

Contemporary accounts of go-go in the mid-1980s underscore the community support and enthusiasm demonstrated by younger black citizens of D.C. It is significant that even in 1984, sympathetic voices in the local media noted:

> One of Washington's best-kept secrets isn't hidden in a Congressional closet. Go-go is out in the open, strutting down Eastern Avenue, running through Anacostia Park, sauntering down C Street. But it's still a local phenomenon, receiving little media attention or music industry response, even though it draws thousands to concerts. Twenty thousand showed up for a recent go-go concert at the Capital Centre . . . Rare Essence routinely pulls in

9,000 kids for a one-night show. Go-go fests draw upward of 20,000 fans, despite $12 ticket prices. Trouble Funk sold over 70,000 copies of "Back Up Against The Wall" in the spring and is readying a follow-up, "Shoo Be Do Wop" for a June release.[24]

In 1983 and 1984 go-go spawned night-long parties at the Black Hole and Penthouse clubs located on Georgia Avenue NW near Howard University. On the waterfront in Southwest D.C., Cherry's on Atlantic Avenue, go-goers moved to hot new dances, such as Happy Feet, the Whop, Inspector Gadget, and the feigned clumsiness of the Jerry Lewis. They came to hear Trouble Funk "drop the bomb" or argued whether E.U. or Mass Extention had "cranked" the hardest the night before.

But even as early as 1984 music observers both inside and outside of D.C. expressed sincere, thoughtful, and prophetic doubts about the ability of go-go to make inroads into the popular music scene outside of our nation's capital. In an article by Jeff Zeldman in the *Washington Weekly,* John Simon, a Washington music attorney, observed that "Go-go is a great live sound . . . but few bands have produced a sophisticated enough sound for the major companies, so they remain pretty skeptical—if they've even heard of it. Translating go-go music to vinyl is an obstacle."[25] Local engineer and producer Tom McCarthy echoed his sentiments: "You have to basically record the band live. For Chuck Brown, we caught a jam and edited it properly to get the feeling. The number didn't have a bridge or hook or chorus, but it did have a groove, the power. I'm not so sure that it can translate that well to radio."[26] Finally, Michael Barackman—Arista Records' A&R director in the 1980s—observed that "Go-go is a new, very exciting trend, one that's becoming more and more to be reckoned with. But though it's blossoming, labels need to hear material that could sell beyond the 75,000 mark . . . The key from a national perspective is material—songs that could break a band on the radio . . . I don't mean go-go can't retain its . . . authenticity. It has to keep those ingredients that make it special and not become homogenized."[27]

But the winds of change were blowing down the streets of D.C. One of the more informed writers at the *Washington Post*, Richard Harrington, wrote two long pieces about the local go-go scene. He quoted Max Kidd, who said that "nobody realizes it's happening!" Harrington countered—perhaps somewhat hyperbolically—with the good news:

Nobody, that is, but the A&R men, producers, even record company presidents who have been flocking to Washington to grab those bands still available, and the BBC documentary crew and foreign journalists who are descending by the taxi-load, and the reporters from magazines as disparate as *Rolling Stone* and *Playboy* who are working up pieces about this home-brewed music.[28]

By the spring of 1985 go-go had become big enough that it finally captured the attention of a major outside force: Chris Blackwell of Island Records. Looking for a counterpart to the highly successful film about reggae and Bob Marley, *The Harder They Come,* Blackwell brought his considerable commercial clout to the District of Columbia. Taking Max Kidd, Trouble Funk, and other members of the local go-go community into his fold, Blackwell produced a controversial film, *Good to Go,* and an Island-released soundtrack album of the same name. Because this particular event in the history and development of go-go is so complex and pivotal in telling the story of go-go, *Good to Go* — along with Bruce Brown's *Streetwise* and Def Jam's flirtation with the music — will be discussed in detail later.

The film was released in 1986 and received very mixed-to-negative reviews, especially locally, where it was decried as wrong-minded. The comments of Rare Essence guitarist André Johnson typify the response of most members of the D.C. community: "The people who made *Good to Go* lost track of what they really wanted to do. People focused more on the violence in the movie, as opposed to the music and the partying. They had a lot of good partying scenes in the movie, but people focused more on the rape by the gang and the dude smoking boat [PCP]."[27] Whiteboy's sentiments are echoed by Chuck Brown: "I never thought nothing of that movie, with all that violence. What does all that shooting and cars turning over have to do with the price of scrapple? It has nothing whatsoever to do with go go. People who did that came from out of New York and didn't know what they were doing.... In *Good to Go* the music was good, but the damn script could go."[30]

In fact, the soundtrack accompanying the film remains Blackwell's most praiseworthy legacy in the go-go field. Most of the groups that appear on the soundtrack were closely allied with Max Kidd, either because he served as their manager or producer or just through years of association. The record contains wonderful performances by Trouble

The Go-Go According to Snowboy

Go-go became a craze here, particularly in London through the "warehouse" parties of the early to mid-'80s. The warehouse parties were, literally, in warehouses that were either abandoned or were hired out and were totally illegal. They went on all night and you brought your own alcohol in to drink (obviously there were unpriced bottles of beer for sale at extortionate prices occasionally) and you risked having your sound system and records confiscated by the police, which happened occasionally. Ironically the "Black Sound of Washington" was being played at first by white trendy post–New Romantic clubber/DJs who were playing that kind of funk alongside the Clash, rockabilly, James Brown, and electro like the Jonzun Crew and Soul Sonic Force. The odd rap tunes such as Fearless Four['s] "Rockin' It" also got played. You must remember that we also had a huge scene of soul, jazz-funk, and boogie in the U.K. and I guess the as-yet-unknown-named go-go sound was perhaps a little too retro for the masses that were into state-of-the-art modern Black music.

The main warehouse parties were called "The Dirtbox" and the main DJ was a guy called Jay Strongman. He was well into that sound and as years went by he got recognized as one of the first to push it. I had been collecting a few go-go records like the "Drop The Bomb" and "Let's Get Small" and "Super Grit," 12-inches by Trouble Funk, just because I loved the sound. We still didn't know, at that point, that it was called go-go. There were a few rumors around amongst that warehouse crowd about the name and the sound, also band names, such as E.U., Hot, Cold, Sweat, and Trouble Funk, were spoken about in the "right" circles.

Where I live, near Southend-on-Sea, Essex (approximately 40 miles east of London), I was DJing at this bar called Whispers and this crowd of warehouse clubbers came in and I was playing "Let's Get Small." "Is this Trouble Funk?" "Is this go-go?" "Where did you get this stuff?" Ironically, I was picking up these 12-inches in bargain bins where no one wanted them! Don't misunderstand me. I had no influence as a DJ whatsoever and this was a year before I'd made my first record, but the WORD was out. Kurtis Blow['s] "Party Time" came out and... BANG!!! It was a huge record here in the U.K. and all of a sudden everyone was talking about go-go. Record papers such as *Record Mirror* (especially writer James Hamilton), *Blues and Soul,* and *Black Echoes* were writing about it and reviewing all the new go-go releases. All the big club DJs were behind go-go and it seemed like it was going to be huge.

Trouble Funk and Chuck Brown came over to play live at the 2,000-capacity Town and Country Club in London and an essential go-go compilation called *Go Go Crankin'* came out on Island. The buzz was enormous! Chuck Brown's "We Need Money," Little Benny's "Who Came To Boogie," along with Redds & the Boys's "Movin' And Groovin'" all charted and just added fuel to the fire. On our national television station, the B.B.C., the very influential and intellectual programme *Arena* did an incredible hour-long documentary on go-go which was made so well the excitement was unbearable. All these bands, dances, venues, people like the DJ "Moonman" and the sax player C.J. who was taking us through the scene, it was TOO much!

Meanwhile I'd been learning percussion and was given an opportunity to make a 12-inch single. This was in 1985 and my friend, Bill Bailey, as a project, wanted to start a label, demo a track on it, record it and get it distributed and reviewed, just to see what the process was. He had no intentions of doing any more than the one record and that's exactly what he did. (He's now DOCTOR Bill Bailey, with a doctorate in nuclear physics!) After a career so far of 10 Latin jazz albums and 16 singles I'm very proud to say that my first 12-inch was a GO-GO one! Yes, Bill asked me. So there I was, obsessed with this *Arena* documentary (that I'd watched probably 30 times) and my collection of go-go 12-inches, so I tore the songs apart to see what made them work, and I demoed this song called "Bring on the Beat." I was really into the J.B.'s at that time (still am) and was interested in giving my song a little more J.B.'s and a little less P-Funk. Go-go has a lot of those Clinton-type keyboard and horn hooks which I was never too keen on. So out comes "Bring On The Beat" by Snowboy and the G.L. Band on ARC records; the U.K.'s first go-go record. *Record Mirror's* James Hamilton's (probably the first U.K. journalist to document go-go), review said that "it is a little lacking in dynamics, but a brave effort" and there was a fantastic article in *Blues and Soul* on me. My local radio station, Essex Radio, played it once every night for three weeks on Dave Gregory's *Soul Show* and he also interviewed me, but we never played out live. It was a studio project. Bill Bailey drove round every black music record shop in London and Essex trying to sell it and eventually, using references from the *Arena* documentary, he actually went to Washington, D.C., and gave copies to Moonman and Douglas Records and got a copy to Max Kidd. Max says he still has it and I'm honored.

Years later when I was more established as a percussionist/recording artist, these big DJ/recording artists called Cold Cut saw "Bring On The Beat" on the wall of a collector's record shop in London, called Reckless, and they heard it and said "I didn't know Snowboy knew how to play go-go percussion" and they phoned me and booked me to feature go-go percussion on a record on Big Life featuring the reggae singer from Black Uhuru, Junior Reid, on vocals. I went into the studio and they let me get straight on with it. I did 12 percussion overdubs and, in fact, if you manage to pick up the remix (the one with the yellow cover) one of the tracks is just all my percussion and the drums! Anyway, so it came out as Cold Cut featuring Junior Reid entitled "Stop This Crazy Thing" and the year was 1988. It got to No. 21 in our national charts.

I feel, at least in the U.K., the reason for go-go's demise was that there were too many long live concert performance 12-inches coming over which couldn't be played in the clubs and were a little boring after a while, I'm afraid. I've read in interviews with go-go artists that they feel their records are OK but go-go is about playing live with the audience response and the continuous non-stop go-go groove, and that's where they felt they were strongest. I'd always hoped that more 12-inches would have come out with shorter, straight-to-the-point songs and let the bands worry about extending them out live. After all, funk 7-inches are an ideal length at three-and-a-half to four minutes, for instance. Personally, I'm still a big go-go collector and fan and look forward to the inevitable rise again of this ultimate party funk.

Mark Cotgrove
November 2000

Funk, most notably the title track and a strong and lively version of "Drop The Bomb," as well nice selections provided by Redds and the Boys; Chuck Brown and the Soul Searchers; E.U.; and Hot, Cold, Sweat. You can tell this is no local production just by looking at the credits: it lists nine engineers and nine studios (ranging from the Fallout Shelter, U.K. to the Airdrome in California), including two mobile studios! D.C., where are you?

If nothing else, Chris Blackwell's interaction with the go-go community did focus some national attention on the music. The years between 1983 and 1988 were the most fertile period for go-go outside of Washington, D.C. The best-known names in go-go—Chuck Brown, E.U., Trouble Funk, and Rare Essence—were finally getting some substantial gigs outside of D.C. and its nearby environs. New York City called, Los Angeles called, Detroit called. In fact, the music was catching on outside of the United States. T-Bone, a Trouble Funk percussionist, observed that "at that particular point, go-go was real hot...especially overseas. We was playing overseas on a 35- to 45-day tour and playing every night in different places."[31] Richard Harrington echoes these observations:

> It's already the rage in England, where articles on go-go
> inundate the music weeklies. In London, a studio band
> calling itself the DC Allstarz cut a pale version of Chuck
> Brown's "Bustin' Loose." Little Benny's "We Come to
> Boogie," available in only a dozen stores in Washington,
> went to the top of England's disco and R&B charts, sell-
> ing 150,000 copies overseas.[32]

In addition to Island Records's efforts, the newly vitalized Junk Yard hooked up with Def Jam while Polydor looked over and eventually signed Rare Essence. Rare Essence toured quite a bit and they were happy to be working so much, but their experience with Polydor was less than satisfying. The band ran smack dab into corporate America and its quest for the lowest common (though highest sales) denominator. André Johnson recalled: "We signed with Polydor and did a single, and they didn't do anything with it. As a matter of fact, it wasn't even a go-go single. It was some type of party record that was bordering on disco. We sent them countless songs, trying to get them to put a record out...Eventually we decided to do the pop record so we could get out of the contract and go on about our business."[33]

Aside from these two unhappy deals with Def Jam, go-go largely remained at arm's length from the national record companies. It seems pretty clear in retrospect that folks from outside of D.C. did not truly understand that go-go is more than just music that you can capture in a studio and then unleash on an unknowing public. Spike Lee had a better notion about black youth culture and music when he spotted E.U. at a special birthday gig at the 9:30 Club in Georgetown. E.U. enjoyed a great deal of exposure, notoriety, and fun from their appearance in Lee's film *School Daze,* but that was back in 1988 and this commercial exposure was fleeting.

D.C. AND HIP-HOP

Hip-hop has emerged as an integral part of life in Washington, D.C. Hip-hop in D.C. was inevitable not only because it was an emerging trend in American popular culture but also because the city is so overwhelmingly black. To be more precise, the District is about 75 percent non-white. The Latino population, particularly of Salvadorians, is substantial and growing, but most residents are black Americans with strong familial roots in the tobacco-growing counties that constitute rural eastern Virginia and North Carolina.

The District of Columbia generally offers a progressive and liberal political atmosphere. The Democratic primary for mayor, city council, and other elected offices serves as the city's de facto election. This political reality is one of several facts that keeps the issue of statehood for the District of Columbia off the table; especially during times when the House, Senate, or presidency is controlled by the Republican party. On the other hand, the progressive political landscape helps to create an atmosphere that fosters change.

Hip-hop (and by extension go-go) in D.C. is further fueled by a solid black middle class with disposable income; one that can afford to fill the Convention Center for a rap concert or an appearance by local singing star Toni Braxton. D.C.'s hip-hop community found an early and strong ally in the form of Howard University, one of the older and stronger historically black universities. Howard University's reputation is such that it attracts students from across the United States, as well as many other parts of the world.

While black Washingtonians quickly and thoroughly embraced hip-hop and became part of the hip-hop explosion, the District of Columbia remains a unique place. In the nascent days of hip-hop, New York City was at its hub with a rainbow of groups—Latinos and gays, in particular—contributing to its development. Before long, hip-hop in Southern California (especially in Los Angeles) was associated with gangstas. In order to understand go-go, you need to know more about the District of Columbia and the role of the music within the city.

Go-go is quite properly associated with the African musical culture of Washington, D.C., and remains the only original musical genre—black, white, Hispanic, or otherwise—born in the District of Columbia. Duke Ellington was born in the city but he didn't originate jazz, though he did nurture it as a band leader, composer, and pianist. Go-go is clearly a District product and is a product of the streets rather than of the cultivated elite or of the academy. Therefore this music—along with hip-hop culture—is associated (rightly or wrongly) with the negative attributes of African American urban culture.

The truth is that it is difficult—impossible really—to separate go-go music from its cultural background. Washington D.C.'s (black) life informs and helps to shape its rhythmic impulse, the lyrics of its songs, its audience, and the ways in which the music is presented and consumed. You won't find go-go at the Kennedy Center (at least not very often), so people go to hear Junk Yard Band at the Black Hole or Da Zulu Club. And major record labels won't touch it, which is why P.A. tapes and local entrepreneurs are so important. Even local radio stations rarely play go-go, so our tape machines or CD players work overtime cranking out the Northeast Groovers or Trouble Funk.

Rap and hip-hop and go-go coexist in D.C. More to the point, rap and hip-hop have certainly influenced go-go, especially since the late 1980s. This is when the second generation of go-go bands—such as JYB and the Huck-A-Bucks—began to mature. Born in the '60s and '70s, their members are just young enough to never remember a time when hip-hop did not exist. An even younger band, such as Jigga, came of age when rap was predominate and everything else was old ... Stevie Wonder, Earth, Wind & Fire, and Diana Ross were artists of your parents' generation.

This shift in musical preference is profound and quite noticeable in the go-go bands formed since about 1987. These bands differ from the first generation in two noteworthy ways. The first is the spareness of their instrumentation. The pioneering go-goers were touched by funk and soul; brass and reed instuments, along with a full rhythm section (à la Trouble Funk or Mass Extension) were standard. Younger/newer bands eschew this instrumentation in favor of an electronic keyboard or synthesizer with an expanded percussion section that usually includes a full drum kit with congas, timbales, and other pitched and unpitched percussion instruments. The more recent go-go bands are very much in touch with the sound and essence of hip-hop in their structure: a multi-faceted vocal component backed by dense layers of percussion. String, brass, and reed instruments are largely absent from younger bands.

"Lead talkers" in go-go are another fairly recent innovation that is directly linked to rap. A lead talker is essentially the frontman, the primary vocalist, and the principal rapper for the group. Singing is important, but it takes a backseat to rapping in the more recently formed go-go bands—occupying much the same position as in hip-hop. Bands usually informally designate one of their members as the lead talker—a term that as far as we can determine is uniquely D.C.

The close and symbiotic relationship between go-go and hip-hop (don't forget that both are forms of black popular music) goes back to the early 1980s when some hip-hop artists such as Grace Jones became interested in go-go. Jones embraced some of the genre's elements on her recording of *Slave to the Rhythm*. In New York City and Los Angeles, producers began to use go-go samples or morphed go-go rhythm tracks onto rap recordings by Doug E. Fresh, Run-D.M.C., and even the Beastie Boys. This was particularly true with Junk Yard during their brief and unhappy tenure with Def Jam in the late 1980s. You can hear the influence of Junk Yard Band on several of Def Jam's artists, especially those under the wing of local music promoter Hurbie "Luv Bug" Azor. As JYB's then-manager, Moe Shorter, stated: "I know my music...and Salt-N-Pepa's 'My Mike Sounds Nice' got our tracks. Them cans and buckets in the background, that's ours, man!"[34] This is the same man who around the same time essentially co-opted Pleasure—the city's only noteworthy female go-go band.

Although they were aware of the borrowing techniques employed by many of the rappers, go-go bands also booked some of the early hip-hop groups into the city. Rare Essence, for instance, was the first band to bring Grandmaster Flash into the city at the end of the '70s. One of the early shows at the Club Lebaron resulted in a failure for the rappers as the D.C. crowd was not "down" with this form of hip-hop and wanted to hear go-go. Trouble Funk's percussionist, "T-Bone" David recalls:

> We did a lot of shows with the rappers. When we were out
> on tour, a lot of the guys, like Public Enemy before they

even got started, would be at all our shows. They would sample a lot of our stuff, too...and they'd slip it in. It would be way undercover, but you know your stuff when you hear it. Kid 'N Play, on "Rollin' With Kid 'N Play" used the bongo part that I did on [the] *Saturday Night Live* [album], and they just stuck it in and said one of their guys was playing percussion. One time, we were playing the Capital Center [*sic*], and I saw Kid. I said, "Man, don't be stealing my stuff, man." He was kind of embarrassed about it, but he knew they had took it.... I told him, "If you need some percussion, man, call me. I'll give you the real thing—you won't have to sample it."[35]

AFTER THE GOLDRUSH

By 1990, D.C.'s systemic support system for go-go had altered. All of the controversy surrounding drugs, violence on the streets that was misdirected towards the music, and the disappointments related to Hollywood and go-go had taken its toll. Not everyone suffered; Chuck Brown was rolling along and funk-influenced groups such as E.U. were still going strong. And the younger hip-hop-related bands—like Backyard and Northeast Groovers—continued to attract a crowd of young men and women who remained loyal followers in spite of the controversy. The usual clubs, such as the Black Hole, operated most nights and the interest in the music in the community remained strong.

But despite these positive signals, the interest in the music had waned and go-go was suffering. There were fewer gigs for groups wanting to play outside of go-go's immediate birthplace. Sure, the jobs at Norfolk State University or at a club in Richmond, Virginia, were still available, but the gigs overseas (especially in western Europe and Japan) became scarcer and the pay remained static. And when a group like Rare Essence crossed the ocean the band was not always booked back-to-back nights or at the largest black music festivals; the gigs tended to be at smaller clubs and the band was not always the headline act.

Charlie Fenwick suggests that go-go has remained D.C.-based largely because of the musicians themselves:

> The problem is basically that...they created a business out of it in D.C....All I ever did was play music. So

when I was, say 18, 19 years old, I could go out and make 500 dollars a week playing music. What happens is these companies come to D.C. to E.U. or Rare Essence and offer these people a budget. But how can you offer somebody a budget [to go on the road] that's making thousands a month at home; to go out on the road to get two percent or three percent of record sales when they could sell P.A. tapes here for 10 dollars a pop.... You see, it's not rewarding enough for them to make it go where it really needs it to go.... Everybody that's here in D.C. does their own thing and they make money; it's kind of hard to get them to kind of shut down what they already do and start over.... A lot of people think that when you go national, you go out there and make all this incredible money, but it ain't that way.[36]

And fewer major record companies were knocking at the doors of go-go bands and their managers. Island dropped all of the go-go acts they had used for *Good to Go*, while Def Jam sat on Junk Yard's contract. They did nothing to promote the band, even in light of their local success with "Sardines." E.U.'s career was boosted due to their appearance in *School Daze*, but this shot of juice only lasted so long. Chuck Brown's more fluid career placed him in front of larger record companies, such as Mercury, but his associations with multinational labels proved to be fleeting and not very satisfying.

By the early 1990s, go-go artists were once again looking towards the District for their bread and butter. Local gigs and recording for local, independent record companies once more became the staple for all of the bands. This shift of events was by no means entirely negative. During the 1990s the established bands survived by performing several nights a week and recording the occasional compact disc or cassette. And new bands, such as Proper Utensils, Suttle Thoughts, and Optimystic Tribe, occasionally emerged from the neighborhoods of Northeast and Southeast D.C.

Early in the twenty-first century, go-go remains entrenched in D.C. The daily details and rumors—Where is Junk Yard playing on Thursday night?; When is that new Backyard P.A. tape due out?; What club will emerge to replace the Ibex?; Did you hear about the weapons charges against Ghengis?; Is Donnell really leaving RE?—may change, but the essentials remain the same. Go-go is still black popular music in Washington, D.C. (albeit more hip-hop- than funk-related these days) and it still attracts a cadre of hardcore fans as well as people who come to go-gos on a more casual basis. The one constant (besides the beat and Chuck Brown) is that go-go remains at the heart of D.C.'s black community— and white folks remain largely in the dark.

2 · Going to a Go-Go

It's over 95 degrees on a hot summer's night in downtown Washington D.C. and inside the hanger-like space of a local dance hall the temperature is even hotter! Thousands of eager teenagers are partying down to the percussion-fueled funk of Chuck Brown and the Soul Searchers, the Capital City's No. 1 band. The big beat rocks the hall as the kids chant back in response to Chuck's calls and dedications from the stage, from the soulful jazz of "Harlem Nocturne" to the hip-hop of "The Show," the Soul Searchers keep the D.C. dance rhythm movin' and groovin'! Two and a half sweat-soaked hours later the concert is over, the Godfather of Go-Go has done it again, an exhausted but happy crowd pours out in the night air.[1]

Jay Strongman, notes for Chuck Brown's Live '87 *album*

The uninformed often assume that go-go is synonymous with hip-hop culture, and to a degree this is true. Hip-hop has become ubiquitous, influencing the expressive culture of younger black—and increasing numbers of teenage white—Americans everywhere, including in the District. Even though go-go sometimes comments on contemporary issues, most notably drugs and poverty, hip-hop's observations on the social scene are louder, more persistent, and far more pervasive. Go-go's true underlying purpose is not to serve as a social sounding board, though it does partially fulfill this function. Instead go-go provides a creative outlet for local black citizens to express themselves in unique and powerful ways. It furnishes local black citizens the opportunity to shout out "I'm black, I'm creative, I'm proud, and I'm representing D.C.!" These shout-outs most often occur during live performances.

BEYOND THE BEAT

On the surface, go-go appears to be dance music, pure and simple. If you can keep your rump from bouncing while Trouble Funk, Huck-A-Bucks,

Jigga, or Chuck Brown are on the bandstand, then the odds are good that you are either deaf or dead. Perhaps more than any other form of contemporary vernacular music, go-go *must* be experienced live to really comprehend its power and the immediacy of the rituals that accompany the music. Go-go music, after all, takes its name from an event—a gathering of like-minded (mostly) black Americans coming together to celebrate. It's a communal experience best understood in the context of its performance. Unlike Western classical music, go-go cannot be reduced to a score, nor is it as tightly scripted or controlled like a performance by "Weird Al" Yankovic. Nor does it indulge in the over-the-top excesses of a performance by an "alternative" rock band like Rage Against the Machine or Korn. Go-go has established its own performance rules that are well-known, understood, and adhered to by the musicians and fans alike.

Go-go is not only non-stop, but also largely improvisatory, with only the hint of a play list established at the beginning of any performance. A go-go proceeds largely on gut instinct as the band reacts to and interacts with the crowd. Make no mistake about it—at a go-go the distinction between the audience and the band is very narrow indeed. There is an ongoing dialogue (much like in a good marriage or any other close, cooperative venture) with give and take and call and response helping to establish the communication necessary for an intimate and satisfying experience. In strong contrast to a performance by a folk-pop artist like Jackson Browne or Tracy Chapman, where the audience is warmly appreciative and enthusiastic but rarely overbearing, go-go crowds are always "in your face" while interacting with the band. Because the go-go community is largely racially segregated and most of its adherents reside in close proximity, the members often know one another well, so go-gos tend to be social as well as musical events. The fans let you know what they want to hear and how good a job the band is doing; they express themselves vigorously and loudly, in no uncertain terms. Go-go fans, in short, are demonstrative, not at all shy, and overwhelmingly black.

Remember, Washington, D.C., is a city divided along very distinctive geographical, economic, and racial lines. Public events like go-gos are subject to people's perceptions about them and the musicians who perform at them. The fact is, many people simply do not find the idea of a go-go event very inviting. If people outside the go-go community think about go-go at all, they perceive it as a "black thing." For one thing, the bands play at clubs in less than savory parts of the city. More to the point, these musical events are not part of D.C.'s cultural mainstream—the clubs do not advertise in the *Washington Post,* you don't hear about go-go events on local television spots, and go-go flyers are not usually found tacked up on telephone poles in upscale Chevy Chase. For a whole host of reasons, go-go advertising is as ghettoized as go-go's performance venues. The bands and clubs would love to have a more racially diverse (and larger) audience, of course. But the truth is that most non-black Americans rarely venture into the parts of the city where go-go clubs are located. Furthermore, most go-go bands begin playing late at night and many of the clubs let out between 2:00 A.M. and 6:00 A.M.—hours that are too late for most people.

These factors lead to the perception that go-go events represent a "closed space" to the non-black population. The clubs are not private, of course, but those from outside of the go-go community rarely go to hear Backyard or E.U. at Breeze's Metro Club or Celebrity Hall. Most non-black citizens of the District of Columbia don't even know where these clubs are located. As an African American musical phenomenon go-go already has to worry about race, but it also wears the mantle of low-class or blue-collar music. None of these factors engender an increasingly diverse audience, and go-go remains ghettoized.

PENTECOSTAL CHURCHES AND GO-GO CULTURE

In some very fundamental respects, a go-go bears striking parallels to an African American Pentecostal church service. Both events, for example, tend to be long, extending for hours with no predetermined endpoint. Nor do they hand out neatly printed programs detailing the event when you enter a Holiness church or as they check your ID when you come through the door at Deno's Club in Northeast. A go-go and a sanctified church service also blur the clear demarcations that separate performers from the audience. Band members often comment that if the crowd is emotionally, vocally, and demonstrably involved, then the go-go is a success. Sanctified church members would probably state it differently—they might say that the Holy Spirit was absent from that day's service. The result, though, is essentially the same—an unsatisfactory and disappointing experience. In other words, both a go-go and a Pentecostal church service succeed only when the majority of the people in attendance fully participate and become integrated into the event. When all of the elements are present—the band is crankin' or the Holy Ghost is present—the end result is more than positive—it can be downright transforming.

Even some of the nomenclature used by Pentecostal churchgoers and go-go devotees resonates. The Northeast Groovers might shout out "Are my soldiers out there?," while the members of a Church of God in Christ (COGIC) temple sing "We are soldiers on the battlefield for my Lord." In either case, they are calling out to the converted. This is a vocal affirmation that the people in the house or in the temple are true believers who understand and have come to answer the call. Likewise, when the Groovers inquire "Are you ready to bounce?" or "People, do you want to party?," the COGIC equivalent is "Do you feel the Spirit?" Pentecostal preachers like Rev. D.C. Rice, who made records for Vocalion between 1928–1930, recorded sermons with titles like "We Got the Same Power Over Here" and "I'm Gonna Wait Right Here Till He Comes." Junk Yard would phrase it differently, asking their adherents to "Clap To The Beat" or to "Let It Ride Socket Beat," but they are asking the same essential question: Are you here to share in the power of this experience?

These are intimate affairs that value face-to-face contact. Even in the most cavernous temple or a huge hall like the downtown Convention Center, the people literally come together in celebration. They bounce and sway together; they move their hands above their heads in unison ("Raise your hands in the air!"). It's very physical—often a sweaty and funky experience. Participants want to experience the familiar; they find solace in observing the rules that prevail at a go-go or Holiness service. Part of the attraction is that you never know exactly what will happen. At a sporting event fans hope a last-minute touchdown or ninth inning, game-winning home run will provide an unexpected thrill; go-go or Pentecostal participants hope that E.U. will crank or the Holy Spirit will visit them while the brass band from the United Holiness Temple's Mass Choir is performing. This possibility (the prospect of a transcending experience) remains part of the event's appeal—you can only show up, participate, hope, and anticipate that something truly special will happen.

Go-goers and the Sunday crowd at a Holiness church gather together to demonstrate their adulation and appreciation of the people they came to honor. They do this in a very public and unabashed fashion, using their bodies as well as their voices. Adoration is a critical component of these performance events—fingers are pointed, hands and signs are raised. People pay particular attention when the (holy or profane) dancing becomes spirited. Sometimes the crowd opens up to spotlight an individual's movement; at other times the crowd moves in closer— perhaps in an attempt to capture some of the group's energy. The ability to bring a group of ordinary people into an ecstatic state is highly valued. A group or a minister with an established reputation draws the largest, most devoted, and most committed crowds, which will stay until the very end of the event in hopes of a transforming experience. In Washington, D.C., adherents come both to local temples and go-go venues in search of spiritual transformation.

Of course, a Pentecostal church service and a go-go are not precisely equivalent events. In a sanctified temple, worshipers' actions are based on a combination of the strength of the Holy Spirit and an omnipresent, unyielding belief in their faith that comes from experience and revelation. A go-go proceeds more on feeling (often very rooted and strong), which exists on a level below the unshakeable rock known to those who are saved. Both are collective experiences united in the power of song and communal "shouting"—both to others in the audience and to the members of the church—as well as ritualized movement. In his excellent book about Pentecostal worship in present-day North Carolina, *Fire in My Bones,* Glenn Hinson's descriptions of Holiness singing and related practices are reminiscent of go-go.[2]

Many of D.C.'s faithful attend the United House of Prayer for All People, the Church on the Rock of the Apostolic Faith. Although this church is not unique to Washington, D.C., our nation's capital strongly supports the United House of Prayer for All People. The church was founded in 1919 by Charles Manuel Grace, aka "Daddy Grace," who was then living in eastern Massachusetts, near Providence, Rhode Island. The House of Prayer soon spread southward and became especially strong in New York City, Virginia, the Carolinas, and Georgia, as well as Washington, D.C. The charismatic Grace was sometimes accused of demagoguery, but the church has thrived since his death in 1960. Both Daddy McCollough and Daddy Madison (Grace's immediate successors) continued to emphasize worldly financial success, resulting in the building of grand temples. Nonetheless, the House of Prayer remains firmly placed in the Pentecostal spirit, where ecstatic speaking, shouting, and dancing are essential. The music heard in these churches is performed by brass ensembles known as "trombone shout bands," consisting of several trombones, a sousaphone, tuba, drums, cymbals, and other percussion. Shout bands provide the music for all church occasions, from the service on Sunday to funerals and baptisms. Today there are approximately 132

United House of Prayer for All People houses of worship in 27 states. Two of the church's most highly regarded musical groups, Madison's Lively Stones and the Kings of Harmony, are based in Washington, D.C., and the intent of D.C.'s shout bands is the same as with any Pentecostal church — to help transform folks so that they reach an ecstatic state. This transformation is furthered by the use of repetition, which helps to heighten the experience. When the people sense the spirit and the crescendo builds, the music gets "hotter." The release that follows the climax often results in a collective sigh.[3]

This use of a variety of simple repeated musical or structural motifs is also commonly found in other forms of African and African American music (John Coltrane's *A Love Supreme* provides a perfect example). It helps to define and reinforce the relationship between the performers and the audience. Repetition has been so integral to Holiness and go-go events that people not only expect it, it surrounds them, much like their African ancestors. Without the repetition that helps to "bring on the feeling," both a Holiness service and a go-go would lose much of its power and its appeal.

In the House of Prayer, musicians are not financially compensated for playing; their payment is the spiritual pleasure that comes from helping to spread the teachings of the House of Prayer. These musicians believe that financial rewards can in no way provide compensation for doing God's work. Many go-go musicians also perform for the love of what they do. Although some are financially compensated, money is not really the motivating factor. Even the top bands have members who cannot make a living playing music alone. Less well-known musicians probably end up investing more into forming and maintaining the go-go group than they earn by performing. Go-go musicians will also often assert that they have shunned record deals from major companies in order to continue to play the music as they know it.

A comparison between the formal band structure in the House of Prayer and the informal structure in the go-go proves interesting. Approximately 10 to 15 years ago in the House of Prayer, five bands were considered the top groups in the "kingdom." These were the Sons of Thunder and the McCollough Invaders, both from New York City; the Kings of Harmony from Washington, D.C.; The McCollough Tigers and the Angels from Charlotte, North Carolina; and the Happyland Band from Newport News, Virginia. Wherever these bands appeared, highly spirited services ensued and everyone knew that they were hearing the best "shout music" in the House of Prayer. There was always uplifting and joyous competition between the bands. Each band enjoyed being selected to play during a major program by Daddy McCollough, the leader of the House of Prayer. Being considered a top band in the House of Prayer meant that you would be willing to spend many hours on hard work and practice to maintain your status. The failure to strive could lead to a band falling from the hallowed position at the top.

Conversely, in the go-go 10 to 15 years ago there was fierce competition between the big four — E.U., Rare Essence, Chuck Brown and the Soul Searchers, and Trouble Funk. Each band would consistently try to outdo the others by coming up with new songs or gimmicks to keep audiences hyped. During the mid-1980s, with "Go-Go Live" shows at the Capital Centre, bands worked hard on their sets, looking for surprises and new hooks to excite the audience.

In both the House of Prayer and the go-go, there are always bands that represent the second tier. These groups constantly strive for recognition and work hard to improve their status. During the mid-1990s the second-tier bands in the House of Prayer included the Madison Hummingbirds, from Portsmouth, Virginia; The Sounds of Zion and the Angels, both from Charlotte, North Carolina; and the Bronx New Heaven Band, from Bronx, New York. These bands created innovative new sounds. Historically, the bands in the House of Prayer have played in the three keys: A-flat, B-flat, and C-sharp. Ronald L. Stephenson (a member of the McCollough Invaders Band of New York) notes that these keys are the most comfortable for brass musicians. As a result, many of the bands transposed most of their songs to these keys. The second-tier groups, however, began to explore other keys, especially E-flat, E major, F major and F-sharp. This innovation allowed musicians in the House of Prayer greater avenues of expression and an expanded repertoire. Today, the Sons of Thunder (Charles C. Stephenson, Jr., played in this band as a teenager) still receive respect and support for their reputation as the most skilled senior band in the House of Prayer.

Meanwhile, in the go-go community, the influence of contemporary music dictated a changing of the guards. With the exception of Rare Essence and Chuck Brown and the Soul Searchers, the most popular bands fell from the top and were replaced by newer bands: Junk Yard, Northeast Groovers, and Backyard. These new-school bands brought a style that was much different and "less musical" than E.U. or Trouble Funk, who were now the elder statesmen of the go-go circuit.

While the foundation of go-go is driven by the percussionists, who establish the beat, in the House of Prayer, the shout bands' music is root-ed in the spirit and the inspiration is drawn from God. These bands emphasize three-part harmony made up of baritone, first tenor, and sec-ond tenor lines all pulled together. Call and response is used within the band as the lead trombone player feeds off the entire ensemble, creating a spiritual journey (a shout) that is key to Pentecostal religions but absent from go-go.

The House of Prayer musicians of today are more versatile than their fathers or uncles for one basic reason: they now study music theory. By increasing their knowledge and skill, they have expanded their musical horizons, becoming even better craftsman. Once, shout band musicians played solely from the heart and the spirit, but today, their natural talent and the power of the Holy Ghost is combined with formal music study.

ANATOMY OF A GO-GO PERFORMANCE

To really understand and appreciate go-go, you have to get down and get funky. But since most of you readers will be unable to hear Junk Yard perform "Ruff-It-Off" at Deno's on a Thursday night or enjoy Chuck Brown steaming the crowd with "Back It On Up" during a Saturday night gig at the Legends Night Club, let's wend our way to a go-go, summer of 2000 style. The venue is the 9:30 Club in Northwest D.C. It's August 4, 2000, and E.U., Trouble Funk, and Chuck Brown share a dynamic triple billing. It is an uncommon opportunity to hear three of D.C.'s finest in one night at one place.

It's midnight and the temperature is unseasonably cool for August. The 9:30 Club, which usually books white rock acts as wide-ranging as Guided By Voices, Karl Denson's Tiny Universe, The Pretenders, They Might Be Giants, Queensryche, Lords of Acid, and Cowboy Junkies, hosts African American acts regularly but infrequently. Maceo Parker usually shows up twice a year and they do go-go double and triple bills several times a year as well. The enthusiastic and knowledgeable crowd has grown large enough that moving near the stage requires considerable effort. Everyone wants to be up close when the "Godfather of Go-Go," the music's acknowledged progenitor and a savvy showman, Chuck Brown takes the stage.

"Wind me up, Chuck!" chants the crowd over and over again as Mr. Brown ambles around the stage slapping and grasping outstretched hands. The hands and fists are already in the air, waving and appealing to Chuck for recognition, much in the style of West Africans who encourage their musicians to a higher level with these salutes. Gathering requests for "Run Joe," "Go-Go Swings," "Bustin' Loose," and "Woody Woodpecker" written on WKYS-FM paper fans, napkins, and scraps of paper, Chuck smiles and carefully places the papers on his guitar amplifier. Most folks in the crowd know that their requests are superfluous—they are standards and form the core of his live performances—they are sure to hear these and many more familiar tunes from the master's repertoire.

Brown takes the stage as the closing act in this tri-part go-go extravaganza. It is unusual for three such powerful and well-known bands to play one venue on the same night, and the troops (die-hard fans) are out in force. The starting time is also early; sometime between 11:00 P.M. and midnight is a more typical hour for go-go to begin bouncing. The time allotted for the sets (E.U. from 9:15 P.M. to 10:00 P.M., Trouble Funk from 10:15 P.M. to 11:15 P.M., and Chuck Brown from 11:30 P.M. to 12:45 A.M.) is optimistic and the short sets mean that the bands must come out crankin' if they are to catch the crowd's attention.

E.U. opens the gig, playing a solid set from 9:30 P.M. to 10:15 P.M. Sugar Bear, as usual, holds forth on bass and lead vocals. He fronts the band and his singing on "E.U. Freeze" and several other songs that contain passing musical references to "Da' Butt" are the highlights of the set. Ju Ju, a chocolate-skinned, slightly built but strong man, anchors the band from behind his drum kit, thrashing his well-trained and experienced arms and hands. Possessed by the beat, Ju Ju swiftly and efficiently mesmerizes the crowd. He's a true powerhouse behind his drum kit, and is the first of the musicians that night to be the direct recipient of the hands held aloft (as they so often are in West Africa), swaying with the rhythm and paying homage to a particularly moving musical moment. Go-go patrons are not just slaves to the rhythm; they acknowledge a masterful passage or performance by pointing and waving their hands directly at the musician producing it. Tonight, E.U. is assisted by Tony "Too Sharp," the Legends' regular conga player, who adds to the manic drive supplied by Ju Ju.

By 10:00 P.M. the large dance floor is filled with mostly black American patrons (roughly equal parts male and female), though white faces form a noticeable minority in the crowd. And these white folks seem to be familiar with the music—many of them shout out requests and some even know how to shake their butts in a way that places them in the mainstream of their fellow groovers. Because of its location and reputation, white patrons attend the 9:30 Club's go-go bills in greater numbers than any other venue in town. A crowd with so many white fans would really raise eyebrows at Deno's, but at the 9:30 Club it is the high percentage of black patrons that is out of the ordinary!

While the crowd waits patiently for Trouble Funk to begin (a child care snafu causes them to come on at around 10:45 P.M.), old-school go-go blasts over the club's sound system. After one false start, the band assembles on stage and runs through a quick sound check. It is difficult to miss Big Tony Fisher, Trouble's massive (about six feet six inches and around 300 pounds) bass player, vocalist, and raconteur. He's a veteran of the go-go scene and provides some of the most powerful singing that you'll ever hear at a go-go club. His towering presence onstage was the highlight of the live performances in *Good to Go*. You know that Trouble Funk is old-school when the band's trumpet and trombone players get up on stage and warm up by playing the bridge to Dizzy Gillespie's "Night In Tunisia"! They are quickly joined onstage by no less than three percussionists, lead guitarist Chester Davis along with keyboardists Robert Reed and James Avery. After only about five minutes of warm up, Trouble Funk is ready to rock the house with a blend that is uniquely go-go but gives strong nods to James Brown, Tower of Power, and George Clinton.

Ten of Washington's (actually, Oxon Hill, Maryland's!) finest keep the patrons bouncing for nearly one hour as Trouble Funk drops the bomb on the Southeast crew, gets "small," and even gives us a taste of "Trouble Funk Express." In about 55 minutes they go through their (and the crowd's) best-known numbers, as tight as a wedding band on a hot summer night. They acknowledge some of their fans: "Tanesha's in the house tonight, everything's gonna be alright, she came to boogie, she came to boogie, y'all! Willie's in the house tonight, everything's gonna be alright; he came to boogie, he came to boogie, y'all!" Their set is one continuous medley of tunes, with individual selections lasting between 8 and 15 minutes depending upon the crowd's level of interest and energy. The band is both hot and crankin' tonight, about as good as we've ever heard them. Big Tony is the band's leader on stage and he moves them through their paces with an ease and grace that belies his size. Trouble Funk represents old school go-go at its best; the band is exceptionally well rehearsed without sounding stale, tired, or contrived. All of its original members are still with the band (after nearly 20 years) and they clearly enjoy playing this packed hall located only a few blocks southwest of Howard University in Northwest. Although Trouble Funk mostly plays in D.C., they still tour regularly (occasionally overseas) and their next out-of-town gig is about one month away in Richmond, Virginia.

Before Chuck and his fellow Searchers come on stage, Go-Go Rudy from WKYS addresses the crowd: "Who listens to the go-go show on KYS on Sunday nights?" He plugs not only the station but also his 1 ½-hour show, one of the few of its kind on local airwaves and the only one to routinely play selections by the more long-running, established bands like those playing tonight. The crowd seems to understand and appreciate Rudy's point—plenty of 'em pump their fists and chant "yeah" at just the right time.

Both E.U. and Trouble Funk are first-class, long-established go-go bands, but Chuck Brown is the acknowledged master. His set is paced like that of a highly trained prizefighter at the top of his game. Completely in touch with his crowd, Brown turns up the heat when he wants to, but even when he is not in overdrive, the "Godfather of Go-Go" keeps the music flowing. Brown turned 66 (or is it 67?—Chuck won't tell!) in the fall of 2000, but he retains the grace and vigor of a much younger man. His band is small—keyboards, trumpet, tenor sax, bass, percussion, and drums (Ju Ju again!)—with Chuck supplying the vocals and electric guitar. They are obviously well rehearsed and completely at ease with Brown's eclectic repertoire, which this August night includes Muddy Waters's "Mannish Boy" and "Moody's Mood For Love" in addition to the requests that Chuck has already acknowledged.

In many ways, Chuck Brown's 9:30 Club set typifies go-go in the new millennium. He plays to the accompaniment of "the beat," but also incorporates other genres of African American music, such as jazz, blues, and funk. This is not so different from the way another—much younger—of D.C.'s most popular groups, Backyard Band, looks to hip-hop for its inspiration. At the 9:30 Club tonight, the overwhelmingly African American audience, most of whom fall into the 20–40-year-old category, knows the music and the performers well. They know how to move and pump their fists—how to behave in this musical and social context. Most importantly of all, they support go-go by coming out to hear it live (the only way to fully appreciate it); they show up and stay until the end. By 1:30 A.M. (very early by go-go standards), the show is over and it's time to go outside into the pleasantly cool night.

SONGWRITING

No matter what level of industry support go-go enjoys, it is always supported by D.C.'s black American community. Go-go survives through a combination of gritty determination, a long history of entrepreneurship, and a strong sense of artistic expression, as well as a large dose of mother wit. But it is also held back in its search for more widespread commercial success—both locally and nationally—by several important, interrelated factors.

As mentioned earlier, even in go-go's hometown, it is rarely heard on the radio. This is a serious problem. The usual caveat is that most go-go performances are too long to play on the radio. In our twenty-first-century world, where few musical selections are more than three minutes long (this statistic actually goes back to the era of the 78 rpm record!), go-go performances really do seem to go on and on and on. But as Junk Yard and E.U. demonstrated with "Sardines" and "Da' Butt," it is possible for go-go to garner airplay with the right song.

The fact that a few go-go tunes have received major airplay underscores the importance of the songs performed by go-go groups. Original songwriting is one of the hallmarks of go-go. Listen to any go-go performance (either live or recorded) and you quickly realize that most of the songs are original, written by the entire band or by individual band members. For example, most Trouble Funk material is written and arranged by keyboardist Robert Reed and bass player Tony Fisher. The writing credits on the Huck-A-Bucks Band & Show's *Chronic Breakdown* attribute all but one of the album's 12 selections to "Roy Battle, Joseph Timms, Ricky Yancy and the Huck-A-Bucks." Backyard takes this cooperative, even socialistic spirit to an extreme by attributing its selections to BYB on most of its compact disc releases.

The exception to this rule is Chuck Brown, of course. A more experienced and versatile musician than most other go-goers, Brown casts a wider net than any of his peers. Brown's own musical roots and personal aesthetics reach far back beyond funk and soul to encompass blues and jazz. A typical Brown set, which is reflected on the *Chuck Brown: Greatest Hits—Back It On Up* compact disc (Raw Venture VPA007-2), mixes original material such as the proto-go-go anthems "Bustin' Loose" and "We Need Some Money" with songs from outside of the go-go mainstream. Even more than blues (T-Bone Walker's "Stormy Monday" and Muddy Waters's "Hootchie Coochie Man" form the core of his blues covers), Brown is attracted to jazz. Specifically he likes the "standards" in the jazz repertoire, most of which were written between 1930 and 1960 and can be heard at jazz clubs and piano lounges around the world. He draws upon D.C. native and musical genius Duke Ellington for his idiosyncratic performances of "It Don't Mean A Thing (If It Don't Have The Go-Go Swing)," and he often includes such warm and comfortable chestnuts as Rodgers and Hart's "My Funny Valentine" and Fields, McHugh, and James Moody's "Moody's Mood For Love."

Go-go performances are usually non-stop, but a Chuck Brown performance stands apart in ways other than just repertoire. Most bands— from E.U. to Backyard Band—construct their sets with lengthy performances of individual songs bridged by percussion segments. The percussion interlude is sometimes accompanied by speech, rapping, or some other form of verbalizing. Chuck's sets follow the same general format, but he constructs an evening's performance more like a suite of songs than a mere series of tunes connected by the beat. This, too, is reminiscent of Ellington, whose extended works like "Black, Brown, And Beige" or "Such Sweet Thunder" are less well-recognized than many of his individual selections, many of which are now standards. One major difference, though, is that Ellington composed those pieces as longer works, while Brown puts individual selections together in a coherent manner. Nonetheless, Brown has a knack for putting together a set that adheres or flows more smoothly than any other go-go band.

Since go-go is largely percussion-driven and the bands are very interested in establishing a groove, the importance of the song lyrics is downplayed. Liaison Records's Tom Goldfogle points out that because they are focused on the live performances that remain their bread and butter, most go-go bands under-emphasize songwriting, especially as it relates to the matter of singles and radio airplay on commercial outlets: "I don't think the bands write material for singles. I don't think the bands are focused on such issues. Chuck would be an exception and I think that Rare Essence would be an exception [though] they may not be thinking singles, but they are crafting songs [particularly Donnell Floyd] and they *are* songwriters."[4]

The structures of most go-go songs are not very complex; they are usually built upon contrasting sections based on rhythmic shifts. They are often cast in a verse/chorus format, which encourages the band (and often the audience) to participate in the singing. "Bustin' Loose" by Chuck Brown follows this format; the chorus line of "I feel like bustin' loose, bustin' loose" is as well-known as any in the go-go world. Because many go-go performances consist of medleys, the individual selections (truncated from their usual length) essentially constitute sections. A case in point is Junk Yard's "Rippa Medley" from *Always in the Pocket,* which mixes four songs — "Block-Block," "One Leg Up," "Let The Beat Go," and "Uh Oh" — into one seamless 6:05 selection.

"Uh Oh" by Junk Yard presents an interesting case of the least complex but one of the most effective and widely used song structures in go-go. It begins with a syncopated cry that is repeated for eight bars. People speak, call out, and sing in many layers over the "Uh Oh" refrain. There is a short break (not quite long enough to call a B section) that is purely percussion before the vocalizing begins again and the song ends. Junk Yard uses a similar format in one of their other standards "Ruff-It-Off." The principal difference is a slightly longer and more instrumentally complex interlude; otherwise the structures of the two songs are virtually identical.

In a live performance, the exhortations to party and the cries of "Who's in the house?" remain critical elements, but they work less well when they are put on a recording. The downfall of go-go's writing is a lack of new material coupled with too many songs that lack a narrative drive — that tell a compelling (or even interesting) story, or at least develop a coherent story line. There are exceptions, of course. Rare Essence reminded the public of their songwriting ability in the late 1990s with such selections as "What Would U Do For The Money?," "Overnight Scenario," and "When The Beam Is On Your Head."

More often, though, the songs are breezy, often fun, but lyrically light-weight fare; for example the Huck-A-Bucks' "Who's Ready," "Tiddy Balls" by Junk Yard, or "Bounce To This" by Northeast Groovers. With their themes of grooving, sexual innuendo, partying, and an invitation to join in the good times, the songs represent the majority of original material performed by go-go bands, and they also reinforce the relationship between go-go and other, older forms of black American music. The various ties between go-go and hip-hop, funk, and soul are quite clear. The rowdy and uncomplicated partying spirit is displayed by a group like Pure Elegance when they suggest that you "put your one leg up and put your booty on the floor." On "Mandingo," All-N-1 implore their fellow go-go heads to "shake your hips to the left and to the right." Much of the rest of this selection is devoted to the recognition of community members who are in the house.

Outright sexuality is the theme of "Tiddy Balls," one of Junk Yard's most popular selections in the mid-1990s. It is performed not only with vigor but with a self-aware leer: "shake your titties up and down." This over-the-top song emphasizes the sometimes salacious nature of go-go. Go-go is rarely as misogynistic and mean as some of the tougher rappers (including Puff Daddy as well as the notorious white wannabe Eminem), who are often not only mean-spirited but cruel and nasty. Instead the sexuality in go-go performances is expressed in a more tongue-in-check manner, much like the older blues men like Blind Willie McTell or Frankie "Half-Pint" Jaxon, whose songs were laced with innuendo and sexual references rather than pliant or overtly profane statements.

Sexuality in go-go is also expressed by the crowd. Along with the raised hands that wave the band on and make signs representing certain sections of the city or crews, go-go music invites the crowd to move, shake, and throb. Go-go venues are often so tightly packed that it is difficult to move, and dancing is usually kept to a minimum. Perhaps inspired by songs such as "One Leg Up," "Bounce To This," and "Shake It Like A White Girl" the often young (under 30) patrons' dancing creates a salacious undercurrent. These and other songs are a call to not only come together but to celebrate your sexuality, which recalls earlier black music styles. In the late 1920s, pianist Clarence "Pine Top" Smith exhorted dancers in south side Chicago clubs to "dance that boogie woogie," and his fellow blues pianist Romeo Nelson suggested that after-hours club dancing was the time to "shake your fat fanny."

Because the majority of go-go band members and their fans live in similar circumstances, most go-go performances emphasize their commonalities. When Backyard's "My Block" alludes to the issues of hustling, the police, and the dreaded knock on the door by "the man," the band is speaking for their neighbors, friends, and family. Junk Yard's "The Word" is built around the problems of everyday life: ill-treatment at the welfare office and the inability to sell an older car because of its poor suspension system. "Sardines"—"them funky things"—also by Junk Yard, further exemplifies the down-to-earth nature of go-go lyrics. This connection with their audience is largely accomplished through innuendo and inference, rather than a well-stated and lengthy narrative. For example, Carl Jones's "Movin' And Groovin'" implies that kids in the 'hood should "move" in constructive ways. The men (and they are almost always male) who write go-go songs know that their listeners understand these references without them having to go into detail and explain the problems and issues, because it is part of their daily lives.

Paradoxically, go-go songs only occasionally address great social issues or notable incidents within the black community. This is simply tangential to the go-go songwriting aesthetic. For example, the issues related to District City Council member Frank Smith's efforts in the late '80s to blame go-go for violence on the streets and his attempts to install curfews based on these claims were never directly addressed by the bands in song. Equally noteworthy, no go-go songs were written about the drug problems experienced by former D.C. mayor Marion Barry, neither his plight nor his subsequent renewal. These two issues represent very juicy topical material ripe for the go-go song spinners, but everyone passed on the opportunity. They were the buzz of the community but neither issue was addressed musically.

"D.C. Don't Stand For Dodge City" represents perhaps the only truly noteworthy exception to this observation. And it's an anomaly in another way because of the song's performance by an all-star group featuring Chuck Brown, Sugar Bear, Little Benny, and André Johnson, known as The GO-GO Posse. This topical 1988 song, written by Square One, J. Mitchell Bebbs, Jonathan R. Smith, and Darrell Johnson, decries the violence found on D.C.'s streets. Its stance is typified by the verse performed by Sugar Bear:

> Now in and of itself, crime is bad enough.
> But here's a major problem that we've got to snuff.
> These weapons seem to float around so easily,
> That it makes me wonder how it came to be
> That everyone is walkin' 'round the neighborhood
> With guns or knives and that ain't good.
> From high school deals to violent crimes
> And the final provocation known as homicide.

Junk Yard and Rare Essence, both of which really blossomed in the late 1980s, remain two of the only bands in the city that regularly write songs with social commentary. People may come to party with them, but they can also contribute wry and pointed commentary about what they see around them. In the late 1980s, D.C. grooved to "The Word," Junk Yard's reproval of President Reagan's redirection of funds to the defense industry at the expense of social welfare programs. More recently, RE asked the question "What Would U Do for the Money?," asking their audience to think about what they might do to make ends meet. Both bands occasionally address some of the issues that they see around them: drugs, poverty, disenfranchisement, and the poor job opportunities in the 'hood.

SINGING AND VOCALIZING

Singing in go-go is also highly democratic, almost communal. Most groups feature a vocalist—Sugar Bear from E.U. and Buggs from Junk

Yard come to mind—but the band members share in the singing chores. Depending on the selection, the group might feature one of several vocalists, and most of the other group members participate in the ensemble singing. The ensemble singing is usually not precise or crisp, but it is emotional because the go-go aesthetic calls for the singers to chime in as the spirit moves them. Moreover, it is almost always in unison rather than two- to four-part harmony. The ensemble singing is also often punctuated by cries ("I can't hear you!?!?" or "Who you representing?") and exhortations to other band members as well as people in the audience. People join in as they get "the feeling." The call and response is not only between the audience and the band but also within and among the band members themselves. The cries of "yeah" ring out spontaneously as the band members improvise over the beat.

The vocalizing associated with go-go also displays ties with other, long-established older aspects of African American expressive culture. Junk Yard provides several good examples of this, many of which can be heard on their album *Junk Yard Reunion: Live At Martin's Crosswinds Ballroom* (JY2040-2). "Hee-Haw," a song about the band ("Let's go out to hear Junk Yard") calls to mind the tradition of black gospel quartets exhorting their listeners to come out to hear them. That well-established tradition was first documented on records by the Birmingham [Alabama] Jubilee Singers in 1926 on their performance of "Birmingham Boys" (Columbia D-14154). Another tie to older African American culture is the use of an animal imitation. The "Hee-Haw" of the title, sung by Buggs, recalls the importance of such imitations among black performers of the past. For example, the virtuoso fox chases performed and recorded by harmonica wizards such as Sonny Terry, Peg Leg Sam, and Freeman Stowers, whose 1929 Gennett recording "Sunrise On The Farm," consists of a monologue interspersed with animal imitations.

The opening of "Ruff-It-Off" is nothing less than a call to arms. It is a series of rough-and-tumble growls and howls by the band members that signal the listener: "Hey, pay attention, I'm fixin' to say something you should hear!" Shortly after the band has you sitting straight up and paying attention, they move into a contrasting B section. Its synthesizer wash, which has a gently understated and free rhythm reminds one of a quiet interlude in John Coltrane's "After The Rain" or "Welcome." With its rubato rhythm, the B section provides a striking relief from the heavy syncopation of most go-go selections. Three-quarters of the way through the piece the singers trade off the lead vocals in a manner reminiscent of the "hocketing" style of musical organization that is sometimes used by West African Pygmies. Near the end of the song, the band cries out to the audience "Remember me, remember me." It's as though they had reinterpreted and recast Jesse Jackson's cry of "I am somebody!"

REPRESENTING FOR D.C.

"Representing" is an important part of the expressive culture at a live go-go program, and it is integrated into each performance. Representing is also highly symbolic. Olympic athletes wear the colors of their country and celebrate winning a medal by parading around with their national flag, while some football players celebrate a particularly inspiring touchdown by spiking the ball or dancing in the end zone. Black Americans, in particular, celebrate public events with special vigor and creativity. The very act of calling out precise locations and neighborhoods brings specific attention to D.C. This naming ceremony usually calls out sections of the city that remain unknown to most tourists and would remain forbidden territory even if they had heard of them. The same process also calls out to specific individuals from D.C., Maryland, and Virginia, permitting the bands to highly particularize their comments and observations. It is a very important personal touch that means a lot to the people in the audience and to the bands as well.

Of course, shout-outs are not unique to go-go and D.C.; they are also part of hip-hop culture. Some scholars suggest that they are tied to the Jamaican practice that expresses public appreciation and respect for people attending a musical event.[5] This might be the case in D.C. (the Caribbean community is large and well-established enough), but the practice also seems to be tied to the church practice of recognizing members—and their deeds—from the pulpit.

Liaison Records's *Always in the Pocket* compilation opens with an introduction by WPGC-FM personality DJ Celo, one of the only local radio personalities who mixes go-go with hip-hop. Celo's the master at mixing go-go live on the air. His invocation—"Coming to you live, I said live from the Capital City, it's the Supa Funkregulator, DJ Celo, representing for D.C., Maryland, and Virginia, East Coast, West Coast, everybody. . . . I'm about to put it down on the one and two for the phat go-go mix. If you don't know about the go-go, keep your ears locked, 'cause we about to school [you]!"— typifies the strong identification that he, and so many others whose voices we don't have the opportunity to hear, has with go-go, black culture, and D.C.

The roll call, most often initiated with the oral formula "Who's in the house?," remains a staple of a go-go performance. This call and response is transformed into the printed word in the liner notes of compact discs in the form of printed shout-outs. These are public announcements of support and thanks for support in the past, and they are repeated until the band recognizes a long series of individuals and crews in the house representing for different sections of the city. These long roll calls underscore the fact that go-go thrives on repetition in both word and rhythm.

Calling the roll (another example of public display) is the job of the band's "lead talker." The lead talker fulfills an important role in a go-go band. He demonstrates his ability to communicate not simply by reciting a litany of names, but through his rhyming skills, his judgment of when to place each name in the roll, and the timing of the display within a go-go performance. Big Tony of Trouble Funk, for example, is quite adept at recognizing people in the house during the course of a song like "Who We Goin' Put On Display," which is usually performed at or near the beginning of a Trouble Funk set.

The role of the lead talker is not limited to the verbal—it's also a physical act. He serves as the main interlocutor between the folks on stage and those in the pits. When Ghengis of Backyard Band shouts out "Put your hands in the air, shake them like you just don't care!," his exhortation is accompanied by gestures echoed by the audience. He's signaling the other participants to join him in a visual call and response as a sign of solidarity that helps to unite everyone in the house. This motif is repeated throughout a go-go show and has become one of its essential elements.

In its use of a lead talker, go-go is similar to ju ju. Ju ju refers to contemporary bands in West Africa, many of them from Nigeria, performing popular music that is as percussion-driven as go-go. Like go-go, ju ju is perceived to be lower class (blue collar at best) music, and many of its patrons are "clerks, traders...and laborers."[6] One of the differences between the two kinds of music is in the percussion: go-go is conga-based, while ju ju bands utilize the talking drums. Another minor difference is that ju ju bands usually perform in local beer gardens also called hotels that serve as a combination "tavern, dance hall, and brothel"[7] rather than in venues like the clubs in D.C. In addition to performing at local beer gardens, ju ju bands most often perform in a specific cultural ceremony called an *ariya*. A wedding or the start of a new business would be two occasions for an ariya.

The hours during which go-go and ju ju are performed clearly indicate a similar impulse. Chris Waterman writes:

> Ju ju performances begin in earnest around 10:00 or 11:00 P.M.... The music continues for six or seven hours, with only one or two pauses. The momentum of the celebration must be maintained, so that guests do not lose interest... and leave for home.... A ju ju performance begins with an instrumental introduction, during which initial adjustments in aural balance are effected. The captain sings solo phrases... segments of which are harmonized by the chorus. He also initiates extended call... and response sections.... The song texts performed by leader and chorus are complemented by surrogate speech phrases played on talking drums or, to a lesser degree, guitar, bass guitar, or congas.[8]

Ju ju bands are typically not paid as such; they are rewarded by the people they place on display, who compensate them individually. Most of the time these people literally walk up and pin money on the musicians in a ritual known as "spraying." This ritual can only be performed while the musicians are playing, and it provides the musicians with most of what they earn by playing. Spraying comes in spurts, sometimes in response to particularly moving musical passages. Hosts who throw exceptionally lavish ariyas are also sometimes similarly honored. Chris Waterman carefully points out that hosts are sprayed "to show generosity. Individuals suspected of throwing parties in order to exploit their guests are scrupulously shunned."[9] A similar ceremony occurs occasionally in African American culture with gospel groups who are not paid for their performances, but are compensated by individual churchgoers, who walk up and place money in the musicians' hands or pin it to their clothing.

While both go-go and ju ju use talkers, they function in somewhat different ways. The talker for a ju ju band—known as the captain—finds out the names of prominent people who will be in attendance at the event, and over the course of a long ceremony he literally names these individuals as a way of paying homage. The information regarding the guests is sometimes supplied by the host, sometimes by the band's manager. The captain then speaks well of the guests using some of the same type of rather generic oral formulas that you would hear at any go-go.

Check Out Receipt

South Bowie Branch

www.pgcmls.info

Sunday, December 13, 2015 1:53:58 PM
46581

Item: 31268107159747
Title: The beat! : go-go music from Washington,
D.C.
Material: Book
Due: 01/03/2016

Total items: 1

*** Pick your holds up at South Bowie Window(SBW
)! Ask us how ***

611

Call and response is also part of the presentation of the captain, with the guest responding to the praise given during the ariya. According to Waterman, a successful ju ju performance exerts "pressure to join the dance, rock majestically up to the band, and initiate a spraying sequence..."[10] Our guess is that a visitor from Southeast D.C. would not understand the particulars of an ariya but that its spirit and the essential elements of ju ju would resonate with familiarity.

Back here in the United States, we are confident that a D.C. go-go fan would feel entirely comfortable at a small New Orleans club featuring one of the city's younger brass bands. The parallels between the two genres are strong. Both brass bands and go-go:

1. Are locally-based
2. Are male-dominated
3. Are performed by African American musicians
4. Favor call and response
5. Often perform late at night
6. Engender interaction between the band and audience

While you often find white patrons attending brass band performances in New Orleans, perhaps the most dramatic difference is that these brass bands enjoy greater recognition outside of the Crescent City than go-go does outside of Washington, D.C. The new generation of brass bands, which has enjoyed a renaissance since the mid-1980s, has received attention across the country, and groups such as the Dirty Dozen Brass Band and Rebirth Brass Band routinely perform in Europe as well. Moreover, some of these bands have recorded for large independent labels like Rounder Records and it is easier to find brass band recordings than go-go recordings in record stores throughout the United States.

The go-go bands know they need to place folks on display, but not because they will be directly compensated—this will come indirectly through the paid admission to the go-go. The bands follow the roll call because it has evolved as part an oral tradition tied in with the event. Placing people on display or calling the roll is an important element of a go-go and the bands certainly understand its significance. They want to not only acknowledge their audience, but also sometimes to pay homage to the city itself, and finally, to women. Here's an excerpt from a Pure Elegance performance of that quasi-macho anthem "Mighty Mouse":

> Before we go any further, I want to send this one out to
> all my soldiers from the east side, the Southeast side of

the river. Then I want to take it on over to the north. The Northeast side of the river. Just take it uptown, man. To all my sexy ladies out there, you always got a Mighty Mouse in your life. It's no bullshit.

Talkers determine who to place on the roll call based on two factors. The first is who they expect to be there; then they look around to see who is actually in attendance. A good talker also has a message in addition to the roll call itself: he might impart such important information as the band's next gig—just to make certain that at least some of their troopers will show up. Sometimes the talker will send out a public service message like "use a condom" or "don't drive if you've been drinking alcohol." Over the years, Chuck Brown and, more recently, James Funk have become the acknowledged masters of go-go talk. Many believe that Buggs from Junk Yard is among the best of the second generation of talkers, while others think that Ghengis from Backyard is the best of the talkers to emerge in the '90s. As long as no one "ruffs-it-off," the gig will be good.

Sometimes talkers display a distinctive sense of humor in their discourse. This seems to be particularly true of some of the younger groups. Here is a brief example by Optimystic Tribe's talker during the course of "One Way Ticket To Hell." It is quite fun-loving, both in its wordplay and in the sense of parody:

It's for the 1-411 crew. My man, Pat Boone, he's in the room. Pat Boone, hey Pat Boone. Guess who stepped in the room? Also for my dawg, OT. Hey 411 Crew, the family's forever. The 411 Crew can get it together, you'all. What's up G Street? What's up G Street crew? Freak Daddy, riding in a Caddy.

Instead of being shouted out from the bandstand, the names are transferred to print as a roll call. The locally produced Big City Record Empire release of the *GO Ju Ju GO* album by E.U. (BCR-0011) from the late 1980s includes not only a "Special Thanks To" section but a "Roll Call" that includes "Landover Hustlers, Seat Pleasant Crew, Uptown Georgia Ave. Crew NW, Glenarden Crew, Dunbar, Coolidge, and Bowie State." Any resident of the D.C. area will recognize these locations and can easily identify the last three as local schools. Physical Wonders' *Return of Da Phyz* (PA1022-2) from 1996 thanks dozens of people in a list that's as local and down-home as one could imagine. Their shout goes out to producer "Reo Edwards, Stan's Skateland, everyone at Dairy Queen" as well as other bands in addition to "D.J.'s Cool, Flexx, [and] QMA." Their notes close with this emotional cry: "P.S. Keep the beat going D.C., if not ours, then any other band. As long as it's from the City."

Along with the public acknowledgments, these notes underscore not only the sense of place—the identification with the District of Columbia and the other members of the go-go community—felt by the bands, but also suggest the cross-breeding and impact of hip-hop and DJs with go-go in the late 1980s and 1990s. As the 1990s unfolded go-go was increasingly willing to venture outside of D.C. to embrace music other than funk and its Godfather, James Brown.

Group names further reflect go-go's democratic presentation. With exceptions such as Chuck Brown, who leads the Soul Searchers, and Little Benny (Harley) and the Legends, go-go band names tend to downplay the individual in favor of group identity. A few of the bands, such as Northeast Groovers, Northwest Younguns, and Petworth—have chosen D.C.-specific names. The majority of them, however, have stuck with less distinctive and more generic names such as Experience Unlimited, Proper Utensils, Physical Wonders, Backyard, Ayre Rayde, and Huck-A-Bucks. This doesn't mean that posters for individual programs don't remind folks that such go-go stalwarts as Sugar Bear will be present or that a DJ like Kool will be performing. But the fact remains: go-go bands generally bill themselves above the individual talents.

The bands are quite happy to call attention to themselves in other ways, one of which is in the packaging of compact discs. The aforementioned *Junk Yard Reunion* release reminds people that the band was once a "Def Jam Recording Artist" as well as of its participation in the WAMMIES (the Washington Area Music Awards). It also clearly states that Junk Yard has appeared at such diverse venues as Wolf Trap Park, the Capital Centre, and the Black College Weekend Tour.

IT'S POLKA TIME!

Despite the fact that it is multilayered and highly syncopated, the rhythmic pattern of go-go serves much the same function as the 2/4 meter that underpins polka. Polka is usually played at a faster tempo than go-go—just over 100 bpm is about right for polka, whereas go-go feels comfortable in the high 70s. Polka also accents the second beat of the pulse, while there is a strong feeling of duple combined with triple meter in go-go, with the accents falling at some very unexpected points. The rhythmic underpinnings of polka and go-go (and disco, for that matter) permit performers to adapt many songs to their genres.

Despite all of the obvious differences, listening to Chuck Brown reminds one of polka music. You can successfully play almost any song to the 2/4 polka beat; this has been done in many "ethnic" (many of them Eastern European) communities around the United States by artists as diverse as Lawrence Welk, "Whoopee John" Wilfahrt, Lil' Wally, and the masterful pop music satirist, "Weird Al" Yankovic. It is no coincidence that "Weird Al" is a third-generation Pole, learned accordion at an early age, and includes selections such as "Polka Your Eyes Out" and "The Alternative Polka" on his brisk-selling and very clever albums. Similarly, Chuck Brown—the master of adaptation in go-go—demonstrates that you can make almost any song into a go-go piece by placing the beat behind it. Witness his versions of T-Bone Walker's "Stormy Monday Blues," the standard "Misty," and Louis Jordan's chestnut "Run, Joe," as well as his take on Stevie Wonder with "Boogie On Go-Go Woman." It works!

In the world of Chicago polka music, Eddie Blazonczyk and the Versatones are the equivalent of Chuck Brown and the Soul Searchers, and you can substitute Happy Richie and the Royalaires or the Krew Brothers for Trouble Funk and E.U. They are not only the progenitors of a local vernacular musical style, they are part of a close-knit community. On that August 2000 night at the 9:30 Club, several people wanted their birthdays acknowledged. Both Trouble Funk and Chuck Brown were only too happy to oblige. Brown even went a step further, incorporating all of the birthday requests into a long version of "Happy Birthday," then mentioning that his own 66th birthday was coming up in that fall. Of course, there were the usual shout-outs for folks in the house and crews representing their neighborhoods. One can easily imagine similar greetings of recognition coming from the stage of Mickie's Hall where—when he's not on tour—Eddie Blazonczyk brings out his troopers in force!

DOWN WITH THE KING

Go-go is associated with late night clubs, booty-shakin' "honies," and the secular world in general. However, the sub-genre of gospel go-go has been part of the community since the 1980s. Instead of playing at the Ibex or the Legends Night Club, gospel go-go is heard at churches and church-related events throughout the Metro region. The fall 2000 itinerary of one of the area's most active bands—the Submission Gospel Go-Go Band— included an October 1 fundraiser to help support the Cheer Explosion All Star Cheerleaders trip to Las Vegas for the Cheerleaders National competition, an October 27 "Youth Explosion" at the Israel Baptist Church, and a performance at Ebenezer AME's young men's retreat in Leesburg, Virginia, on November 10.

Gospel go-go groups are dedicated to promoting the word of God through music—they form a music ministry with a distinctive D.C. beat. According to their mission statement, Submission Gospel Go-Go Band wants to "create an atmosphere where young people can have the opportunity to have fun, fellowship, and hear the message of the gospel of Jesus Christ along with affording them the opportunity to give God praise in their own way." The band consists of "ten Christian young men with an ear, mind, and soul for ministry. Their music is a combination of an urban go-go sound and uncompromised Gospel message." In the past the band has not only performed for local churches and youth ministries but at the BET Gospel Explosion at Paramount's Kings Dominion, located about one and one-half hours south of D.C.

THE INTERSECTIONS OF GO-GO AND RAP

Hip-hop artists first paired up with go-go bands in the early 1980s. Kurtis Blow was one of the first rappers to come into the go-go fold. Local writer Jeff Zeldman noted that "Blow, America's leading rapper...calls go-go 'a revelation.' He put his money where his mouth was when he brought in Experience Unlimited to back him on his recent 'Party Time' release."[11] The 1987 Trouble Funk album *Trouble Over There* (Island 90608-1) not only includes Blow, but also the master of the funk bass, Bootsy Collins. Despite the *Good to Go* debacle, Trouble Funk maintained their ties to Island Records and *Trouble Over There* has to be one of the best-distributed go-go albums. Its downfall, however, is that the record is over-produced and includes a large contingent of musicians from outside of the mother ship, D.C. It is not a horrible record, but *Trouble Over There* is not only faceless, it's not really go-go. The female chorus on "New Money" (produced by Bootsy Collins) and the album's Euro-tech, highly processed percussion simply sounds out of place. The Kurtis Blow–featuring "Break It Up" comes across as rather generic funk-based rap. All told, *Trouble Over There* lacks the energy of a good go-go record, is largely devoid of the distinctive rhythmic attack and complexities demanded by a critical go-go audience, and simply sounds too synthesized.

Although the mix between hip-hop and go-go was rather uneasy at the beginning, some elements of hip-hop have become part of the go-go aesthetic. The use of lead vocalists who rap—like Buggs of Junk Yard—rather than sing more melodically—like Chuck Brown—is quite acceptable in the early twenty-first century. A newer, younger band like Jigga not only features a lead rapper, but is pared down to an essential unit of multiple percussion supported by a synthesized keyboard. The fact that Jigga and Backyard eschew lead guitarists and horn players reflects the shift away from instruments that characterizes so much of contemporary hip-hop. But the fact that these bands continue to perform songs that identify with D.C. and employ a battery of live percussionists who still maintain "the beat" flies in the face of mainstream hip-hop and rap artists.

DJs have appeared on many of the compact discs released by go-go bands since the mid-1990s. Their role is a curious one. They don't rap, per se, rather they serve as interlocutors, voices that tie together the selections on the compact disc. This occurs largely in the studio, even on records that were recorded "live." It is perhaps best illustrated by a Liaison compilation called *Supa Funkregulator Celo Presents... 'Always in the Pocket'—The Best of D.C. GO-GO Volume 3* (L 1228-2). This collection, which includes selections by All-N-1, Pure Elegance, Junk Yard, Northeast Groovers, Backyard, and Huck-A-Bucks, contains studio and live selections recorded in clubs in and around D.C., but also "vocal drops." These pithy spoken interludes are provided by 15 individuals ranging from DJ Flexx, Big Chris, and DJ Rico to Jas. Funk and Chuck Brown, and are mixed in as part of the post-production process. Like a sensitive percussionist, the drops added punch to the selection. They also add another sonic dimension to the songs and reinforce that go-go is D.C. music with its roll call and shout-outs.

DJ Celo (a jock at urban powerhouse WPGC) also mixes hip-hop and go-go live on the air during his popular show. The "Supa Funkregulator" is a homeboy who grew up with go-go. His work on *Always in the Pocket,* consisting of remixing and scratching (providing both the rhythmic drive and slightly out-of-synch repetition associated with the style) previously existing recordings and adding the vocal drops, reflects his radio persona and style. The vocal drops represent yet another example of the importance of shout-outs in go-go, and their contribution typifies this aesthetic. This mix also underscores another of the truths of go-go in the early days of the twenty-first century—it not only emphasizes "the beat" but the fact that contemporary go-go bands are looking for a sound collage that flows from one song to another.

In a live performance, bands accomplish this simply by maintaining the beat while the lead talker facilitates the switch from one selection to another. A go-go mix by Celo (whose style and approach still represent a minority within the go-go community) that is released on a compact disc re-emphasizes specific references through repetition. His remix of Pure Elegance's "One Leg Up" reinforces the song's refrain as well as several of the timbale breaks. The vocal drop by James Funk (on this particular selection) reminds us this is not your father's go-go, but a post-hip-hop version. Celo's seamless mix from this track to the next selection, "Hey Ho" by Northeast Groovers, is accomplished by matching up very similar rhythmic patterns. During the course of "Hey Ho" the Supa Funkregulator emphasizes the ritual of go-go by his repetitive use of the spoken phrases "That's a pocket for ya!" and "Let's clap your hands, everybody!" It is an interesting live performance mixed through the filter of the technology and sensibilities of a new century.

Rappers (D.C.-style) are part of D.C.'s go-go scene, though only in the new-school bands such as Junk Yard and Pure Elegance. Go-go rappers generally perform as singers first; rapping remains a secondary—though important—role for most of them. Rapping is clearly subordinate to singing in go-go bands; its funk (with soul touches) roots are difficult to replace entirely with hip-hop aesthetics. There are several notable rappers in go-go: Ghengis and James Funk come most immediately to mind, but Lawrence West (better known as "Maniac") stands out as one of the more colorful, entertaining, and inventive singer-cum-rappers in D.C.'s go-go scene.

West first emerged as a member of the Peacemakers back in the '80s, before moving on to Rare Essence, the Groove Masters, the Legends, and then to A Touch of Essence. In 2000 he reinvented himself once again as the leader of Maniac & The Soldiers. Having played at places as diverse as the Cave Yard and the Howard Theater, he has performed at nearly every go-go venue in town. Ms. Mack got him into Rare Essence when they were short a singer. Lawrence West became "Maniac" based partly on his reverence for local DJ "Maniac" McCloud and also on his own unpredictable and zany stage presence: "I'm crazy...in a good way. I will try anything on stage if I think people will like it."[12]

Indeed, Maniac is known in D.C. as a rapper with a proclivity for simple yet memorable rhymes who emerged in the late 1980s. Maniac himself describes his rhymes as "hooks," implying that they are as important and integral as a melody or a line from a text that sticks in your memory. Some are closely tied to funk and hip-hop jargon: "We want you movin'—we want you really groovin'!" or "If I see y'all freakin' in the freakydeek zone...." Others, such as "What do you do when you're home doing nothing?," stand as entertaining and thoughtful nonsense. [13] All are delivered with Maniac's typical verve and flashy humor. The point is that go-go rappers do more than vocalize and help set fashion trends—they also sing and (in the case of Maniac) connect to the audience through their use of humor.

Not all of go-go's vibrancy and energy comes across via either P.A. tapes or compact discs. Go-go's power is dissipated in this transition. In order to really understand go-go, you need to experience the music in the context of a live performance, with bodies swaying and hands in the air, the drummer grooving the beat, the bass amp booming, and the lead talker communicating directly with the other participants. Only then can you feel the power and get it in your soul.

3 • Band Profiles

CHUCK BROWN: D.C.'S NATIONAL TREASURE

You cannot discuss go-go music without acknowledging the contributions of Chuck Brown. You cannot have an intelligent conversation about the origins of go-go without mentioning the contributions of Chuck Brown. And, finally you cannot even begin to talk about the incredible talent that Washington, D.C., has produced without adding Chuck Brown to that list. Washington, D.C.'s musical giants include Marvin Gaye, Duke Ellington, Mary Chapin Carpenter, and Me'Shell Ndegéocello. Throughout history Washington, D.C., has always been respected for producing great musical talents who had to leave the confines of home in order to find stardom. As a matter of fact, a criticism of Washington has been that entertainers could not make a living here and that you would have to leave in order to "make it."

Although many of the great talents did have to leave D.C. to find stardom, Chuck Brown not only found success at home, he moved to the nation's capital where he invented a new form of music. Known affectionately as the "Godfather of Go-Go," Chuck pioneered this music in the early 1970s. Since then he has released nearly a dozen albums and has won many local music awards. However, Chuck would probably say that his most satisfying rewards have been to contribute to his community and to witness the growth of an art form for which he is largely responsible. Not only is Chuck Brown a valuable local resource, but he should also be recognized as a national treasure for his musical accomplishments. History is replete with arguments regarding who started other uniquely American musical styles such as jazz, the blues, and rock 'n' roll. The argument can be extended to include the development of rap and hip-hop, and many artists and individuals can be mentioned as the innovators of that form of music. You can assert that Afrika Bambaataa, or Grandmaster Flash, or Kurtis Blow, initially defined rap and then hip-hop. However, in Washington, D.C., most folks would answer the question, "Who started go-go?" with one name—Chuck Brown.

I feel blessed to have witnessed the growth of Chuck Brown. I was not in Detroit when the Motown sound was developed, nor was I in Memphis when the great singers like Al Green emerged from that city. I didn't live in Philadelphia during the height of the Philly Sound's popularity. But I did observe history being made right here in Washington, D.C., with Chuck Brown. It started in 1970 when I first heard Chuck Brown perform as the leader of the Soul Searchers at the LeGemma Ballroom on F Street in D.C. The Soul Searchers began their musical journey in 1968, and had evolved to become Chuck Brown and the Soul Searchers by 1972. On that night in 1970, the Soul Searchers took the stage and Chuck led them in song, playing a jazzy but funky guitar. They were playing the latest rhythm and blues songs with a precision and feeling that I had only witnessed once before—when I heard the Young Senators perform. But this evening belonged to the Soul Searchers, and the youthful, well-dressed audience was mesmerized by Chuck's band's musical mastery.

R&B DAYS

At the beginning of the '70s, the Soul Searchers were rated as the number two band in Washington behind the sizzling hot Young Senators. The Young Senators were riding high after the release of "The Jungle," which rose to number one on local and regional R&B music charts. As a result of "The Jungle," the Young Senators got an opportunity to meet Eddie

---

* This chapter was written primarily by Charles C. Stephenson, Jr.

Kendricks of the nationally acclaimed Temptations. Jimi Dougans, a leader of the Young Senators, recalled his meeting with Kendricks:

> I met Eddie Kendricks through an associate who recommended us to him as a potential back-up band. I was given Eddie's phone number and upon calling him I was surprised when he answered the phone. He later came out to hear us play at the Monday Night Go-Go at Bryne Manor Knights of Columbus Hall and he asked me whether or not the group would agree to back him up. I said yes without even talking with the guys.[1]

The fierce band rivalry between the Soul Searchers and the Young Senators eased only because the Young Senators accepted Eddie Kendricks's offer to tour with him after he left the Temptations. This was a golden opportunity for the Young Senators, but as a result of their departure on a world tour, Washington became the city that the Soul Searchers ruled.

During this period in Washington, "the go-go" meant the dance hall, party, or function. A case can be made that the first go-go band was actually Tommy Vann and the Professionals, who played the go-go circuit, including Bryne Manor. Jimi Dougans remembered: "Tommy Vann and the Professionals were an all-white band that played all-black music. They were the first band that I would call a go-go band. I know that blows your mind, but it is true. The first go-go band was white—now that's interesting."[2] In these early days, the music didn't have "the beat," but the bands were called go-go bands because they played at the go-go. Chuck Brown defined the early go-go: "The word 'go-go' has been around since the '60s, Smokey Robinson had the tune 'Going To A Go-Go' and it was more or less like a function. I was around with the Young Senators, Sidewinders, groups like Scacy and the Sound Service, The El Chorals, Tommy Vann and the Professionals."[3]

During the late '60s and early '70s, D.C.'s bands performed primarily Top 40 songs—covers of popular records played on the radio. Patrons would go to a go-go expecting to hear the latest tunes played professionally by various bands. Chuck commented: "Going all the way back to the other groups, we were go-go bands at the time, I would say, but we were doing like the Top 40. Original music wasn't incorporated at the time. We were doing all Top 40—as many Top 40 as we could possibly do in one night—25–30 songs."[4]

In tracing the development of go-go in Washington you must go back to the '60s. Live bands were always popular in this city; young adults would flock to clubs to see them perform. A group's popularity was based on their ability to best interpret and perform a Top 40 record that would drive the audience to dance all night long. These same bands would also perform at "cabarets" that were the centerpiece of social interaction. Various social clubs and civic organizations would utilize cabarets as a means of raising funds, and bands such as the Soul Searchers and the Young Senators became essential groups in this formula.

I believe it is very important to understand Chuck's connection with present go-go groups as well as with "old-school" bands of the past that paved the way for today's sound. Back in the early days, the competition between groups was tremendous. Each group worked seriously on developing its sound and fine-tuning its repertoire each week in order to maintain the audience's interest. The Soul Searchers came up with a device that would keep the audience dancing the night away by playing continuously, linking songs together. Chuck explained:

> It began to be continuous when I started dealing with the percussion. I left a group, the Los Latinos; I had been playing with them for a while. They were a Latin group that preferred funk. They gave me the idea of the percussion [bridge]. Between songs, bands used to stop and go into another song or talk to the audience. That was way back in 1964–65. I put my group together in '66 we rehearsed for about six months before we played anywhere and then we started playing in '67.[5]

There you have it; Chuck began developing what was referred to as "the beat" in '67 as a device to keep the audience dancing between songs. The first time I recall hearing "the beat" is when I first heard the Soul Searchers perform (in 1970) and Kim Boy was the drummer. I remember Kim Boy as a very skilled drummer who played a steady beat with precision and swing. Kim Boy would later set the standard for all drummers in Washington. He was not a showy drummer, but a very effective one who allowed the music to happen around him. As the drummer, he was the heart of the action.

So from the first time I heard the Soul Searchers I can recall that Kim Boy kept the group flowing. After a song was complete, Kim Boy would continue playing a beat that was similar to that played during the song. This "breakdown" would continue until Chuck would strum a tune on the guitar, which indicated that it was time to start a new song. During the percussion breakdown, Chuck would talk to the audience. He would acknowledge the presence of certain fans; he would give a shout-out for a birthday or even promote the next performance of the Soul Searchers. This talk or rap would later become a centerpiece of go-go, and it remains the visual and musical focus of each band's performance today, as Chuck himself observed:

> Later on, as it caught on as the years went on, we didn't stop between songs anymore to talk to the audience. We talked to them while the music was still playing, letting the percussion go on. And that way we had a chance to communicate and the audience gave us some ideas. Our fans would come up with some hooks and it ended up being "call and response." Back and forth you see. That's how that go-go started.[6]

It is very interesting to note that Chuck's musical influences are broad and diverse. Chuck is an admitted jazz and blues enthusiast. He considers gospel, the blues, and jazz to be his musical foundation. Chuck grew up listening to music of the '20s and '30s. He mentions Blind Boy Fuller and Bessie Smith as early musical influences. Like Art Blakey and the Jazz Messengers, The Soul Searchers have built a reputation for being a collection of the best professional musicians in town. The alumni of the Soul Searchers is a who's who among the music industry. Past Soul Searchers include: Ricky Wellman (a drummer who also played with Miles Davis); Donald Tillary (trumpet); and Hilton Felder (keyboards). The fact that Chuck could attract the best musicians around town was a testament to his ability to judge talent and to the respect that was shown for his leadership. The fact that talented musicians make up the band has been a key element in the continued success of the Soul Searchers.

LIFE PASSAGES

Chuck Brown's life passages are not unlike those of most African American males born in the Depression era. Born in Garysburg, North Carolina, in 1933, Chuck moved to Washington, D.C., when he was three years old from Gaston, North Carolina. While growing up he would return periodically to North Carolina where he picked cotton, plowed, and cut pug wood. Tired of farm life and of having to work very hard for little money, Chuck attempted to join the service when he was 13. Being too young to join the military, he instead had to settle for digging ditches in order to earn a living.

As a youth, Chuck had to tolerate the injustice and racism of that era. Because of his trying circumstances, he often found himself attracted to street life and attributes the lure of the streets to his personal growth and development. Chuck explained:

> Well, it comes from the streets, you know, like I'm an old ex-street kid. I grew up in the streets. I left home at the age of 13 and I tried to battle my way through life to find myself, you know. At that age, there isn't too much.... You got to go out there and experience it for yourself. No one is going to teach you, you know. So I've been through a lot of ups and downs, a lot of hard times as a kid. I've had all kinds of jobs; I even tried boxing for a few years. I was a pretty good sparring partner, could have been a contender.... [7]

Street life finally caught up with Chuck and he began to go in and out of penitentiaries for robbery. After joining the Marines at age 17 (a stint that lasted all of 11 months), Chuck was back on the streets and found himself in Lorton prison during the early 1950s. He was to serve four years in Lorton for assault with a deadly weapon, which ended up as murder because the guy he shot later died after six months in the hospital. Chuck maintains that he acted in self-defense. It was in Lorton that he reached back to his younger days—when he had played piano at the Mount Zion Holiness Church of God—and started playing the guitar. Chuck listened intently to Sister Rosetta Tharpe but described his early style as similar to that of the jazz guitarist Charlie Christian.

Chuck was obviously talented, and he delighted his fellow inmates and guards with his musical talents. He credits this period as being partly responsible for straightening out his life, saying: "A place like Lorton is not only a place, in terms of paying a debt to society, but it is designed to help one rehabilitate himself. That's what happened to me. I became an entertainer at Lorton, as far as hitting the stage—playing my guitar and making noise. I was encouraged by a lot of inmates, the officials and all. They gave me my parole . . . I played my way out of there. I got a job, got married, raised my kids and during that time I was playing a little music."[8]

It is now obvious why Chuck has such a touch with everyday people from all walks of life. The Soul Searchers for many years were the favorite band of the so-called hustlers and the fast crowd. This may have been because Chuck knew how to relate to the "brothers" on the street. He was one of them and had a feeling for what it took to entertain them. So during the '70s, Chuck ruled Washington, D.C.; after the Young Senators decided to leave D.C., the Soul Searchers inherited the throne as the top band and did not relinquish the title for a decade. They played as the top band in all of Washington's hot spots, including the Ebony Inn, Pitts Red Carpet Lounge, Masonic Temple, Panorama Room, Burgundy Room, Maverick Room, Club Lebaron, and LeGemma Ballroom.

SHORTY'S IN THE HOUSE TONIGHT!

Chuck built on his popularity to push his group further. He would use the fact that he had developed a loyal following to his benefit by recognizing his fans while he was playing, calling out, "Shorty is in the house tonight, say what!" or "We have Michelle from Southeast in the house this evening." This helped to further the group's popularity because people would flock to the go-go with the expectation of hearing their name shouted by Chuck.

Over the years it has always been evident that Chuck absolutely loves doing what he does. He now continues to play not because he has to, but because at age 67 he still loves to perform. At a Chuck Brown performance you will almost never see fighting or violence of any kind. During the period of increased violence in Washington, D.C., Chuck refused to play in the traditional go-go venues because of the high incidence of street violence. He would say that something was wrong with society when young people were preoccupied with violence and drug abuse. Because he believes the audience members are all his children, you could sometimes sense that Chuck felt partially responsible for what was happening at the go-gos. He made the following statement to describe the positive impact his music has on young people:

> It motivates them . . . puts something on their minds. It
> motivates them like the audience participation; it's a

family sort of thing—one great big happy family. While they're in, they're dancing; they don't have any fighting or violence. . . . Like I said before, in terms of getting a message in the music thing. If you play music and put the right kind of feel behind it—the kids will dance to it and then they begin to listen . . . listen to the lyrics and it tells a story. All the old classic songs . . . can be used in terms of the go-go feel. You keep the kids busy, keep their minds out of the fire, they don't have no reason to get into the negative thing that people have been talking about.[9]

As the Godfather he has treated all of his young the same. (When I say his young, I mean the go-go bands that can directly attribute their existence to his influence in some way or other.) As an example, Chuck was very generous in sharing himself with E.U. in the early years. I can recall Chuck allowing E.U. to open for him during one of his runs at the Panorama Room. Opening for the Soul Searchers at a go-go was like performing at the Apollo prior to a James Brown performance. Chuck did not have to give E.U. this opportunity, but he did. He would always take the time to talk with the group and share pointers on performing and the music business. I have always thought that Chuck picked Sugar Bear as one of his musical heirs in order to keep the groove going when he decides to retire from playing. Recently, Chuck said: "Sugar Bear was my little brother, man. He would open up for people like the Chi-Lites and the Ohio Players. That little boy, man, he used to rock the house. He was nothing but 16–17 years old then. The older he got, the better he got. So he was one of my motivators."[10]

Maybe he forgot that he was responsible for giving E.U. their first break, or perhaps it was insignificant to him because it was a natural way of life for him to help younger bands. He does, however, recall how he gave James Funk an early break:

James Funk got started because I had James playing records for me on my breaks. So finally I gave him a mike. I said, "James, talk to them cute little girls out there. Take this mike, boy." He took the mike and started talking. I said, "Speak clear, use good diction so that those girls can feel you. They want to feel you, son. Talk to them a bit." And he did. I said, "Keep this up and you'll end up on the radio one day." Where is James now? With me, still, and on WPFW.[11]

So through the years, Chuck did not have any reservations about sharing his knowledge and advice with fellow musicians. This is rare among musicians because of the competitive nature of the business. I believe that Chuck would revel in the idea that a band had replaced him in performing. I say this because all of his actions point to the fact that he feels he cannot leave the business because it is still a work in progress. If you talk to Chuck long enough you will come away with the understanding that he does not believe that bands today are performing at the level of the bands of the past. Chuck observed: "The purpose of the music has been defeated.... I don't know how to say it without offending other musicians, but where are the other bands? It's just noise out there. Some of these young [go-go] musicians have never learned to play their instruments."[12]

While Chuck does appreciate the fact that younger bands perform go-go music, he is also interested in spreading the style among more established musicians: "I've been working on it, trying to get a certain sound across and the other bands picked it up and I'm up and I'm hoping that it will spread among the old, famous musicians...classical artists."[13] He seems to feel that the link may be broken because groups today do not have a full understanding of go-go's roots.

We know that the current go-go bands are not as popular as the Soul Searchers were during their heyday, perhaps because there are so many more go-go groups than there were in Chuck's era. During the emergence of go-go only a few bands acted as innovators of the music. Although there was a plethora of groups who played at go-gos, there were only a few who played go-go music or "the beat." Today, a majority of the popular bands do indeed play go-go, perhaps resulting in poorer musicianship. Little Benny Harley responded to a question about the sound and future of go-go as follows:

But as far as other bands, the ones that say "hoo-ha, wuu-uuuh!" All that? That's nothing. You got to make music. People don't want to hear that. When you go up the East Coast, once you go cross Maryland, people are going to say, "Get that junk out of here. It don't make no sense.

You're not saying nothing. You're just talking and playing the beat. That's not go-go." Maybe to them, that's what they want it to be. That's why I started this group [The Legends of Go-Go]. Because I'm like...you all [killing] the go-go. And Chuck ain't going to be around forever.[14]

Through the years, the Soul Searchers released several top-selling records. Their first release was a 1971 album on the Sussex label entitled *We the People*. This release, which included guest vocals by Bill Withers, proved to be a modest success and is touted as the first go-go record, mostly because it was the Soul Searchers' first recording.

During the following two years Chuck looked for a sound. He was searching for the element that would bring what would become go-go together. He would continue to experiment at the go-gos themselves in order to see what would work on a live audience. In 1973, Chuck had finally come up with an approach that would become the basis for the new go-go sound. The release of "Blow Your Whistle" that year followed on the heels of a local craze—kids riding bicycles and blowing whistles. "Blow Your Whistle" successfully tapped into a local happening that helped to spur record sales. This was an important innovation because it was art imitating life, and it started a trend that spread throughout the go-go movement. Other bands also released records that reflected what was happening in the community or at go-gos. E.U., for example, released "E.U. Freeze," which represented a local go-go dance craze.

However, "Blow Your Whistle" was followed by the national hit, "Bustin' Loose," in 1979. "Bustin' Loose" emerged as the go-go national anthem, and the most popular go-go release to that date. "Bustin' Loose" was not only a local go-go smash, it was also a foot stomping, finger-poppin', and head shaking hit record across the nation. The record was number one on the *Billboard* rhythm and blues charts for over two months and also made a dent on the pop charts as a top 20 hit. This incredible success would eventually lead to the single going platinum and the album reaching gold status.

Because of the remarkable success of "Bustin' Loose," by late 1979 go-go was international in scope. This record was used on countless movies, television shows, and commercials. Today, the song is still periodically heard on television, and is played at least once a week on the now-popular old-school radio shows, such as the nationally syndicated Radio One program *The Tom Joyner Show*. "Bustin' Loose" raised the bar a few notches for other groups to follow. Chuck even re-recorded the song in 1996 for a national television advertising campaign for Black & Decker. In addition, Schlitz Malt Liquor licensed the original "Bustin' Loose" track for a national television and radio campaign. Chuck fondly remembers the development of "Bustin' Loose":

> I was uptight when I cut "Bustin' Loose." I was trying to figure out what to do. That was the disco era. Now, go-go started catching on in '76 over at the Maverick Room, and I played "Bustin' Loose" for two years before I cut it. I had to change a few drummers to get that tune like I wanted it, and I changed a few musicians to get that tune like I wanted it. Matter of fact, I changed damn near the whole band to get that tune like I wanted it. After I played it for two years, I got married to it. I didn't want to record the tune, but my producer said, "If you don't cut it, man, somebody's going to steal it." I just had that feeling that if it was pushed right, it was going to be fairly big. I can't say I didn't know it would hit, because I did. Then, when it was released, it was a gigantic hit.[15]

INTERNATIONAL RECOGNITION

The success of "Bustin' Loose" would lead to national and international tours for the Soul Searchers. Many thought that with the appeal of "Bustin' Loose," the Soul Searchers would follow the road of other successful acts from Washington, which was to leave town and not return. I am certain that the lure of fast dollars and bright lights were a temptation to Chuck. Legend has it, however, that the bright lights were not enough to make Chuck abandon Washington. Through the years, Chuck has toured around the nation and the globe. In the summer of 1992, Chuck Brown and the Soul Searchers traveled to Japan for a two-week tour, performing in Tokyo, Osaka, Nagoya, and Yokohama. That same year, three Chuck Brown CDs were released in Japan on the JIMCO label. Chuck completed a European tour in April of 1993, playing in five different countries to coincide with the European release of *This is a Journey...into Time* on Minor Music. Regarding one of his earlier trips to Europe, Chuck commented:

> Europe has always been very enthusiastic about American music. As long as I can remember, black artists, white

artists, all American musicians have all been very well received when they go over there. This country is used to our music...used to what we are doing. The European audience is responsive, even if they don't like you they'll show you some appreciation. They'll clap for you and all that. D.C. don't do no whole lot of clapping. They've listened to it for so long.[16]

For all his musical accomplishments, travels, and national and international attention, I recognize Chuck as the official ambassador for go-go, as well as the "Godfather of Go-Go"—titles that reflect his legacy. I was elated in the summer of 2000 when I was asked to join Chuck Brown and Rare Essence on the Mall of the Smithsonian for the Festival of American Folklife. This was an important moment because it was a kind of compensation for all the years of misunderstanding and lack of recognition of go-go music by Washington officials. It was even more gratifying when Anthony Gittens, Director of the D.C. Commission on the Arts and Humanities (DCCAH), stated that this evening represented the largest attendance of a single event in the history of the festival.

Standing on the stage that evening I could not help but think about all the trials and tribulations that the music has had to overcome during the course of the last 30 years. To finally be accepted by your own city and country as a legitimate art form is an incredible feeling. Chuck Brown deserves as many tributes and awards as can be bestowed upon him, because he is truly a great person. For his achievements, the DCCAH decided to honor him for all he has done to promote local music and talent. On December 11, 2000, the DCCAH presented Chuck with a Special Recognition Award at the 16th Mayor's Arts Awards, which were held at the historic Lincoln Theater in Washington, D.C. Chuck was given the award for his contributions to music and for the innovation of go-go music, which has brought national and international attention to Washington, D.C. This is indeed a significant award from a city that has finally grown to love and appreciate Chuck for all he has done and brought to this city.

While writing this chapter it became apparent to me that it would have to remain incomplete. Part of one chapter in a book does not offer enough space and pages to truly talk about the wealth and breadth of Chuck Brown's contributions to D.C.'s music. What is needed is a book devoted entirely to this talented musician—which could be followed up with a full-length movie. I am convinced that a full-length movie about the life and times of Chuck Brown will do more to explain go-go music than any other movie about go-go that could be produced. Hopefully, this book will serve as a token tribute to Chuck Brown. I am very proud and honored to know Chuck and to appreciate all he means to this city and nation. Macon, Georgia, may have James Brown; Detroit may have Smokey Robinson; Oakland, California, has Sly Stone; and Minneapolis has Prince, but I would not trade any of them for D.C.'s Godfather of Go-Go, Chuck Brown, say what now!

RARE ESSENCE: FROM INNER CITY GROOVERS TO THE MOST WICKEDEST BAND ALIVE

Rare Essence is not a household name throughout the United States, but ask most any music fan that has resided in the District of Columbia some-time after 1976 about them and you'll probably receive a very different response. Rare Essence, or RE, as they are known by their most enduring fans, has funked, rocked, and grooved go-go enthusiasts from all across Washington, D.C. This band has played for mayors, other politicians, and the sons and daughters of presidents in venues ranging from the Robert F. Kennedy Stadium to the Black Hole to Sidwell Friends High School. RE has exerted far more influence on young musicians and young audiences than any other go-go group in history.

Please do not misunderstand. We all know and respect the fact that Chuck Brown is the Godfather of Go-Go. Chuck created "the beat" and made the music popular throughout the Washington metropolitan area. But it was the combination of the Soul Searchers and Rare Essence that is primarily responsible for go-go's success. I have always maintained that if Chuck Brown is the Godfather of Go-Go, then the members of Rare Essence are the first-born "Godchildren."

Despite all of their musical achievements and the vast popularity afforded them by their fans in Washington, D.C., national success has eluded RE. Why is this the case, and how can "the most wickedest band alive"—as they like to call themselves—continue only to groove the inner city of Washington, D.C.?

ROOTS

Rare Essence began in 1976 as the brainchild of James Funk. I knew James Funk as a DJ who played records at Soul Searchers gigs. He also played during the Space DisGo that I promoted at the Panorama Room during the early 1970s. I remember James as a serious observer, one who always seemed to be preoccupied with the music. He was a very good DJ who had a knack for rocking the house and had a keen sense of what the people wanted. So it was no surprise to me when I heard that he was the leader of a new group of guys in Southeast Washington D.C.

I can vividly recall when I first heard about Rare Essence. E.U. was practicing and Sugar Bear, the bass player, was going on and on about this young band that had a very appealing sound—"Hey, this band in Southeast is making a lot of noise and they are going to be very popular. I have seen them draw huge crowds and I see the folks getting off to their music."[17] Sugar Bear was always known as the E.U. scout because he enjoyed reconnaissance work—going out and listening to other groups so that he would have a handle on what the competition was doing. During one of these outings he noticed with great excitement the existence of Rare Essence. Not only did he notice them; he also predicted their rise in popularity. Sugar Bear based his prediction on the fact that Rare Essence was playing "the beat" in a style similar to that of the Soul Searchers.

It is interesting to note that this evaluation occurred in the late 1970s, during a period of musical reassessment by the groups in Washington. This reassessment was brought on by the disco craze, which caused a dilemma for the bands because the audience's tastes were swiftly changing. The audience no longer wanted to hear "message music"; they just wanted to party. "The beat" allowed them to party, and the Soul Searchers, although criticized by many bands for playing "the beat," became Washington's most popular group. James Funk obviously was paying attention to the changing taste of the audience, because when he brought Rare Essence on the go-go circuit the fans called them the "Baby Soul Searchers." Sugar Bear was not the only one to notice them.

He was correct about them, too. Rare Essence almost immediately generated a buzz throughout the city and started developing a loyal following. It was not long afterwards that E.U. changed its style of playing to incorporate "the beat." Despite my objections as well as those of others in the group, this change had to be made in order for the band to continue functioning. I can honestly say that Rare Essence's initial impact on the local music scene was dramatic because they engendered a musical change.

During Rare Essence's development it was obvious that they were different from other groups of the time. They developed an organization that was far superior to that of their counterparts. I might add that James Funk not only borrowed from Chuck Brown, he also borrowed from E.U. During the mid-1970s, E.U. was the most organized band in the city: the members owned a record store, promoted themselves, recorded themselves, marketed T-shirts and bumper stickers, had buttons for the fans, and so on. James Funk undoubtedly also paid attention to what E.U. was doing and thought to improve his group; by 1980, Rare Essence had become known for its organization as well.

A PROFESSIONAL ORGANIZATION

Under James Funk's and Ms. Annie Mack's careful stewardship, RE developed into a professional business operation. Unlike many bands, the members of the group spoke in one voice and very rarely engaged in idle gossip or chatter. They placed business first and were very clear on their purpose. This was perhaps the single most important factor responsible for the success of RE. RE became a corporation owned by some members of the band as well as others who comprise management. Decisions about RE's business are decided by the corporation; as a result, no one person has too much influence. I have always respected this organization, because it allows for intelligent and rational decisions to be made on behalf of the group and its future.

As the manager of Rare Essence, Ms. Mack (that is how she's always addressed or mentioned) emerged on the scene with a splash. As the only female player in the go-go business at that time, she sought and quickly received the respect and attention of all. During an interview, Ms. Mack responded to a question about RE's business organization:

> I guess it's more or less like they say: when you plant a seed and you shape it the way you want it to go.... When I started working with them, before I started working with them, I had a terrible attitude. You know, I really did. I didn't take from nothing from anybody. But when I started working with them I wanted them to be a certain way; I wanted them to always get respect. And I carried myself with the respect that demanded respect. And I wanted them to carry themselves so that they would not be questioned.... And a lot of that kind of helped them and helped their whole situation. And then we learned later that we should be paying taxes. Then we

had to start paying taxes. And we were the only group paying taxes. And we were paying taxes and the whole nine yards.[18]

Clearly, Ms. Mack provided the business brains for the group. She learned quickly and forced the industry to deal with her and the band fairly. It did not take long for Ms. Mack to figure out the essentials of running a go-go band; by 1980, Rare Essence was the top band in Washington—a status that has not changed in 2001.

I have been a fan, a competitor, a partner, and an observer of Rare Essence for over 20 years. I have watched them grow and maintain their musical hold on the city during this span of time. Rare Essence is definitely a phenomenon without equal. I am certain that in some other city in the United States there exists a band that can play in different venues for seven nights a week. I am certain that there exists a band that can survive the rampages of death and drugs and still continue forward. And finally, I am certain that there exists a band that can continue to fill venues without songs playing on the radio or videos playing on BET or MTV. Well, maybe not; however, Rare Essence continues to move forward despite all the stated odds.

I went to hear Rare Essence play for the first time in many years one Saturday near the end of 2000. I needed to hear them as inspiration for me to capture their essence for this profile. Judith (my wife) and I were thoroughly surprised and mesmerized by RE's continued mastery of go-go. Without a doubt, RE is the essence of go-go. They rocked over 300 people who came to Club U that night. It was evident that partying was the order of the evening as young adults grooved into the wee hours of the morning. Not once was there an incident of violence or any kind of disturbance. The folks were enjoying themselves to the max.

Picture, if you will, the Club U, with low ceilings and therefore excellent acoustics . . . an awesome sound system with six massive bass speakers on each side of the stage putting out a deep, rich, pulsating sound . . . state-of-the-art 24-channel boards that can mix the sound of nine musicians into a funky groove in unparalleled fashion. Now imagine that all around you are people dancing—mostly without a partner, because at a go-go you do not need a partner in order to groove. Add on top of it the presence of young men and women from throughout the Washington metropolitan area who are looking good in the latest fashions and getting off to the sounds of RE. So, picture yourself having the time of your life, just enjoying the music without a care in the world.

The Young Senators when they were the back-up band for Eddie Kendricks, formerly of the Temptations (1971 promotional shot from Motown Studios in Detroit, Michigan).

Suttle Thoughts relaxing on a playground.

This Trouble Funk album cover brings one back to the mid-1980s.

Blurring the line between performer and audience, Trouble Funk bass player/vocalist Big Tony.

Trouble Funk in a promotional picture circa 1990, during a period of their national and international success. Photograph by Nick White.

An old school poster for a program at Club LeBaron (ca. 1982) held up by a new school go-go fan.

Rare Essence's "Hey Now," was produced by Chuck Brown and released in 1988 by D.C.-based I Hear Ya! Records. RE then consisted of (*front row, left to right*) Quentin "Footz" Davidson, Milton "Go-Go" Mickey Freeman, and James Funk, as well as (*back row, left to right*) Andre "Whiteboy" Johnson and Donnell Floyd.

When Rare Essence performs, it's clear that percussion remains the heartbeat of go-go.

A close-up and revealing portrait of Chuck Brown (aka "The Godfather").

Chuck Brown and trombonist Greg B, who has toured with Prince, among other bands, share a moment on stage.

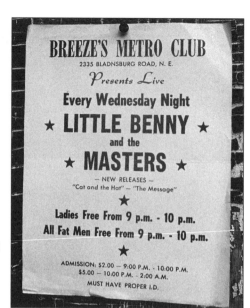

BREEZE'S METRO CLUB
2335 BLADNSBURG ROAD, N. E.

Presents Live

Every Wednesday Night

★ LITTLE BENNY ★
and the
★ MASTERS ★

— NEW RELEASES —
"Cat and the Hat" — "The Message"

★

Ladies Free From 9 p.m. - 10 p.m.

All Fat Men Free From 9 p.m. - 10 p.m.

★

ADMISSION: $2.00 — 9:00 P.M. - 10:00 P.M.
$5.00 — 10:00 P.M. - 2:00 A.M.
MUST HAVE PROPER I.D.

Breeze's Metro Club's unconventional offer appears on this "All Fat Men Free" flyer from (ca.) 1987.

Dozens (of the hundreds) of P.A. Tapes are displayed on the wall of the P.A. Palace store.

"Hand Dance" is a local term for a D.C.-style swing dancing, which underscores the fact that musical aesthetics from earlier decades don't always comfortably mesh with newer traditions.

A go-go crowd salutes both the Washington Monument and the music.

Before performing outdoors, Junk Yard Band members bow their heads in prayer.

Donnell Floyd and Go-Go Mike of Familiar Faces blowin' on stage.

Members of Mambo Sauce discuss voting rights for the District with the media.

Mambo Sauce drummer, Patricia "Twink" Little, in a characteristically playful mood.

Mambo Sauce on stage and representing for the District.

A go-go groove is unique in that there are no basic steps. There is no right or wrong, because it is a feel and a movement to the drums and a call and response to the band. "Are you tired yet?" is the question the audience must answer with a resounding "No!" While Donnell and Whiteboy lead the band, Go-Go Mickey supplies the funky accents on the congas and the rototoms. He is, of course, syncopated (and in sync) with the drummer, who supplies a steady beat, a beat that cannot be broken or interrupted because the drum beat is the heart of go-go—take it away and the party dies. Now add the spice of the guitar and bass and the overtones of the keyboards, and you have the sound of Rare Essence, "the most wickedest band alive."

Seeing RE perform is indeed a treat. The group's energy and command is not equaled by any other band in Washington. They lay down a funky groove and command that your body move, sway, sweat, and bounce. The sound of the drums and the bass hits you directly in your heart. The lead vocals supplied by Donnell, Whiteboy, and Ms. Kim Graham are exceptional. The "ruff" (rough) phases have the attention of everyone in the club, although it is not necessary to actually *see* the group perform—you come to feel the groove, not see it. At 30 dollars a pop, you get your money's worth.

While witnessing Rare Essence on that Saturday night, I was reminded of what James Funk said regarding the influence of George Clinton and James Brown on his music:

> George wasn't really at one time doing much of nothing but conducting. He might have been signing hooks and things like that but he wasn't basically doing much but basically conducting. And I like the way he always got into a groove, and just stayed there, you know just grooved for however long he wanted...you know, "hit me, horns," like a James Brown "hit me," put it right there, you know, make something real simple so big. You know what I'm saying? And I kind of like the way...their grooves came on. James Brown did it but he did it more formatted than, I would say, George Clinton did. So I just like the way...that's what basically turned me on.[19]

This helps to explain the RE groove, which can grab and hold you for an entire evening. The basic element that James Funk created years ago still remains a crucial element of the group today. Although James Funk is no longer a performing member of RE, his legacy endures.

WHY?

If RE is so good, why doesn't the band have a major record deal? This is a good, fair question, but the answer should and must come from the record industry. For many years, this band has displayed its ability to "handle its business." RE has constantly been a major player on the music scene in Washington. They have produced many 12-inch singles, albums, compact discs, and music videos. They have produced local hit after local hit, including "Body Moves," "Hey Buddy Buddy," and "Overnight Scenario." Yet they still perform without a major-label record deal.

The lack of a major record deal does not seem to bother RE; they keep moving forward. The band has been a major factor in go-go music in four decades (since the '70s)—a tremendous feat. RE has the uncanny ability of staying current with its music. So many groups have come and gone, but RE (along with E.U., Trouble Funk, and Junk Yard) remains on the circuit. Consider the role played by groups like War, Earth, Wind & Fire, the Commodores, and Mandrill, which were popular when RE first started performing, but are no longer performing. It is a testament to RE's greatness that they have managed to keep audiences entertained from one generation to the next, seven days a week in live performance. This is a great achievement that must not go unnoticed. In this day and age of computers and instant everything, RE has somehow kept its position as the top band in Washington (Chuck Brown is in a league of his own).

Leadership and organization are the underlying cornerstones of the band's success. After James Funk left RE and Ms. Mack decided to retire, André "Whiteboy," Johnson and Irving "Captain" Brady took over the reins without missing a beat. Under André's leadership RE continued to meet the challenges of the music business. André has been able to utilize the various talents within the band; for example, he encouraged Donnell Floyd to emerge as a songwriter and lead vocalist, which has helped to maintain the band's popularity.

The team of André and Donnell is responsible for producing many of the band's CDs and music videos. Observing from afar, I have developed a great amount of respect for their leadership. Donnell never likes to be recognized as a leader of RE, but anyone doing business with the group or affiliated with them knows about Donnell's positive influence on RE. André and Donnell are also responsible for ensuring that RE keeps its edge. Musically, they are always looking for ways to maintain the group's popularity. Whether this means adding a female band member or incorporating hip-hop or rap hooks, it will be done. Currently, I would say that the band still maintains the old RE groove—just with added spices and flavoring on top.

Despite the influence of André and Donnell, just one or even two members cannot accept full responsibility for RE's success. The success of the band goes back to its corporate organization, which guards and controls the group's every move. The corporation not only strictly guards the band's business interests, but also its creative direction. This is almost unheard of in the recording industry, let alone in go-go.

The corporation's support has helped RE to navigate through incident after incident. In addition to the death of drummer Footz, the band has survived the departures of several other popular members, including James Funk, Little Benny, and most recently Donnell Floyd, who began 2001 with a new band called 911. RE's popularity has not diminished as the band moved from one leader to the next. André commented about his own ascension to a leadership position:

> But nobody else was going to and they was all looking at me because I was the band leader at the time and I was one of the managers, so it was like, "Well, you got to do it," so I had to do it in order for us to keep going. But I depended more on Donnell, Derek, and some of the other members, whereas Funk really didn't. For example, it would be three people from the band ready to start playing a gig, Funk would start playing. I wanted all ten of us there prior to playing.[20]

Let's revisit the question: Why, despite all that RE has accomplished, are they still just playing in Washington? Over the last 10 years or so RE has developed relationships with many accomplished rappers and hip-hop artists. In an effort to promote go-go shows, RE was the first to bring Grandmaster Flash into the Washington, D.C., area. In an attempt to broaden its appeal, on at least one occasion the band has recorded with popular rapper Doug E. Fresh, developing a relationship with him that continues to this day. Unfortunately, all of this work has gone for naught because all the gimmicks have come up empty in the national perspective. Add to this the following comment from André about the hype surrounding

E.U. following the release of "Da' Butt," the national hit tied to Spike Lee's film *School Daze*:

> All of a sudden everybody was interested again, because they had a national hit record... André Harrell from Uptown Records was calling, after a show we did at the Apollo.... "If you're interested, I can just shop you right now. Columbia's interested; I think I can bet Artista's interested." So we was like, "Yeah, André, go ahead." In the process of that, André kind of lost focus, because MCA came into the picture.... So then André came out with Guy. He had Father MC, Mary J. Blige... and then he picked up Puffy.... Puffy started to do some things with us. He tried to help us get some producers to come down here, because André wanted to use a hip-hop producer with a go-go beat. We tried that a couple of times and it didn't really work, and Puffy ended up going to New York.[21]

The big deal continues to elude go-go because major recording studios want to produce it to their liking. This obviously misses the point. Over the years RE has made repeated attempts to partner with various major labels, only to be left unsigned. This reality has not stopped the artistic success and stamina of the band, because they continue to strive in other areas and accomplish what most groups with major deals cannot — a constant performance schedule.

As their popularity grew, the drugs and violence epidemic that hit D.C. in the late '80s and early '90s made RE prime fodder for the press and local activists. As the drug trade and its associated violence increased in Washington, so did the scrutiny of the band. News story after news story would single out RE gigs as the epicenter of violence and killings. For example, in the fall of 1987, the *Washington Post* labeled a fatal stabbing outside of Celebrity Hall the "Go-Go Slaying." Then, in December of the same year, three bouncers where shot during an altercation at Cheriy's Club and the *Post* headline read "A Go-Go Club Shooting." These reports began to affect business. They caused the go-go industry to respond, but not in unison.

Any intelligent person would know that RE alone was not responsible for the national increase in drug abuse and violence, and how it manifested itself in the streets of the nation's capital. But it was easiest for the media to point the finger of blame at go-go, and then at the most popular go-go group, which was Rare Essence. Although RE was the target of the media assault on go-go, they did not join with other groups to participate in the Go Go Drug Free Project in 1986. The project was organized to combat the growing negative media and to record an anti-drug go-go song, which was written in collaboration with the groups who participated: Chuck Brown and the Soul Searchers; E.U.; AM-FM; Redds and the Boys; C.J.'s Uptown Crew; Mass Extension; Little Benny and the Masters; Hot, Cold, Sweat; Ayre Rayde; and Junk Yard Band. City officials, anti-drug activists, and arts activists joined these groups in their efforts to curb drug use.

By 1987 the continued harassment meant that venues no longer wanted to host go-go shows and the future looked bleak. RE was forced to join forces with other go-go bands and participated in a second anti-drug project, D.C. Don't Stand For Dodge City, which was sponsored by G Street Express and CD Enterprises.

In spite of all of the above efforts, the members of RE had to be convinced that the band's image connected it with drugs and violence. As a result, RE started to urge its audiences to conduct themselves in a respectable fashion, because not to do so would threaten the future of go-go. There is no doubt that the active participation of RE and the other mentioned bands in addressing the issues of drugs and violence helped to curtail the problem in Washington.

I believe that RE is the key to the perpetuation of go-go into the twenty-first century. I believe the future is theirs more so than Chuck Brown's, because they continue to be a weekly (sometimes nightly) major factor in Washington. RE performs in the tradition of Chuck Brown, E.U., and Trouble Funk, but today they bring in elements of hip-hop and are often referred to as "The People's Band." It is their responsibility to pass it on for bands after them to follow. Because the future of go-go is so cloudy, it ultimately hinges on the ability of RE or another band to translate their popularity into a major record deal, with promotion and monetary support. RE is the heir apparent to Chuck Brown as the ambassador for go-go; however, time is an enemy. The band must make a move within the next couple of years in order for the legacy of go-go to continue.

EXPERIENCE UNLIMITED — MISSED OPPORTUNITIES

This is the most personal profile for me to write because of my affiliation with and affinity for the group involved. I first met the guys who were to become members of Experience Unlimited in 1970. At that time, I lived across the hall from André Lucas, the group's conga player. André, or "Pops," as he was called in the group, allowed the group to practice in his parents' apartment. The original crew consisted of Gregory "Sugar Bear" Elliot (bass); Ronald "Preacher" Roundtree (drums); Donald Fields (guitar); and Rufus Lassiter (guitar).

From the rolling hills of far Southeast Washington, D.C., the original members of E.U. all attended Ballou High School. The guys in the band reflected the demographics of Southeast, equally split between female-headed households and two-parent households. Southeast was and is the city's most economically distressed section and was shunned by politicians and other citizens because of its poverty. It was also a place where hard work and perseverance were the order of the day. So, from the beginning, E.U. was accustomed to working hard, facing challenges, and overcoming obstacles.

A good example of this occurred one evening in 1972, when bad luck came upon E.U. All of the band's equipment was stolen, including the P.A. system, bass and lead guitar amplifiers, various percussion instruments, and other miscellaneous items. As the band's manager, I was always concerned about the equipment, and this incident presented quite a dilemma. Unfortunately, the parents of the band members were not financially able to help the group buy new instruments. However, the community rallied around E.U. and steered me to the community credit union to apply for a loan to purchase new equipment for the band. In order to secure the loan I needed a cosigner, and Bret Lucas, André's father, agreed to act in this capacity. As a result we were able to get a sizable discount from Zaverella's Music Store in Alexandria, Virginia, and we purchased replacement equipment for the band. This was an important period in E.U.'s development because it demonstrated the base of community support that E.U. received from the very beginning.

E.U. next found practice space in a community center in the public housing projects of Valley Green. Ms. Vastine Blakney, the director of the community center, offered her support to the band from the beginning. This support eventually spread and the community began to embrace and identify with E.U., a relationship that would last for many years. It was from this base of support that E.U. began to cultivate its following.

From the beginning, E.U. enjoyed a loyal following because of its diversity and unique appeal. Interestingly, the original band was more interested in playing rock music than go-go because they appreciated both Jimi Hendrix and Grand Funk. As a matter of fact, the group chose the name Experience Unlimited because of their respect for the Jimi Hendrix Experience. "Unlimited" was chosen because they did not want to limit the range of their music. Thus, Experience Unlimited was born.

The group always displayed an uncommon energy and charisma. They quickly became an audience favorite because they played with showmanship that was unmatched by the other groups with whom they appeared. They quickly become known for doing the outrageous in an effort to entertain. I remember a 1971 show in Maryland where Preacher jumped off the stage and engaged the crowd by encouraging the audience to clap and sing along. Early on, Gregory "Sugar Bear" Elliot emerged as a crowd favorite because of his style of bass playing. Sugar Bear says that Jimi Hendrix influenced his playing from the start. He wanted to be known as the Hendrix of bass and played with a flair reminiscent of the Seattle-born guitarist. Sugar Bear recalls how he wanted to emulate Hendrix on the bass: "I tried to imitate him on my bass! I was wild back in the days, you know. That's why we started playing; that's where our style came from, playing different, like more rock, and we were playing hard....For young musicians we [were] ahead of our time. We were playing stuff that white groups were supposed to play."[22]

Most musicians in Washington during the early 1970s had the opportunity to play around the city because of the D.C. Recreation Department's Showmobile. The Showmobile (a city vehicle that literally brought live entertainment around D.C.) helped many people—especially the young—deal with the tedium of the hot, humid summers in Washington. Led by Raymond Gray from the D.C. Recreation Department, young groups such as Experience Unlimited were paid a stipend to play around town. Even more importantly, working on the Showmobile gave them valuable experience and exposure as professional performers.

Raymond Gray also directed the Ambassador's Band, an orchestra consisting of musicians from across the city. The Ambassador's Band provided valuable learning experiences for musicians. Raymond Gray and the Ambassador's Band's legacy is an integral (but under-appreciated) part of the go-go legacy in Washington, D.C. Sugar Bear remembers the influences of Gray and the Ambassador's Band:

> The Ambassador's Band, I remember them. You could be part of the Ambassador's and at the same time be part of the Young Citizens Band and the Soul Searchers, and they grew up with that. And they grew up with a certain

kind of discipline. So even if you didn't play in the Ambassador's, you knew of their professionalism. The good thing about Mr. Gray was discipline. He would say we're gonna play at two o'clock and you better have your butt there and that's what the bottom line was. So he got the whole nine yards. Mr. Gray was hard but he had respect. You don't have that kind of caring about your bands today, the way they had back then.[23]

It was the summer of 1973 that afforded Experience Unlimited its greatest visibility. During that time the group literally toured the entire city, playing in public parks and for countless block parties.

By the end of the summer the band was one of the most requested in the Summer in the Parks program. E.U. had become a major player in the city. The band just loved to play. No audience or gig was too big or too small for them and they approached each performance like it was their most important. E.U.'s attitude became well-known to its audience and the popularity of the group soared. Sugar Bear comments that E.U. "was in so much demand we could get about three or four shows in one day. I mean, you start out in the afternoon and the afternoon is like one or two o'clock at a park, at a block party. And then we go to another show at a splash party or somebody's cabaret, and then we would go to our regular night work. We would play the Cream Beaux Palace or the Howard."[24]

Experience Unlimited received accolades for playing with feeling and being real crowd-pleasers. The group's show integrated rock overtones with a dash of Afro-Latin percussion that kept hands and feet tapping, all pulled together with funky horns. Their performances were, without a doubt, some of the City's most outrageous and entertaining. After a summer of touring the city and building an audience the band began to receive more opportunities to play with other popular groups, such as the Soul Searchers, The Aggression, 100 Years Time, and Black Heat.

However, during the group's ascent, the fact that the members of E.U. considered themselves to be a family began to separate them from their counterparts. E.U. developed a real respect and deep feelings towards each other that were felt and shared by their audiences.

Although rock- and funk-based (I find it interesting that black groups that played hard were called funk and white groups who did the same thing were called rock), E.U. possessed a certain affinity for promoting peace and love. The group patterned its music after popular bands such as War;

Earth, Wind & Fire; Mandrill; Santana; and Osibisi—the groups from the early '70s that were experimenting with the boundaries of musical expression. It was no surprise that local bands developed followings based on the type of music they played. Some people loved to dance all night and therefore followed the Soul Searchers; others who had an appreciation of the wild and outrageous may have been fans of 100 Years Time.

The one gig that probably goes down as the group's largest came at a huge August 1973 Anacostia Park program billed as the end of Summer in the Parks. Billed as a battle of the bands, the lineup included, among others, the Matadors, The Shadows Band, and of course E.U. E.U. faced its greatest challenge when it closed this show, which featured the best bands in Washington, D.C. I will never forget the band's preparation and the intensity with which they approached the gig. They were "psyched" for the biggest moment in their lives. Sugar Bear also lists this night as his most memorable musical moment. Despite 30 years of performing throughout the United States with acts such as Earth, Wind & Fire, Gil Scott-Heron, Ohio Players, and Salt-N-Pepa, this local gig stood out. Sugar Bear recalled: "We got over 50,000 people, man! And you couldn't even see the end of them, and they were waiting for us. That was the most exciting time of my life, if you describe it, it was like a championship. It was like playing Orlando and Shaq and Michael Jordan. And people waited all day for us all day. Out of 20 bands who played, we were like the grand finale, you know, the last band. I'll never forget that moment as long as I live."[25]

This gig was the black Woodstock for the participating bands. By this time E.U. (like many of their peers) had a horn section that helped to provide accents that punctuated their music. That evening the horns of E.U. rose to the top. Playing original compositions as well as tunes by Earth, Wind & Fire and Mandrill, the group not only held its own, but they also displayed a professionalism that would become their trademark for many years to come.

MANAGING E.U.

I believe it is very important to share E.U.'s early development and experiences—they will help you to get a grasp on what was happening in Washington, D.C., during the early 1970s. It is also important that you understand the role of the city. The Ambassador's Band, the Showmobile, and the "Compared To What?" sponsored summer-long musical events which were critical in supporting the local bands. This support helped to lay the foundation for the development of go-go. Today it is politically correct to say that it takes a village to raise a child. In the 1970s, the city of Washington, D.C., acted on this proverb.

As the manager of E.U., I had absolutely no experience in the music business and no mentors. I was essentially on my own. Managing a band was not a career ambition or my dream, but it was something to which I was drawn. I always felt that the opportunity to manage E.U. was a signal from a higher power, so I accepted the responsibility. I never had an interest in the music business, although like millions of others, I loved music and could never get enough of it.

For me, managing was more of an effort to give back to the community than a business interest. After the first few years, however, the group began to demand more and more attention; I had to devote all of my spare time and effort to forming a business of a kind I knew nothing about. Quite naturally I made mistakes because I drew upon my experience as a community activist. Many times, my interests and consciousness clashed with the group's business, which was to make money. From the beginning I demanded that the group donate their time by playing for events that benefited the community, in order to help young people accomplish positive things.

Luckily for the group, my strategy did help to propel them to greater success. Aside from the Summer in the Parks gigs, I ensured that we would be part of shows for the city and other high-profile organizations that afforded us worthwhile publicity. E.U. was everywhere! We played for teens, we played for adults, and we even played for political events. The E.U. creed became: Bring us a diverse and expansive audience and we will play!

In 1970, the Malcolm X Day Committee established the Malcolm X Day Celebration, an annual cultural and political tribute to the life and legacy of Malcolm X. E.U. performed at the first celebration and for the next 24 years appeared as its major attraction. The band's popularity helped to raise the visibility of the Malcolm X Day Celebration, and as the event grew in size—over the years, it often attracted as many as 50,000 people—so did E.U.'s reputation; the band developed an image as a "band of the people."

E.U., DISCO, AND THE CITY

In the early 1970s a dichotomy was slowly developing in the city. On one level, local bands were getting support from the city by playing for various communities on the Showmobile. The city's critically important support of local performance groups not only enabled E.U. to play throughout D.C., but also provided us with much-needed, reliable financial backing. Bands learned that performing at clubs did not guarantee an actual paycheck. Often either the promoter did not do a good job in promoting the show, which prevented people from attending, or "it was a bad night." In either case the bands would take a hit, resulting in either no money or a reduced rate. This was one of the pitfalls of being an up-and-coming group— more established acts rarely faced the same problems.

However, as times changed and a new administration took over the White House, policies shifted. By decade's end, support for community services had subsided, including the funds allocated for the D.C. Department of Recreation. This reality eventually caused the end of valuable programs affecting the city's youths, such as Summer in the Parks and the Showmobile. The end of these valuable programs happened to coincide with the advent of disco, which changed the music scene in Washington, D.C., and everywhere else.

Following the path established by other groups, E.U.'s success led to the establishment of a corporation to oversee the business. The band became a self-contained act, owning sound equipment and a truck, and maintaining a sound and road crew. In 1975 E.U. relocated from the Valley Green Community Center to Howard Road, also in Southeast, Washington, D.C. Because the Howard Road location was large enough, we decided to open E.U.'s House of Peace.

The establishment of the record store also allowed me to broaden the band's business. I now had a base of operations from which we could book, promote, rehearse, and plan for E.U.'s success. I was also able to hire members of the group to work in the store and to help promote the band, which gave them an up-close look at the business. The store also led us to trademark the "E.U." name and to the development of a logo and other related graphics by Malik Edwards.

Because of E.U.'s diverse repertoire and abilities, its fan base grew to include not only people from the Southeast neighborhoods, but also the so-called black hippie crew and political progressives. As a result, the band performed six or seven days a week at various venues. For a while E.U. performed weekly at the Dimensions Unlimited Go-Go at the Panorama Room. Dimensions Unlimited, which was directed by Bill Washington, the premier concert promoter in the city, featured national recording artists. Bill Washington took a liking to E.U. and allowed them to perform as the opening act (a plum position) on several of his concerts featuring top acts from around the nation. It was also a testament to E.U.'s popularity during this time. E.U. was also booked by popular social clubs that promoted weekly go-gos at clubs and halls throughout the Washington metropolitan area.

Despite all the attention and popularity that E.U. had attracted it was still difficult for them to get a major recording deal. However, the lack of a major deal did not usually stop D.C. groups from recording, and the band was beginning to perform original material that was the basis for future recordings. From 1974 through 1985 E.U. released several recordings on local labels:

> Led by founder Gregory "Sugar Bear" Elliott, E.U. has been around since 1974 [sic; 1970]. E.U. released what is considered, in Chocolate City, to be the first straight up go-go record: "Hey You" in 1976 on the local House of Peace label (it was penned by T.T.E.D. boss Max Kidd). In 1977 E.U. released its first LP on Black Fire Records...A succession of now out-of-print singles followed. To wit: "Rock Your Butt"/"E.U. Groove" 1979. "E.U. Freeze" 1980, Vermack Records; "Come Party With Us" Vermack; "Just The Way You Like It, Severn Moons" featuring "Ooh La-La-La and Computer Funk"; "Somebody's Ringing That Doorbell" 1982, Vermack; "Party Time" (w/Kurtis Blow) 1983, Mercury; "Future Funk" 1983, Capitol City; "Do Your Thing" 1984, Capitol City; "E.U. Freeze" (remix) 1985, T.T.E.D./Island.[26]

Although we had the ability to produce and record, getting our product radio airplay was a crap shoot. During this era Al and the Kidd Promotions worked hard and was committed to go-go recordings. Under the leadership of Max Kidd, this company attained airplay for most of E.U.'s releases. Max didn't only promote E.U.'s records; he also worked with the Soul Searchers, Trouble Funk, Rare Essence, and other local go-go bands.

THE BEAT ARRIVES

Despite the fact that all was seeming to go well for E.U. in the late 1970s, the music scene in Washington was about to change forever. It was during this era that bands including E.U. were forced to re-examine what they were playing because their popularity was waning. Sugar Bear recalls that "the big bands like Trouble Funk, Chuck Brown, E.U., [The] Aggression were like dying off. Other bands like 100 Years Time were breaking up, but we were still here. And so by us being one of the popular bands, we had to adjust. Get on or get off! Take it or leave it! It had to happen like that."[27]

Disco's emergence constricted the fecund local band scene. Bands no longer reveled in their musical diversity—now groups were virtually required to play with a disco beat. The raging debate among musicians and bands about whether or not to play "the beat" came to an abrupt end when it was evident that the people wanted to dance. It was very hard for some groups to change their style and bands such as The Aggression, Lead Head, and Father's Children did not survive past 1980.

I will never forget the debate that heated up in E.U. I sided with those who did not want to change styles. I thought that it would be selling out—that E.U. would just be sacrificing its unique style in order to make a few dollars. Sugar Bear led the other camp. They countered with the argument that people no longer wanted to be preached to; they wanted to party. He further believed that if E.U. did not change, we would lose our core audience. Sugar Bear recounted:

> The band was like, they were saying it was too commercial...but I said, "Look man, it's about survival.... [If] that's what the people want to hear, we play it for the people. We call ourselves the people's band so we gotta give the people what they want." So it was a big conflict in E.U. People wanted to do it this way, or people wanted to do it the way I chose to do. But I chose right, you know. And that's what caused the turmoil.[28]

Clearly, this was an emotional period for Sugar Bear. It represented E.U.'s first major flap; so major that Donald Fields, the lead guitar player and one of the original members, decided to leave the band as a result. When Donald left the band, it was like the soul of the group moved on. It would continue to change, but it would never reflect the original "family vibe" spirit again. E.U. had crossed the great divide and decided to become a business in pursuit of lucrative record deals.

By the late 1970s, Rare Essence was making some serious noise in D.C. Sugar Bear recalled:

> When I saw them, I thought they had learned from us and Chuck. They had that beat climbing and the crowd pumped up by playing the cover to him [Chuck Brown]. They were working the beat, and talking trash in between. That's when I knew, that's what people wanted. And...even at parties, homecomings, whatever, they wanted to dance. And we got back and I was so excited because I knew we could do it. We had the musicianship, it was just a matter of putting the mess aside and play[ing] the beat. And we did it! But of course some musicians didn't like it because they said, "I ain't gonna play that beat."[29]

By late 1979 E.U. had added the go-go beat to its arsenal. In early 1980, we closed E.U.'s House of Peace store due to lack of sales as well as the lack of interest from newer band members, who eschewed activism in favor of the music business. It was a new day both for E.U. and for music in D.C.

Rare Essence not only caused E.U. to change, they also forced Trouble Funk to restructure its musical style, resulting in a fierce competition between the three bands. These three groups filled arenas that could hold upwards of 20,000 people—an unheard-of phenomenon. Local groups demanding top dollar and filling the Capitol Centre (when they allowed go-go shows) and the Washington Coliseum! Most of these shows were events sponsored by G Street Express, a prominent concert promotion company that took go-go music seriously and saw the potential for national and international success. Over the years, G Street Express would sponsor concerts, videos, and compilation records that featured the leading bands in Washington, D.C.

The early 1980s proved to be a healthy period in Washington for the surviving go-go bands. The enthusiasm for the big three (Chuck Brown was always recognized as the godfather and therefore above the fray) grew and grew. Major record company scouts now looked to Washington and started to make overtures to sign bands to lucrative record contracts.

After several major personnel changes, E.U. (now under the leadership of Sugar Bear) had no problem attracting the best musicians in the city. Sugar Bear secured Ricky Wellman on drums (he had also played with Chuck Brown and Miles Davis); Mike Scott (Prince's guitar player);

Michael Hughes, producer and songwriter; C.J. of C.J.'s Uptown Crew; and Vernon McDonald, formerly with The Aggression. While E.U. was in competition with Rare Essence for the pulse of the city, they continued to be one of the best show bands in town. E.U. also had a knack for finding fads or gimmicks to help promote the band and as themes for record releases. For example, in 1979 they released "E.U. Freeze," which came out of a gimmick that would be used during performances: E.U. would play a funky beat with horns screaming and drive the audience into a frenzy, then Bear would tell the crowd to "freeze, y'all." The "Freeze" became a local favorite and audiences began to request that the band play the tune. This participatory vamp became a part of go-go as it is known today.

When E.U. released the "E.U. Freeze" it was played on WOL-AM, WHUR-FM, and WDJY, and was promoted by Max Kidd. It was the beginning of the raising of the bar of competition among E.U., Trouble Funk, and Rare Essence. Trouble Funk countered with the release of "E Flat Boogie" in 1980, which some thought was a page out of Chuck Brown's soul diary. If you were to go back and listen to the earlier go-go releases you would notice that the records did fit industry patterns. Songs such as E.U.'s 1979 "Rock Your Butt" (which was much earlier than "Da' Butt") were tunes that radio could and did play.

Over a span of several years, E.U. would work with talented producers such as Robert "Shine" Freeman, a gifted producer who learned the ropes working with Kenny Gamble and Leon Huff of Philadelphia International Studios. Shine almost single-handedly changed the go-go scene by improving the repertoire and increasing professionalism. In an effort to restructure E.U., Shine agreed to work with me as a producer in 1981. Shine not only came in and worked with me, he also brought new members to E.U. who had a different flair and a sense of stage presence that added to the group's popularity. Aside from adding new members, we decided to pursue recording as a means of projecting E.U.'s appeal.

Shine made studio arrangements at Philadelphia International Studios and when the group passed through the doors of the studio you could sense that great things happened in the building. The aura of Sigma Sound Studios inspired us. E.U. would record several records using Sigma Sound Studios and Shine as the producer. One popular recording was "Oh La-La-La," which became a local craze—you held up one of your hands and flicked your wrist with the beat. Then the audience would join E.U. in reciting the chorus.

In 1982, Shine, along with Charles Moreland, the President of Galaxy

Unlimited Records (and former non-voting delegate for Washington, D.C.) produced and released the LP *Future Funk*, which became a prototype for his professional vision. Today, Shine is Reverend Freeman, pastor of the Save the Seed Ministries in Waldorf, Maryland.

These were great times; a healthy competition kept go-go popular. Rare Essence, Trouble Funk, and Chuck Brown were formidable foes and rivals for E.U., but friendly banter kept the music alive and well. During the '70s and early '80s, bands tended to be more supportive, and although they were competitive, it was in a positive sense. For example, E.U. had a very good relationship with a group called Symba. We would attend their practices and support their shows as they would ours. We also shared a deep commitment to helping to make the world a better place through the material we performed. By the mid-1980s, however, bands were very much interested in "making the money" and not as concerned about what was going on in society.

THE MOVIE YEARS

By 1985, my involvement with E.U. had become peripheral for many reasons. Sugar Bear believed it was important to expand the band's management and my own career was moving forward, so I did not have enough time to devote to the group. The management of E.U. was now being handled by a team of individuals who formed a company for that purpose. Although I was no longer the sole manager, I did harbor strong opinions as to how the group could succeed, and I continued to book engagements for the band.

That same year, the film *Good to Go* promised to be the greatest single event in history for the advancement of go-go. As an outside observer, I witnessed E.U.'s excitement about the Island Pictures film deal. They were prepared to do all they could to ensure the success of the project. It was obvious that E.U. and other groups would benefit greatly if the movie and the record signing worked out. After over 10 years of striving, the big time appeared to have finally arrived in Washington, D.C. Unfortunately, when the movie was released, E.U. did not appear in a single scene. I was surprised at this development; Sugar Bear says, "I think it was a thing between Max [Kidd] and Island Movies. But they didn't use any footage of E.U. playing. Matter of fact, the crowd shots used in the movie were scenes that we played in. So, I don't remember exactly what happened. I guess it was for the best. As it turned out, we didn't miss anything."[30]

I will never forget the evening I attended *Good to Go*'s premiere at the Warner Theater in downtown Washington, D.C. The excitement of the evening was outrageous; people in the audience were prepared for a major movie that would put D.C. and go-go on the map. However, I was disappointed almost as soon as the film began. As it turned out, *Good to Go* had very little to do with the music and more to do with stereotypical violence and black-on-black crime. I was also very upset with the fact that a white boy was scripted as the savior of people in the so-called ghetto. *Good to Go* turned out to be just another wrong-minded Hollywood portrayal of black life. Fortunately E.U. escaped any damage because of their absence from the screen.

Just as the city was reeling from the disappointment of the Island film, E.U. finally caught a huge break. I was still booking engagements for the group. Ted Hopkins, E.U.'s then-manager, and I had a decent working relationship and I would ocassionally throw shows his way. I had ties to the 9:30 Club, which was one of the few "white" clubs that allowed (and still does) go-go groups to perform. I got a call asking me to find a band for Spike Lee's birthday party. Spike Lee thoroughly enjoyed meeting and hearing E.U. and wanted the band in his new movie, *School Daze*. Sugar Bear recounts: "At that point I stood there thinking that it was much like other situations, you know, 'cause I said okay, we want to be in the soundtrack. But I didn't think that much about it because we had so many guys coming to us with that same scenario. Man, so it wasn't no big thing.... That's why I wasn't even excited about it because I said we'll try another one and see what happens."[31]

In 1989, "Da' Butt" was released on the Virgin Records LP entitled *Livin' Large*. It proved to be the first go-go release to receive national attention since Chuck Brown's "Bustin' Loose" a decade earlier. Propelled by the success of *School Daze*, the song became a national phenomenon. As a result, E.U. was asked to perform and accepted national dates with other accomplished R&B artists. It was a long time coming, but it seemed that go-go was going to reap the rewards of many years of sacrfice.

However, a failure of this newfound attention was the fact that go-go still had to be defined with audiences. Nationally, people did not "get it." Since the public could not identify exactly what go-go was, E.U. was inaccurately billed as an R&B group or a rap act. Still, the band forged ahead, accepting dates as they came in. *Livin' Large* proved to be popular because two other tunes on it were also hit singles. The release of "Taste Of Your Love" displayed the versatility of the group; it was a ballad that featured

Edward "Junie" Henderson on vocals. The next release was more in the go-go flavor—it was entitled "Buck Wild." Sugar Bear maintains that because the national audience was unfamiliar with go-go, it would have been helpful if other groups from D.C. were ready to go on tour to help spread the excitement of go-go. He recalls one attempt to form an alliance of go-go bands for potential tours:

> We arranged this show at the Apollo and we took bus-loads, about three buses went up there from home. And, the fact that it was mixed up with the New York people, we thought it would be a good show. Okay, this was a great experience, they [the Apollo audience] gave Chuck love, you know what I'm saying? 'Cause he came out and did "I'm Bad" by L.L. [Cool J]. Remember that? Essence got the stage next . . . the crowd was digging that. And we were still being E.U. We had our little whatever and we had "Da' Butt," of course. I remember I was happy but it was a sad thing because we were trying to break ground and showcase D.C. in New York. But they only accepted us and Chuck. . . . [32]

Sugar Bear's statement implies that Rare Essence was unsuccessful in winning over the crowd and may have been the reason why another attempt was not made to promote a tour of D.C. go-go groups. He believes the reason why go-go has had such a problem going national is because it is impossible for one group to carry the sound. When rap emerged, multiple groups helped to spread the music and the same was true with the Motown sound. E.U. could not establish go-go nationally alone.

POST-"BUTT"

After the success of their 1989 Virgin Records album, *Livin' Large*, E.U. received many awards and lots of attention for its achievements. You would think that other go-go musicians would be happy and encouraging of their success; when a go-go band is able to make a name for itself, it helps the whole genre because of that attention. What groups should have done during the era in which E.U. garnered national attention was attach themselves to the wagon and proclaim that go-go had broken through. But this is not what happened, according to Sugar Bear, who also noted: "I think the clubs [in Washington, D.C.] didn't give us the support when we was out there to back us up."[33]

Also, despite E.U.'s success, Virgin Records did not know how to promote the band. It seemed that Virgin wanted to take the path of least resistance by considering promoting E.U. as an R&B band, which is not what they are. This internal debate was causing some problems, and by the early 1990s, it was rumored that Virgin wanted to release E.U. to make room for other artists. Sugar Bear told me:

> Virgin wanted to clear the area and make room to sign Janet Jackson. I believe they cut three acts in this process—Ziggy Marley, Red Man, and us. At this moment, it was easy for them to do this because our numbers weren't that great. After the *Cold Kicking* CD, I knew a problem was developing because Virgin wanted to market us as an R&B act. In addition, the A&R department was going through some changes, which meant the guy that signed us was no longer with the company. Everyone was into making money and they never figured out how to market the group.[34]

It gets even more disturbing. Virgin had lost faith in the group. When E.U. was nominated for both a Grammy and a Soul Train award, Virgin Records didn't believe they had a chance and sent the group home! This slight took place one day after Gladys Knight edged out E.U. for a Grammy in the category of Best R&B Performance by a Duo or Group with Vocal. As it turned out, E.U. did win the Soul Train award for Best New Group or Artist, beating out Guy, New Edition, and Levert. Sugar Bear harbors absolutely no ill will about the Grammy, because he appreciated the nomination and believes that Gladys Knight beat E.U. because of her seniority in the business.

After the Virgin Records and awards fiasco, E.U. received a shockingly rude welcome home from the fans and promoters. The promoters questioned whether or not E.U. could draw audiences the way they did prior to leaving D.C., and some fans accused the band of selling out. This charge brought the following response from Sugar Bear: "I didn't like that at all and I used to get in arguments with people who accused us of selling out. I said how could you hate on me because of my dream. I'm finally doing something like a boxer would. You train as an amateur and you want to be a champion someday and I said this is the only way I see that we're gonna get out there to the next level. And if you're hating on me, that's wrong."[35]

I believe that part of the problem in Washington is that bands do not want to venture out for fear they will give up the "throne." It seems to be so serious a sacrifice that bands will not risk exchanging local dominance for a chance at national recognition. Sugar Bear commented: "Somebody had this thing like we wanted to be kings of D.C. Chuck and Essence continued to battle about how they wanted to be the best here, you know what I'm saying? Who's the best band in Washington, D.C.? But they didn't want to give up the chair."[36]

The notion of go-go continuing to prosper both in and outside of D.C. is interesting. Many of us (myself included) believe that go-go's future now rests with Rare Essence. However, I attempted to get Sugar Bear to respond to the possibility of other bands such as Backyard, Junk Yard, and Northeast Groovers becoming the groups to best represent the future of go-go. Sugar Bear responded:

> We're lost. There's no more the rush from the following bands. All the bands imitate each other. Every band sounds alike. They have no more horns, no more bass guitar players, you might see a guitar here or there. Of course you still got the percussion, the beat is still strong. But the front line has been working hard for this rap thing and it has lost total direction of where the roots come from. Most go-go shows are now like a rap concert.[37]

Sugar Bear reminded me about Jill Scott, whose release "It's Love" from the album *Who is Jill Scott?* represents the closest thing to a national go-go record. Although Jill is from Philadelphia, she's obviously aware of go-go's potential and utilized "the beat" in making a hit record. Sugar Bear commented: "It's like a breath of fresh air on the radio. But she's getting more play than Chuck and we got. I'm sure she knows what is go-go music. I don't even think she'd call herself a go-go band. But everybody knows from here to New York, they know what it is. That record gets serious airplay."[38]

The E.U. story is significant, of course, but it is also interesting, because it shows how a band rose from the projects of Southeast and became a nationally known group. Their struggles also show the constant battles they waged in order to continue playing the music. The story shows Sugar Bear and other E.U. members' true love for the music. I focused this profile around Sugar Bear because he is the only remaining member of the band who started in Valley Green and toured Los Angeles, California. This music will certainly endure; E.U. is the Paul Bunyan of the music. The group went out and explored and brought back valuable lessons that (hopefully) bands will learn from in order to spread go-go.

4 • Communities

Another thing about Washington, D.C....you have a high population of blacks, which is almost a separate city. In certain areas, here it is the capital and there are all these tourists, then you have the real city over here. The people have something to say, like, "Hey, this is not just a tourist city. We live here!" Our music is about that. We're really about the street, the people who *really* live in Washington, not the politicians on Capitol Hill or the President on Pennsylvania Avenue. We live here and we're dropping the bomb, or we're getting small, or we're good to go. These are all our slangs and they mean something about the life we lead.[1]

James Avery

Because Washington D.C. is in many ways a city divided, go-go helps to promote a sense of unity within the African American community. It helps to demarcate physical as well as psychological space. For example, upper Northwest (above the National Cathedral) is a "white" section of town, while the extreme Southeast (across the Sousa Bridge) is distinctly "black." Go-go provides many young (and increasingly middle-aged) black residents with both a rallying cry and a common point for musical and cultural references. In ways similar to a church—especially Pentecostal ("Holiness") sects—go-go provides a place for like-minded people to gather. Like church, an important part of its intent—often expressed by way of the performance rituals—is to transport its participants to another spiritual realm through a blend of verbal exchanges, movement, physical interaction, and an essential groove.

The distinctive sound of go-go provides aural evidence of blackness: if you don't appreciate the music (whether it's old- or new-school is of little consequence), can't tell the difference between Chuck Brown and Northeast Groovers, or believe that Chuck Brown is found in a comic strip—then you aren't black. But race is only part of it. You have to be from the city or P.G. County in order to "represent" for the music, because go-go is a D.C. thing. The chances are good that if you are a black man or woman from San Diego or San Antonio, you are not part of the go-go community. In short, if you understand go-go—if you get it—you're marked as both an African American and a Washingtonian.

These geographical and racial limitations are often sadly acknowl- ;
edged by the go-go community. Most wonder why, with the obvious exception of Prince George's County, the music is largely ignored by those who live outside the area bounded by the Beltway. On the compact disc *R.E. 2000* (RE2001-2), the song "We Push" addresses the issue: "You don't really want it—out of D.C.—they don't really want it! North and South Carolina don't really want it! A.T.L. don't want it!" The same disc has a brief selection called "Keep It Real" that is an admonition and a plea not to give up the fight for go-go's recognition.

Clearly, members of the community think that it is very important to represent for D.C. and go-go. Citizens of Washington, D.C., are disenfranchised by law, and much of the city's black population is even further removed from the political process by economic factors. Go-go gives a voice to the black citizens of Washington, D.C.—it's a truly unique sound with which they can identify. If you represent for D.C.—like DJ Celo does by way of his WPGC broadcasts and E.U. does when the band performs at Norfolk State University—then you *are* someone with something to say. Black people in D.C., at least, pay attention to go-go.

NEIGHBORHOODS AND CREWS

The District is divided into four discrete geographic sectors: Northeast, Southeast, Northwest, and Southwest. Within these sectors lie very distinctive neighborhoods such as Petworth, Capitol Hill, and Brookland, which form small communities within the District. The "blackest" section of D.C. is Southeast. The terms "far Southeast," "across the [Anacostia] River," or "east of the [Anacostia] river" are local codes for the blackest and poorest as well as some of the prettiest neighborhoods in the City. As the original home for many of the members of Trouble Funk and Junk Yard, the Anacostia section of Washington, D.C., is arguably the most fertile breeding ground for go-go bands.

Anacostia itself is a mixed bag. Its rolling hills have some lovely detached single-family homes. But if you come over the 11th Street Bridge onto Martin Luther King Avenue, you soon encounter a welter of small businesses, row houses, and projects. Barry Farms is one of the most notorious projects in far Southeast and has been ground zero for many go-go bands since the mid-1970s, when Chuck Brown first "busted loose."

Far Southeast is also home to many "mobs," "posses," or "crews." Crews provide some of the glue that helps to shape the social fabric of black youth. According to a 1998 report: "Today, crews and gangs are neighborhoods, street to street, and block and block. Not all crews are violent but all have the potential to be violent. Some crews are social crews. In certain schools there are over 30 crews.... Some of the gangs set up in Congress Heights, Hanover Place, Paradise, Parkside, Potomac Gardens, LeDroit Park, First Street, "R" Street, and "O" Street."[2] The crews define themselves in many ways, including by the style of their clothing, the color of their clothing, their hand signs and signals, and (to a small degree) graffiti. Ironically the best-known D.C. tagger—"Disco Dan"—is not a gang member, just a creative member of the community. Most of D.C.'s crews are black, but one of the largest—the Brown Union—is largely Salvadorian and is based in Mt. Pleasant.

Interestingly, the rise of female crews has paralleled the rise of go-go. Also largely based in neighborhoods, female crew members, like their male counterparts, tend to be in their teens and early twenties. Some female crews are associated with male crews, but the modest majority of them stand alone, without direct male affiliation. Their names—4th and Kennedy Honies, Wheeler Road Honies, Puff Down Honeys of 14th and A Street, Emery Heights Honeys—reflect not only their gender but their location within the city. Neighborhood identification is especially important for many of these groups. According to urban researchers Brooks and Miller, the Top Cat Bitches "seldom come uptown; stay in Southeast on the Maryland side or hang out on Martin Luther King Avenue and Chesapeake Street." The Lucious Honeys, on the other hand, stay "at Alabama [Avenue] and Congress Park on the Southeast Side." The same study notes that the Butter Nut Honeys "like to go to the 'go-go.'"[3]

Some of the crews are involved with civil causes, such as canned food drives or holding benefits for people who are down on their luck or who have suffered a tragedy like a house fire. Take, for instance, the example set by the Second to None (220) Honies, a female crew that traces its roots back to the late 1980s. Their presence is felt not only on the streets but on the Web as well. Here is an excerpt from their (Internet-posted) mission statement:

> Every community in America faces the continuing chal-
> lenge of providing much needed services with limited
> resources One of the best ways of meeting this challenge
> is through volunteerism. The 220 Mission is to just "GO
> HARD!" To show the world and one another that with a
> little class, a touch of style and uniqueness that we can all
> get along in a peaceful harmonious society. We are out to
> break the stereotypes about black women. We want to see
> improvement of our community, race, and ourselves.

Their site also lists some of the agencies devoted to combating homelessness and dealing with issues related to housing in the District of
Columbia—Christmas in April in Washington, D.C., Mi Casa, Inc.,
National Alliance to End Homelessness, SOME (So Others Might Eat),
and the Washington Legal Clinic for the Homeless. This loose-knit community group is actually part of a larger system of self-help, grassroots
community groups that have existed in urban neighborhoods for several
generations. Jack and Jill of America, for example, founded in Philadelphia
in 1938, has spent more than 50 years working to improve the lives of
youngsters, especially African American children. This mostly volunteer
organization works to this end through education, recreation, and social
programs.

Another female crew—the All Around Honies—shares some philoso-
phies with the Second to None (220) Honies, though their energies are
more focused on go-go music and events. They seek to:

> establish and maintain a level of respect between one
> another. There are too many negative connotations and
> bad publicity directed towards go-go and go-goers. Go-
> go music is a way of life that not everyone can under-
> stand....Your appearance and behavior is a reflection of
> you and what you represent....We try not to put our-
> selves out there to be disrespected, and we give each other
> a lot of attention which makes others curious to find out
> who we are and why we do what we do. We are one of the
> few cliques that don't associate themselves with a lot of
> negative drama within the clubs or the public. Our main
> purpose is to show "Elegance," much "Love," "Spirit,"
> and a lot of "Strength."[4]

Despite the good works of the Second to None (220) Honies and a handful of others, crews are often associated with the distribution of drugs and other related criminal activity—such as carjackings, home invasions, and armed robberies—that takes place across the city (indeed, across the United States). Drug-dealing is perhaps the most nefarious activity with which crews are identified. D.C. mobs have been involved with all types of drugs, ranging from marijuana to crack cocaine to heroin. And drugs can provide a high level of income for a teenager still in school or with limited job skills.

By and large, D.C. crews are social groups whose loyalty is based on their school or neighborhood connections or childhood friendships. They tend to break down as their members enter their twenties and are more likely to have relocated to attend college or a job, to have married, or to have simply become too involved with full-time adult activities to devote time to this part of their social life. D.C. and Prince George's County are filled with crews like 9th Street Dogg Pound, 35 Double O, Oxon Hill Niggaz, 4 Duce (42), Nu Projex, Indian Queen, 7th & Taylor, 640 (Naughty Boyz), and 7 Woodz. Many of these are small groups—any group, no matter how small, can call itself a crew—and many are ephemeral. Nonetheless, crews are important in D.C. because they provide young adults with a way to organize themselves; it's a matter of pride and neighborhood identity as much as a social grouping. Crews are also social groupings that are outside of the normative bounds of school, church, or clubs like the YMCA—another attractive point for some youths.

Most D.C. crew members' dress reflects mainstream hip-hop culture. Designer labels, such as Tommy Hilfiger, Eddie Bauer, Nike, or DKNY, are very important in the 'hood, but many dress more casually in baggy shorts or pants and jogging or basketball shoes, with baseball caps turned backwards or to the side. With subtle and important exceptions (such as a Junk Yard T-shirt), a b-boy from Southeast would not look out of place in the ghettos of Milwaukee, Nashville, or Seattle.

HIP-HOP CULTURE

Hip-hop is social, linguistic, and cultural self-expression, and rap is one of hip-hop's musical forms. Hip-hop evolved in the late 1970s and represents the most important, vibrant form of African American expression since the heyday of "black power" in the previous decade. It is one critically important and widespread reaction to urban life in the post-industrial, post-soul

United States. Hip-hop began in the coastal urban centers of greater New York and the sprawl of Los Angeles and diffused throughout the country, hitting D.C. around 1980. It is a prime example of what cultural geographers call "contagious" diffusion, starting locally but then being spread by way of the mass media as radio, television, and print journalists realized that what was happening in the ghetto held greater implications for American culture in general. Eventually, of course, hip-hop spawned its own media— magazines such as *The Source* and *Vibe,* as well as a cable television network called The Box, which is primarily carried by cable systems that serve urban areas. The D.C.-based and highly successful BET (Black Entertainment Television) trumpets hip-hop culture on many of its programs as well.

But in the early 1980s hip-hop was still so fringe (due to its ghetto heritage and its recent evolution) that it was only reported as peripheral news. At that time it was fighting for press space with such other American phenomena as Valley Girls and the "death" of disco music; time has told us which cultural expressions have had a lasting impact. The fact that hip-hop was viewed with suspicion is underscored by Tricia Rose in her book *Black Noise.* Rose writes: "Hip-hop is a cultural form that attempts to negotiate the experiences of marginalization, brutally truncated opportunity, and oppression with the cultural imperatives of African American and Carribean history, identity, and community."[5] Because hip-hop (like go-go) is so strongly rooted not only in contemporary black culture but in its historical lineage, it found its strength and its launching pad in the fringe netherworld of urban America.

Although rap emerged out of the shadows of soul power and budding "funketeers" (after all, trends in all forms of popular music are cyclical), it is more than coincidence that hip-hop culture established itself just as that liberal president from the South, Jimmy Carter, headed back down home. Carter's administration in some ways represented the vestiges of LBJ's "Great Society," which provided a reasonable safety net. The years of Reagan and Bush (senior), especially here in the District of Columbia, represented a new paradigm: the bifurcated regimes of the Republican-led federal government in tandem with the rise to power of Marion Barry. The fact remains that the hip-hop nation began just as the Republicans answered the call of the majority of the American electorate.

Hip-hop recreates, reformulates, and then extends urban black life for a wider audience (black, white, Hispanic, Middle Eastern, etc.), bringing it into their homes primarily by way of radios and compact discs. Just think...the baddest of the West Coast rappers can politely invade your family room in International Falls, Minnesota; Plains, Georgia; Detroit, Michigan; or Manhattan, Kansas. What a great way to annoy and perplex your mom and dad and impress your friends! And it's safe, too, because you don't have to even see or interact with a real live black person in order to enjoy hip-hop culture. You can learn the latest local gang signs, hear the latest ghetto slang, and enjoy the latest black tunes without leaving the comfort of your own home and venturing onto the mean streets of far Southeast Washington, D.C.

Today those long-established modes of communication are proving to be too slow. Here in the twenty-first century—more than 20 years after hip-hop emerged—you can visit any one of dozens of fresh Web sites devoted to hip-hop culture. Just type in "hip-hop" on your favorite search engine and see where you end up—it's quick and easy, and places you in instant contact with what's really happening across the country and throughout the world. The world in 1980, however, was not able to transmit information as quickly as today, and hip-hop was both localized and just beginning to stir. This local flavor helped go-go to emerge in D.C., but—for better or worse—it has remained a local staple. Back then, you had to live in urban (black and/or Hispanic) America in order to even feel the change on the streets. Hip-hop reflected not only its urban origins but also its constituency. In New York City, for instance, hip-hop was based in black American as well as Latino (especially Puerto Rican) culture. On the West Coast, most notably in Los Angeles, hip-hop's flavor was spiced with Mexican—and to a lesser degree, Asian American—influences. In the District, however, hip-hop has retained its strong black roots.

Because the nationwide mass media both did not understand hip-hop culture and initially treated it merely as a ghetto anomaly, indigenous trends remained largely within the communities from which they originated. "Tagging," or "writing," was largely a New York phenomenon until the media picked up the inclination of (mostly young and male) black urbanites to leave their signature graffiti on the walls of subways or in other public spaces. Despite the vogue for graffiti in some cities, it was less important in others, such as Washington, D.C., where tagging remains a lesser art.

Fashion, on the other hand, quickly became more ubiquitous. This is no doubt due to the interest of magazines and television in acknowledging fresh tendencies in the ways that people dress. By the mid-1980s, loose-fitting clothes (especially baggy shorts and jeans) could be seen on the mean streets of Detroit as well as the summer-swelled streets of the small towns, like East Sandwich, that dot Cape Cod, Massachusetts. The same is true for the three-figure designer sneakers that initially hit the scene on the asphalt basketball courts of Harlem and were eventually touted by such famous athletes as Michael Jordan or Deion Sanders. This "rainbowing" of Nike or Adidas commercials allowed a handful of multinational American-based corporations to proclaim their racial diversity (though one wonders how many of these sales to ghetto youths translated into more lucrative or even executive positions for non-white employees).

Dance is intimately associated with hip-hop. Dance (indeed, movement in general) is integral to African American music and has been since Africans arrived on these shores. The importance of dance has been further reinforced by the waves of new Americans, such as Jamaicans and Cubans, who arrived as part of the African diaspora and brought the rhumba, skank, and other polymetric-inspired dances with them. In the South, dancing—most of which is highly improvised (sometimes idiosyncratic) solo or group dances—has been an indispensable component of musical events ranging from fife and drum band concerts in the hill country of Mississippi to funeral parades in New Orleans. During the 1930s the incredible athleticism of lindy-hoppers and the smooth sliding steps of Cab Calloway inspired a more urbane generation of blacks who had joined the Great Migration and ended up in the urban North. More recently, James Brown's onstage movements in the late 1950s and 1960s clearly set the stage not only for funk and rap but for black-inspired dancing into the twenty-first century.

Because they are so closely intertwined, music and movement can not really be separated in black American culture. This is especially true of hip-hop, when the gymnastic styles known as breakdancing as well as the robotic movements of waack dancing broke out of the ghetto and into the American mainstream. Dance historian Katrina Hazzard-Donald describes some of the most important, and largely male, components of hip-hop dance:

> Hip hop dance is clearly masculine in style, with postures assertive in their own right as well as in relation to a female partner. In its early stages, hip hop rejected the partnering ritual between men and women; at a party or a dance, hip hop dance was performed between men or by a lone man [much like the step dances of fraternities]...the

male does not assume the easygoing, cool, confident pol-
ish characteristic of earlier popular-dance expression
[especially swing]. Even in its early stages hip hop dancing aggressively asserted male dominance...and it does
appear to celebrate male solidarity, strength, and compet-
itiveness; themes that might be expected to emerge via the
social dance in an era of high black male unemployment
and of scarce jobs for which men are increasingly forced
to compete with women.[6]

OH, LADIES!

The lack of women participating in the performance, promotion, and
management of go-go is painfully visible. For example, nearly all of the
contributors to the TMOTTGoGo Web site, run by Kevin Hammond, are
male. Most message-posters on its active bulletin board are also male, with
the exception of René Dickerson, who is a very regular contributor.
Excluding Ms. Mack, who managed Rare Essence in their first few years,
women are all but absent from the ranks of managers. Cheri Mitchell han-
dles the keyboards for the Hip Huggers and women occasionally sit in on
percussion instruments at local gigs, but once you get Pleasure out of the
way, it's simply not possible to name a truly significant female go-go band.
To paraphrase James Brown, go-go is a man's world.

Even the language of go-go is male-oriented. Go-go talkers, for
example, use masculine terminology when they are on stage and recognizing people in the audience. Except when they are speaking directly to
women, like when they shout out to a female crew, they refer to people in
the audience as "dawgs" (a reference not only to men but to a particular
black fraternity), to their "troopers," or even their "man." For that matter, the use of "nigger" in the community usually refers to a male, while
"bitch" connotes a female and in a very pejorative way.

It's not that women have no interest in go-go; you see plenty of women
attending go-gos at the Icebox and at other local venues, and they also purchase their share of P.A. tapes and commercially issued compact discs. But
while women consume go-go in various ways, few participate in its presentation or in its business end. "Honies" is the colloquial term for women, and
some honies do very public and positive community work with other members of their crew. Female crews are not only territorial, but also provide a
social network through which women—especially younger girls—attend

go-go events. Many of the teenage girls flock to go-gos in the company of their crew, their contemporaries, and friends from the neighborhood. Initially, at least, the girls remain segregated from their male counterparts.

You see many girls and women at go-gos, dancing, talking with their friends, and grooving to the music. As mentioned earlier, dancing is an important ingredient at a go-go—an integral part of the interaction between the band and the patrons. If that call and response (in its broadest meaning) is not happening, then the go-go is simply not happening. This is a rare occurrence, but it does happen. Most go-goers simply groove to the music, but there is a tradition that developed in the late 1980s of display dancing, especially with Junk Yard Band. It is solo dancing (for example, to the "Funky Hoedown" or the "Hee-Haw") that bears some of the hallmarks of hip-hop; it is very athletic, improvisatory, sometimes acrobatic, and calls attention to the dancer's vigor and prowess.

Solo go-go dancing is mostly male and the majority of the dancers are in their teens. You occasionally see women dance like this but it's almost always younger men you see doing the Hee-Haw. Maybe black women in D.C. don't like to place the spotlight on themselves in such a context, or maybe they are brought up to be less overtly competitive than the men. When asked why so few women dance like this, women sometimes respond that most girls don't like to get all sweaty like boys! Perhaps it can be viewed as a preening process for males, one that women eschew but men value because it brings them very public notice in much the same way that a spectacular slam dunk brings respect and attention to b-boys on the court.

That go-go is a male dominated musical genre (even more so than rap) is beyond dispute, but the nagging question remains: why? There are no easy answers to this conundrum. The conventional wisdom is that, much like jazz and other forms of twentieth-century African American vernacular music (and also like much rock-inspired pop music), these are not roles that women choose to occupy. Charlie Fenwick, one-time manager of Pleasure, observed this of women in go-go: "It's hard to find them and keep them. Once they want to get married, you know, and have a family and all that. . . . A guy can go out and get married and have a family and still perform, but women can't."[7] Whether this is simple rationalization, personal bias, or an observation based on some deeper understanding of black life in the District, Fenwick articulates what a lot of other male go-go heads told us.

Some other thoughts about the dearth of women in go-go. . . . Unlike, for example, fiction writing, a craft for which women ranging from Jane Austen to Maya Angelou have been recognized, go-go requires that women appear in public, late at night, and largely in the company of men. Perhaps D.C.'s black female performers have found other outlets—like gospel—to express their musical creativity in a less threatening atmosphere. Because they have so few forebears in go-go, it is also possible that the women are uncertain if there is an audience for female go-go performers.

On the other hand, black women from Bessie Smith to Dinah Washington to Aretha Franklin to Whitney Houston *have* enjoyed a prominent position in twentieth-century black popular music. These are powerful, successful women and they stand as important figures as well as role models for other black performers. Black women, in fact, have played a more significant role in shaping American popular music than have white females (even with Janis Joplin or Madonna in mind) in the rock-oriented world of popular music that has existed since the mid-1950s.

Pleasure emerged in 1988 as the first all-female go-go band. Most of the band members were in their late teens when they got together with the help of Charlie Fenwick, and initially they came under the sway of another Fenwick-led band —Hot, Cold, Sweat. Michelle Peterson, Pleasure's most visible member and their leader, recalls that they "became like a family" after doing so many dates with Hot, Cold, Sweat. She was particularly influenced by their rapper, Slick Rick, who helped her come up with the nickname "Sweet Shell."

A keen and thoughtful observer of go-go and its sexual politics, Sweet Shell suggests that professional jealousy played a major role in the rise and fall of Pleasure:

> Well...90% of the members in the band were musicians who were already in the music circuit. However, we were new to go-go....Things went fine with it until our name began to grow more and more throughout the industry. I found that with some people, it had almost become personal. I mean, go-go is such a male dominated circuit, and here is this all-girl band that come[s] out and just start[s] doing things other groups had been trying to achieve for years. I guess it became hard for some to swallow.[8]

Commercial and artistic success came to Pleasure rather quickly and in less than a year, they were well-known around the area. A personal connection helped to lead them to a new management situation. This change also led them to venues way outside of D.C. and to perform music outside of go-go:

> Claudia (Malcolm), our keyboard player, had some type of connection with somebody who knew Herbie (Love Bug) Azar [sic], manager of Salt N Pepa.... Finally, she came to us and explained Herbie's interest in using us as a back-up band for Salt N Pepa's tour. Claudia and our drummer Shawney (LaShawn Dandy) were the main ones in the band who were really "gung-ho" on going national. The rest of us, especially Lil' Boogie (Natasha Proctor) were really close to Charlie. But at the same time, anything that happened in the band, they would all look at me ... they all assumed I was the leader of everything.[9]

The band members eventually decided to go on the tour, which greatly disturbed Charlie Fenwick, who Peterson characterized as "hurt," "upset," and eventually "bitter" over the band's split with him. The commotion quickly spread around the community and in a few days the band members went on WOL (D.C.'s "black talk" radio station) to explain what had occurred. The contentious situation created a royal mess; with one exception (Lil' Boogie) the band agreed to split and come under Luv Bug's aegis. But it did result in another D.C.-based female band—Precise— that included some go-go in its repertoire:

> Herbie had us all come to his home in New York, where we met his staff, went to different parties and mingled with a lot of celebrities there. We were all excited. There, he explained to us in detail how he planned to use us on the tour with Salt N Pepa. :... However, we didn't want to just sit around waiting. We still wanted to play. That's when Precise was born.[10]

Although Sweet Shell eventually left Salt-N-Pepa's fold (her young son, Marcus, and a desire to get out from underneath the shadow of her better-known employers called her back to D.C.), she didn't lose her

Women and Go-Go

Real people listen to and appreciate go-go music. Teenagers, pre-teens, men, and women, all listen to go-go music. Most of us are black, but soon, hopefully, the genre will expand to all races. I guess the reason why it is considered "black music" is because it was born in Washington, D.C., also known as Chocolate City, for the most part.

The reason I mentioned women is because I happen to be one, thank God. I am a woman who happens to love and appreciate go-go music. I happen to be a woman involved in music. I also happen to be a woman at the go-go. My being a woman should not be an issue in go-go, but it is. Go-go is a man's world, a man's music, according to men. They may not say it, but they think it for sure. I'm here to dispute that, to debate it, and to prove that the men are wrong about the women in go-go, as well as some other things surrounding the music.

I have encountered many kinds of offensive behaviors being involved in go-go music. I've been called a freak, a bitch, a groupie, a wannabe, etc. etc., but I take it all on the chin while I give it back to those haters that spit the venom in my direction, hence the name Soldierette!! I am one of the few women involved in go-go music today, and probably, hopefully, will not be the last. I am Soldierette!! and I'm here to stay.

Now I won't even part my lips, or my pen, to say that all men think the same about the women at the go-go, but I will say there is a vast majority... who do. Historically, women have been found at a go-go dancing and behaving in a manner that is unfitting for women, in society's eyes. Personally, I believe that some women at the go-go are there to find their "dream man" and some are there to "pick up" a man, but there are also others, like myself, notwithstanding my involvement with the music, who are there to see the bands and listen to some funky go-go music. I am definitely not looking for any of the aforementioned at the go-go.

What I have encountered while there, though, is the attitude and behaviors from men that I am one of those who wants to be touched and felt up, and basically, treated like trash. I ain't the one. I most assuredly let these men know my feelings about this behavior. How I do love to dance, but my dancing does not entail my palms being put on the floor and my derriere being posted up in the air, against some stranger's groin. This is not a position that I would want to be caught dead in. Being in this business, though, allows me to know or get to know, a multitude of different men. If they have met me, they know that I command respect, from everyone, especially men. They also know that I'm a huge go-go fan and am willing to do whatever it takes to help the music get the respect and recognition that it deserves. I have spoken to various audiences about the music that I love. I take it everywhere I go. I play it everywhere I am. I give it away. I write about it on the Internet and in articles written for various publications. As of this day, I've been asked to write for an internationally published urban magazine. Guess what my subject matter will be? I don't even have to tell you. I push the music at every chance I get because I want people to know about and to love it, as I do.

How did a woman in her mid-thirties get to be involved in go-go music, you ask? For starters, I was born and raised in Washington, D.C., and my brother was a go-go DJ in the early '80s. I am also the child of musicians that worked in Washington, D.C., and around the world. My grandfather and his two brothers, my uncles, were all saxophonists in the '40s, '50s, and '60s. They were in a group called The Three Saxes for Lester. My remaining uncle performed at nightclubs and private parties for many famous faces such as Robert Redford, Pearl Bailey, and many others. He has since retired for health reasons. My father was a vocalist in a couple of national acts, The Phantones and The Maskman and the Agents. I was the baby in the family during the times of all this stardom and could not escape the live music being played at home, the musicians calling and knocking on the door, and everyone traveling somewhere, all the time. I also had my keyboard lessons to learn, that is until someone stole them while we were moving. I was so hurt by this, I didn't want another thing that someone could take from me, which included keyboards. Now, I wish I [had] continued with my lessons.

Go-go has a major shortage of female musicians and I'd be ready right now to step up to the plate and show 'em how women could make it funky. I haven't figured out yet why there are so few women involved, except to say that traditionally little girls were not enrolled in instrumental music in grade school. We were always encouraged to enroll in cooking, sewing, and typing classes while the boys took shop, sports, and band classes. Also, there is that "man's territory" that exists at the go-go. You can't see it or touch it, but it's there. Men think, consciously or subconsciously, that go-go music belongs to them and therefore, women are there for one reason, to be freaked and felt up and prodded. Maybe that's why women are not involved in the music, I'm really not sure. That can only be discovered through speaking with every female musician in the area. Trivia seems to play a big part in the scene also. If you don't know who played with who back in 1980, you're not a true go-go head or fan. [Go-go] trivia is a man's game, just like football, basketball, and baseball trivia. Men claim these activities as well. This dilemma probably expands over many genres, and not just go-go.

I now manage a variety of bands in the city, as well as the Web site, www.soldierette.com. I have started, single-handedly, Soldierette's Entertainment Management, where I have several acts in addition to a go-go band. This endeavor of mine was seemingly easy, and for the most part it is, that is until I acquired the go-go band. Go-go is so much different from other genres, and it shouldn't be. Go-go probably hasn't reached its full potential because of the differences it has from other genres. There is so much money to be had and made within go-go and so many different types of people pulling at these go-go bands, that it makes it seem as though [there is] not enough room for the hundreds of go-go bands out there. On the contrary, [there's] plenty of room for everybody but they just don't know it yet.

Go-go is promoted in a "local way." Local meaning right in the D.C., MD, and VA area, for the most part. It isn't promoted nationally, in general, as all other genres are. This is a big problem in my eyes. There are too many people within go-go that have local ties and use those ties to gain attention locally. There are no "big time" promoters coming into Washington, D.C., checking out a go-go, and contacting a band to say "Hey, I saw your show and I want to do some work with you, NOW!" It's funny how the rap and hip-hop artists have come into the city, melded in with the locals, then took the music back to their genre, without even giving go-go so much as a nod. There was Salt-N-Pepa, Timbaland & Magoo, and Def Jam Records, to name but a few. Other artists such as L.L. Cool J, Heavy D, and Doug E. Fresh sampled the music. I won't say they didn't pay for it, but whose name do you recognize? Go-go, being local (translation: no big money), sat down, put its head between its legs, and cried. Nothing else was done about it to this day. I'm glad men take claim to the genre in this case.

There are a few other reasons, in my opinion, as to why go-go music hasn't taken off over these almost 30 years now. One would be the fact that some people in the Washington, D.C., area don't want the music to be nationally recognized. Again, that goes back to the issue of men thinking that the music belongs to them. How would it be possible to give something away when everybody from every direction is holding on to it as though it were theirs? The answer is: It's not possible. I think that if bands were to branch out and embrace other genres, as well as each other, not just hip-hop, people would be more willing to embrace our music. We in the go-go community say that we are tired of the go-go bands doing cover songs, but yet, covering hip-hop music is all that we do. There are a few go-go bands that perform their own music, i.e., Chuck Brown, Trouble Funk, Rare Essence, but they are the exceptions. Surely I believe that if we add the go-go flavor to a hip-hop or R&B tune the music will only improve, but...haven't we heard that song before? It gets kind of old over time. I would most expediently jump on an original tune done in the fashion that our go-go bands perform a hit hip-hop tune. There is a serious lack of creativity amongst the go-go bands today. Sure, it can be called creative when a band takes one style of music and changes it into a go-go song. However, it's even more creative when a go-go band creates a song that hip-hop and R&B artists try to emulate. After all, they're on top, we're just strugglin'...tryin' to maintain.

Some say that bands hate on each other. I find that true to an extent but not so much as the fans hate on the band that is not their favorite. Everyone has a favorite and doesn't recognize that all of the bands have something good about them. Fans love to compare and dissect a go-go band. They also love to see a good battle between the bands, whether the musicians call it that or not, it's still true. Surely this author loves to see her favorite go-go band whoop up on another band. There is nothing finer than the top go-go bands in the city on a show together. With the Legends of Go-Go being my favorite, because they crank the hardest, it's a wonderful thing when they sit another band down on their hiney. I don't actually expect the other band to do anything about it. It's all healthy competition for real though. They're all just doing their thing and the crowd determines who cranks, or who puts on the best show, or who hits that old-school song the best. The shows are what make go-go. It wouldn't be as appealing to me if it weren't for the shows, I don't think. It's all good fun though and not to be taken too seriously. This seriousness that some fans have about their favorite band creates animosity between bands and their fans to the point of physical or verbal altercations. This is a very blatant reason as to why go-go cannot spread its wings...nobody likes drama.

Another reason I have found is that the city, Washington, D.C., and its surrounding suburbs in Maryland and northern Virginia, have all but turned their backs on the music. This music was born and raised in Washington, D.C., and is an orphan in its own home. There are political reasons as to why certain clubs or neighborhoods won't allow go-go music to be shared and enjoyed in them. That's the "not in my neighborhood" syndrome. It's like that until the money runs out in a club. When a club is experiencing "slow times," go-go is welcomed with open arms. Go-go music has the ability to attract thousands of people in one night and people with the ability to put on a show like that simply won't. There are too many greedy people within go-go today. There is a serious lack of integrity also. We are untrusting of outsiders, for historical reasons mentioned earlier. We don't know how to be painfully honest. All genres have their "barroom brawls," but go-go has the reputation of being "thug-like." The music nor the culture is understood by the very city it was born in, nor do they try to understand. They do know we love it and will fight to keep it, but they do not care about it nor show any sign of changing. There have been times where an incident would be blown out of proportion for the sake of selling newspapers, all at the expense of go-go music. The powers that be, local governments, neighborhood associations, the ABC Board, and in my opinion, most whites in the area, want to rid this city of go-go music and its culture, black people. Yes, I'm saying it's a black thing. Think about it like this. If we were all white kids attending a rave, they'd block off the streets so we'd have freedom to walk them all night, listening to our music. If go-go were an "acceptable" art form I could have deleted this whole paragraph.

Another reason, in my opinion, as to why this music cannot and has not succeeded to the levels expected of it is that some of the musicians involved are totally unprofessional. This may be the biggest and most important reason. Generally speaking, if our musicians were as serious about getting to rehearsals, getting to the shows, and maintaining their equipment as they are concerned about the "crank" and the "pocket," go-go surely would have surpassed other genres by now. If our musicians would handle their business as though it were a nine-to-five job or something that they would normally deem important, the shows would not and could not fail. There is a limited, very limited mind you, number of go-go bands that handle their business in this fashion. Granted, money is an issue with some as far as maintaining the proper equipment. However, I believe that if you're going to be in a band making money off your music, you've got to keep your equipment top-rate. You've got to get there on time, no matter what. That's with any profession though.

If go-go bands only dealt with clubs and/or promoters who exhibited a wealth of integrity, it would go a long way for them. Sadly, this is not the case though. This is one of the ugly facts of the music industry. It's not just in go-go, either.

Finally, and most definitely important, is the fact that go-go bands are not in this together. Everyone is for themselves. Dog eat dog if you will. Go-go bands say they have love for one another, but try to get them to organize themselves and unite as a genre. It's not going to happen, at least no time soon. There are too many people today wanting and needing to make fast money, the honest way. It would be about time that go-go musicians foresaw something past performing at the local club. It's not hard to foresee when I can see a go-go band performing onstage at a Soul Train Awards show or a Grammy Awards show, or an American Music Awards show, with their own category. Why can't go-go aim for something like that? Why won't they? The answer is: organization. We have none.

I have made attempts to put together the beginnings of what we call "The Go-Go Alliance." This was also done before by people involved in and who love go-go music. It didn't work then because nobody wanted to stick together as a unit. There was one person who stuck it out until there was nothing left, though. Maurice "Moe" Shorter is the man that was there for go-go. He still is. I have . . . several names and contact numbers for bands that are interested in uniting as one organization. Together with Kevin "Kato" Hammond of *Take Me Out To The Go-Go Magazine*, we have been laying the groundwork to organize all of the players. These players would include, but would not be limited to, musicians, record labels, producers, promoters, venues, music stores, organizers, the media, the people with business savvy, the recording studios, and the technical crews involved in go-go music today. This is our vision for go-go. It will work. We just need some time to work it all out. We have most of these titles now, but we want more. This Go-Go Alliance will be a mean, clean, running machine with the goal of forcing go-go onto the charts.

We are, and will remain, in the category of garage bands if we don't make our minds up to do this thing right. It's an insult to the genre but it's the way it is. If no one organized entity can or will speak for the entire genre, inside or outside of the D.C. area, who will? One band doesn't want another band speaking for them and vice versa. So...that dilemma will not be solved until everybody puts down their shields, unswells their chests, and gets onboard, together.

On the positive side of things, I haven't and won't give up. I think that there are people who deal in go-go with lots of integrity. I think there are bands who have their act together. There are also clubs and promoters who have their integrity in check. If the band has its act together, notwithstanding the music, they can demand an honest exchange of business dealings, and get it. I have no doubt in the belief that good begets good or that if you deal with integrity, you've got all aces.

These beliefs, and straightforwardness, that I possess, oftentimes get me, and keep me, in trouble. I can be found daily writing and interacting on the Community Bulletin Board on www.tmottgogo.com. This is really not a pleasant experience for me because of the lack of respect I encounter from male fans. This is a part of go-go that I just deal with. I'm not comfortable with the stalkers I encounter though. As long as people don't take this too seriously, I won't have to react to a bad situation. It doesn't have to be this way, but it is. One day, our black people on-line (and off-line) will learn to respect one another, especially the women. It's all good, though. I give my opinions on anything and everything and I stick with them no matter how much adversity I encounter. Go-go has never seen a woman like Soldierette!! before so they better just get used to me because I'm not going anywhere.

I love go-go music and I think that if the things outlined are checked, go-go music can and will soar, past our expectations. We need and should keep the dialogue going, without disrespecting one another. We should take heed to suggestions that sound logical. We should and need to change our ways of thinking and set out to bring in new fans to the music. We should never hide the problems we have within go-go music because family secrets will always remain just that and our problems will never be solved if hidden. We can never grow if we don't know. We'll continue to make the same mistakes over and over again and the music genre is what suffers the most. We can do this. We need to do it together though. "United we stand, divided we fall" fits very well right here.

"Peace! while 'Keepin' da' Focus on da' Boogie'" is my tagline to my writings. I write this because I want people to understand that we need to have peace in our community and our culture. We need to focus on the party aspect of go-go music and not the negativity that others like to attach to it. If ever I write about or talk about or am at a go-go, keep in mind that I want it to flourish while we party, while it spreads all over this world, peacefully.

Peace! while "Keepin' da' Focus on da' Boogie"

Soldierette!!
October 2000

interest in music and singing. She also stayed close to the go-go community. She was briefly married to Buggs from Junk Yard and often sang with Precise. Eventually she also managed Precise, but the singing/managing gig became too much and she relinquished control of the group to Marguerite Rice, who later turned the band over to Terrance Cooper (aka Coop), the longtime Backyard Band manager.

In the summer of '97, after a long hiatus, Shell was back singing with Precise. Then she was confronted with her grandmother's death as well as a painful romantic breakup. Shell also perceived that excessive drinking and smoking were helping neither her peace of mind nor her health. At the urging of Sophia Pope (a long-time friend and former Precise member), Shell visited and then joined the Holy Christian Missionary Baptist Church for All People, a Pentecostal church to which she still belongs.

Although she doesn't directly state the facts beyond her observation that go-go is a "male-dominated" musical genre, Shell intimates that gender helped steer and shape her go-go career. For example, in a culture where women bear a disproportionate burden for child care, her status as a single mother proved to be a critical element in her decision to leave Salt-N-Pepa. She also suggested that she wearied of guys hitting on her, which kept her distracted from keeping her eyes on the prize. One of the former members of Pleasure, drummer LaShawn Dandy, kept her professional bearings and spent several years playing in the band that provided the music for Arsenio Hall's nightly talk show.

Some folks are more outspoken than others, and Soldierette (René Dickerson) is one of them. Like Hillary Clinton, Dickerson is a lightning rod; she's convinced that most men in go-go, whether consciously or unconsciously, want to keep it the nearly all-male club that it has been since its inception. This attitude is perhaps most clearly demonstrated by some of the messages posted on the TMOTTGoGo Web site, where Soldierette is a very active participant. Dickerson explains:

> Men don't think that women should be involved in [go-go]. That's why I get so much grief on . . . the go-go bulletin board. [Women] are not respected in go-go music in my opinion because you can go to a go-go and just see how they treat the women there. And I think that it is all the way around from the bottom to the top from shows to backstage. . . . I'm so outspoken on that bulletin board . . . because when I'm nice and stay in my place, you

know—the ladies' place—then I get no grief from them. But as soon as I start voicing my opinion and...if I say a cuss word, oh man, they are ready to lynch me. But the guys cuss and they say whatever they want and so there is no problem with being a man. So from my point of view, a woman's point of view...they've never even met me! They just know that I'm a black female who likes go-go music.[11]

Soldierette knows that you have to experience go-go live to really understand what it's like. Like everyone who knows and has lived in the scene, she can suggest which audio tapes or compact discs are worth owning, and she can render her candid opinion of the quality of the videotapes that have documented go-go events. Most of the latter are single-camera operations of amateurish quality, but what they choose to document is significant: "They don't know what they're looking for—they just focus on the band and maybe the tops of people's heads. They shouldn't be focusing on that girl with her hands on the floor and her butt up in the air or this guy over in the corner with eyes closed just boppin' to the music."[12] She notes that at the notorious pool party videos, the spotlight on naked or near-naked women misses the point of the music and the interaction that occurs between the crowd and the musicians.

For Dickerson (and many others), go-go serves as a community nexus. It remains an important gathering point, a forum for people to shout out and be recognized by their peers. She sees it as a place where people will sing "Happy Birthday" to celebrate that rite of passage. It's like a neighborhood bar where many of the people (the regulars) know one another. But not everyone is willing to go by the loose, friendly, unstated but widely understood rules observed by Soldierette and her like-minded comrades. For example:

I'm at a go-go and I'll start dancing. Usually I don't have a partner and then some guy will walk up behind me and he'll start getting too close. I don't need him up on me and I don't want one. I'll say, "Hey, I'm not one of them [loose women, hos, etc.]!"...I think that women are not demanding their respect at a go-go, within the go-go world....I carry myself as a lady and you got half the battle won then....Now I wear what I want to wear but I don't wear something where my butt cheeks are hangin' out all over. And when I dance, I don't have my butt up in the air and some guy on the back of me![13]

Her opinions are colored by her gender but also by her many years of attending go-gos. She lived in Northwest D.C. when she was in her mid-teens: "We used to live off of Georgia Avenue and Farragut Street and my grandmother lived up on Montique Street, which is right around the corner from the Ibex. So I used to go to the Ibex...saw Rare Essence there for the first time, and then E.U. You used to could see three or four bands in one night...for like four dollars, five dollars."[14] Dickerson was also influenced by an older brother who also enjoyed go-go.

These early experiences got her interested not only in go-go as music, but also the business end of it. Although she is a long-time Metro employee, Dickerson is more than simply a go-go devotee. She helps to promote the Legends, a band that employs half a dozen go-go veterans—Little Benny (Harley)'s name is perhaps the most prominent in the band. Like so many of her contemporaries, Soldierette is eager to see the popularity of go-go expand and strongly believes that the lack of contracts with major record labels is a critical factor inhibiting the bands. She's well aware of the contributions of Max Kidd, Charlie Fenwick, Moe Shorter, Coop and the handful of others who have labored to push go-go "so that everybody in the world knows about this music."

CRACK AND GUNS

In Washington, D.C., the divide between rich and poor and white and black is heightened by the city's stature as a national and international tourist destination. People visit the District of Columbia to see the White House or to walk through the Smithsonian's National Air and Space Museum, or to hear a concert at the Kennedy Center. Unless they are here to visit friends, they don't usually come to see the sights in Anacostia, nor do the myriad tourist buses that take tourists around town have Barry Farms on their list of stops. But the truth is that over half a million people live in Washington, D.C., and relatively few of them are directly linked to the parts of the city that the tourists flock to see.

Drugs provide one means of dealing with the city and urban life in general. D.C.'s drug problems were at their worst between 1984 and 1991. Drugs ranging from marijuana to heroin have been part of D.C. (and every other city in the United States) for decades, but there were two new problems—crack cocaine and PCP (angel dust). By 1985, crack, in particular, seemed to be everywhere, and the mobs were thriving. The most public gang figure associated with drugs at this time was Rayful Edmond III. Before he was arrested and tried in 1990, Edmond oversaw an immense drug operation with spidery fingers that stretched throughout the entire city and into the surrounding suburbs. In 1987, the Edmond crew brought as much as 400 pounds of cocaine a week into the city, accounting for about a third of all of the cocaine traffic in the District. Edmond was big time, but there were plenty of much smaller operators with similar *modi operandi.*

That drugs presented a major threat to the city in the late 1980s did not escape the notice of D.C.'s citizens. Little Benny was living in Southeast at the time and recalls the daily challenges offered by crack cocaine. For him, it became a highly charged, volatile, and very personal dilemma:

> You didn't know what was going on! You thought it was the love boat [PCP] they was tripping on, but it wasn't the love boat—it was that crack. 'Cause you could see them ... their nerve system just jumping. You know as far as somebody smoking PCP, they were thinking they was flying! When I started, I was smoking PCP. And I had a little thing I went through ... but I found me. I made sure I got up out of it—got detoxed. I went back to school 'cause I wanted better for my family; it was a phase I went through.... [15]

Much of the controversy and blame swirled around Marion Barry, the mayor of the District of Columbia during the darkest times of the crack infestation. Barry, a respected civil rights leader and longtime local politician, wanted to lead the city towards even greater self-sufficiency, following the path towards home rule that was first blazed by Walter Washington, the first elected mayor of Washington, D.C. But with a bloated, inefficient city bureaucracy working with antiquated computer and communications systems (in some measure a legacy of the federal government's decades of running the District of Columbia as their own fiefdom), Barry was caught up in the maelstrom. It became a firestorm when Barry himself was caught with crack cocaine and arrested on January 18, 1990, and then booted out of office.

Always the street-smart and wily politician, Barry was vitally aware of the importance of go-go. He made certain that bands like Junk Yard were part of the D.C. Department of Recreation's Summer in the Parks programming, which brought music and other entertainment to citizens of Washington, D.C. This ploy not only brought go-go to the city's youth in a safe, daytime format, it also helped them to equate go-go with Marion Barry. At election time, this association doubtless helped to gain the Mayor some added support.

As crack cocaine infiltrated the streets and lives of an increasing number of the District's citizens, violence also blossomed. The District had one of the highest per capita murder rates in the United States during a period that paralleled the spiraling drug epidemic. The screaming headlines in the *Washington Post* both underscored the problems and heightened awareness of the fact that the level of violence was approaching epidemic proportions. These sentiments were echoed in newspapers and in news reports broadcast to the rest of the country. The bottom line for most people was: Visiting your nation's capital can be dangerous to your health.

The truth is that it was far more dangerous for the people who actually lived in the District of Columbia than for anyone visiting the city. The truth is that black-on-black violence was (and is) a much more pervasive problem than the problem occasionally encountered by a tourist from Iowa or Egypt. The truth is that most people visiting the city rarely witnessed or were victims of the drugs and violence. Drugs and violence most often touched the lives of the people who lived in the shadow of the Capitol—not those merely passing through during broad daylight.

As the quintessential symbol of black youth culture in Washington, D.C., go-go music became the most direct target for citizens who were rightly concerned about these issues. Here's the quick and dirty line of reasoning: Black youth = violence, street life, and drugs. Go-go music = black youth culture. So . . . if you can restrict or even eliminate go-go, you can cut down on all of the negative elements of street life. Therefore if we (the city's power structure) can control go-go, we are part of the way to stemming the (perceived) negative aspects of the music. But as Little Benny pointed out, one of the primary flaws in this line of reasoning is that "crack people didn't want to come out to a go-go. Crack people are disturbed . . . they don't want to hear no music—they want to get away from everybody!"[16]

In the late 1980s, violence was rocking and wrecking the streets of the District, but it stayed on the streets and rarely occurred inside go-go clubs. The fact is that clubs like the Ibex or the Black Hole utilized very strict security (either off-duty Metropolitan Police or private security firms). Bringing a weapon into a go-go club was not impossible, of course, but it was quite difficult to get it past the screening—including body searches and metal detectors—employed by all of the clubs.

In a June 22, 1990, *Washington City Paper* article sagely entitled (with an appropriate nod to South Africa) "The Indestructible Beat of the District," Alona Wartofsky neatly summarized the violence directly associated with go-go:

> On April 11, 1987, gunmen sprayed a crowd of hundreds leaving a Rare Essence show in the Masonic Temple on 10th and U Streets NW at 4 a.m. Wounded were 11 people, including a 17-year-old who spent eight months recovering at Howard University. Sure, fist fights between hotheads broke out at go-go shows, just the way they do at rock concerts. But this was something different, and the go-go community was stunned. Six months later, another 17-year-old, Wendell Heard, was fatally stabbed outside Celebrity Hall in the 3400 block of Georgia Avenue NW after leaving a show. *The Washington Post* dubbed it the "Go-Go Slaying."[17]

Over the next 16 months, several other unfortunate and similar events occurred outside go-go clubs. These, too, were quickly, carelessly, and generically labeled as go-go-related. The fact remains that none of this extreme and gun-related viciousness took place in the clubs, but rather on the streets. Furthermore, this violence was drug-related and had nothing to do with the music or the clubs. Nonetheless, as Wartofsky put it, "go-go took the fall."[18]

The assault on go-go did not go unnoticed by the musicians and others in the go-go community. Chuck Brown observed that "the go-go don't have nothing to do with the drug war, but the drug war affects the go-go."[19] Joe Clark, a local promoter, suggested that "Bad people follow go-go and good people follow go-go. When [drug dealers] see someone they don't like or someone who owes them money, they take it out on them right there. They don't care who they hurt."[20] Rare Essence guitarist Andre "Whiteboy" Johnson later echoed these sentiments:

We had fights up at the Howard Theater or the Coliseum.
but those were fistfights; you fight with a guy and the next
week you might see the same guy and y'all might be partying together. It wasn't until the guns came into play that
people were actually getting shot....The violence thing
really put a damper on the business aspect. Now clubs that
were in business with you all of a sudden don't want to do
business with you. Clubs were afraid that somebody might
be shot, the police would come down and take their liquor
license, and suddenly there ain't no club anymore.[21]

Some observers of the go-go scene looked elsewhere for the problem.
Record producer Reo Edwards said that "When the black club has a go-go
band, the police aren't there the way they come out to other places. We pay
taxes. That's the bottom line. This is a business and we pay taxes so why
shouldn't we have police protection? At the Cap Centre they always have
police protection."[22] The implication is clear: the rich and the white get better police protection and quick response, but other folks in the city need
not apply. Of course, the police responded with adamant denials. What else
could they say? No one wants to be accused of being racist or of dispens-
ing police protection based on class distinctions. Deputy Chief Kris Coligan
suggested that go-go had placed a substantial burden on an already
strained system: "We're always there in numbers and strength. And being
there so often, we get a read basically on what groups are playing, as to what
the crowd will be, and what type of disorder or action we can expect."[23]
    "D.C. Don't Stand For Dodge City" represents a musical response to
the situation. The song was performed by a collective fronted by Chuck
Brown (Chuck Brown and the Soul Searchers), Gregory "Sugar Bear"
Elliot (Experience Unlimited), André Johnson (Rare Essence), and Benny
Harley (Little Benny and the Masters) and released in the fall of 1988 by
the D.C.-based I Hear Ya! Records. Each of these vocalists helped to create a unified sonic montage that commented upon the contemporary D.C.
scene, specifically the intense problems with street violence and with black-
on-black crime. But the most telling part was performed by Little Benny:

> I looked into the paper and there I read
> That three were injured and two were dead from
> Crimes motivated by a common tug,
> That five-letter word we know as drugs.

This compelling performance is unified by the refrain: "D.C. don't stand for Dodge City!"

The first direct political actions related to go-go, violence, and the government of the District of Columbia go back to the fall of 1987. Desperate times were upon the city and some citizens were more than eager to pass legislation—laws, regulations, or just plain something—that would help save the youth (read African American youth) of the District. Ward 1 city council member Frank Smith stepped forward to propose an emergency law that would restrict the times when citizens under the age of 21 could be in "public halls"—not after 11:30 P.M. on weekends and 1:00 A.M. on weekends. This strict legislation was intended to restrict the ability of teenagers to attend events of all kinds, but the most direct targets were the go-gos. The city council debated the issue for several months and in December 1987 the curfew became law. But it was not long before the ever-vigilant and always busy council member Smith introduced the District of Columbia Public Hall Regulation Amendment Act, which became law in the District in March of 1988. This time Smith struck directly at the club owners: anyone who allowed minors to remain in their "public hall" during the curfew hours could lose their business licenses to operate in the District of Columbia. And the city council was not yet done whipping the youth of D.C. into shape by limiting their civil rights. The Temporary Curfew Act of 1989, passed by the city council in April, set an 11:00 P.M. to 6:00 A.M. weekday curfew that was extended to midnight on weekends.

Frank Smith defended his actions in numerous television and print interviews. He told Alona Wartofsky:

> It wasn't the curfew, it was the violence that gave go-go a bad name. I never asserted that there was any organized relationship between go-go and this violence....I don't think that it was the music itself or the people, the promoters, or the people in the industry. . . . We have developed a culture in this town where underage-population persons were out really late hours of the night and involved in an atmosphere which seemed to be conducive to violence and confrontation and drugs.[24]

These controversial bills met general opposition throughout the city, and several prominent organizations and many individuals weighed in through public forums. The bills generated many calls to local talk radio programs, the *Washington Post* published a handful of letters, while a relatively smaller number of citizens appeared before the city council. Chris Dunn, representing the American Civil Liberties Union of the National Capital Area, minced no words, stating: "We oppose its passage because it violates the First Amendment, because it is unconstitutionally vague, and because it constitutes bad policy."[25] Writing as a member of the D.C. Commission on the Arts and Humanities, a Washington Area Music Association (WAMA) board member, and a manager of local go-go bands, Charles C. Stephenson, Jr., suggested: "I believe the intent of this bill may be positive, but I seriously believe the effect could be devastatingly negative to go-go music in Washington.... It is a fact that the youth of Washington are greatly influenced by go-go music [and] if this bill passes you will have seriously impacted on a cultural lifestyle indigenous to Washington, D.C."[26]

Not surprisingly during the time that the drug wars raged and the city council busied itself legislating go-go out of business, the go-go community struck back. A bipartisan coalition of musicians, promoters, record company officials, and fans came together under the dramatic, somewhat hyperbolic, banner "Committee To Save Go Go" to fight the power of the potential legislative action. In addition to lobbying the District of Columbia's city council's efforts, the committee wanted to bring a musical message to the streets and neighborhoods of the city. Specifically, they wanted to produce an audio and visual message to

> impact upon the current drug epidemic facing the youth population of the District of Columbia. According to Metropolitan Police Department 1985 statistics, 833 juveniles were arrested for drug possession. It must be noted that arrests for the possession of PCP and cocaine are on the increase in the District and that figures for 1986 could very well be higher than those of 1985. To combat the drug epidemic facing this city's youth, multi-faceted approaches must be employed. Go go musicians in Washington, D.C. have quite an influence upon the youth of the City.... This project proposes to secure a collaborative agreement with the leading go go groups to produce an anti-drug record and video."[27]

The record, *Go Go Drug Free*, was produced and released, but the video portion never came to fruition. This project offered an opportunity to make a clear anti-drug statement, and to culturally communicate that message to the youth of Washington, D.C. It would prove as successful locally as national and international projects like "We Are the World" and "Hands Across America."

In truth, and beneath the surface, the Committee to Save Go Go represented a broad spectrum of the city's African American civic and social activists. The Go Go Drug Free Project provided a common meeting ground for RAP, Inc. (a drug education and rehabilitation program), the Mayor's Youth Leadership Institute (an advocacy group for the city's youth), the Malcolm X Day Committee (a coordinating group for the annual Malcolm X birthday celebration), United Black Fund (a group that provides grants to community organizations), WAMA, and WDJY-FM 100. Chuck Brown and the Soul Searchers; Experience Unlimited; Redds and the Boys; C.J.'s Uptown Crew; Mass Extension; AM-FM; Little Benny and the Masters; Hot, Cold, Sweat; Ayre Rayde; and Junk Yard Band entered into an agreement with these public interest groups to participate in the project on a one-time basis.

Understanding that it was vitally important to hear "the message" from a variety of sources, the go-go community—using the Go Go Drug Free Project—enlisted the help of Mayor Marion Barry. Barry was held in high esteem by many Washingtonians, enough so that he was elected as mayor on four occasions. He was persuaded to donate 10,000 dollars of the city's money to the project, and a rap—set to "the beat"—was written for him:

> I'm Marion Barry and here's my rap
> I won't tolerate drugs in the nation's cap
> Better be clean when you cross the line
> Stay away from drugs and crime
> Take it from the Mayor of Washington
> Being drug free won't spoil your fun
>
> Walk away and don't be shy
> About saying no to getting high
> Life's too short to throw away
> Saying no is not too hard to say
> Never too late to turn it around
> Turn it around with the go-go sound

Drugs will kill and destroy your will
And leave you broke and standing still
Never, never, never be shy
To tell the world that you won't get high

Although the message is overtly anti-drug, the committee needed to raise money to supplement the funds provided by the District of Columbia to fight drugs. The idea was to "broadcast a positive record and video . . . the youth in the District will be targeted for anti-drug education with results that save lives. The project would promote a message to the youth in the current cultural music form that they undoubtedly relate to and appreciate—the go-go."[28] The project brought its message through Barry's rap and video as well as through a series of public events.

One of the most notable of the events was a reception co-sponsored by The Honorable Marion S. Barry, Jr., and the Mayor's Youth Leadership Institute, which was held on September 12, 1986. Held in the Mayor's Conference Room in the District Building, the fundraiser enjoyed the direct support of Ron Clark, Director of RAP (Regional Addition Program), Inc.; Dr. Calvin Rolark, then President of the United Black Fund; Rev. Louis Anthony; and Dr. Reed Tuckerson of the D.C. Public Health Commission. Clark said that "we believe that something creative has to be done to turn back the current drug craze plaguing our community. The local go-go musicians greatly influence our youth. It is our desire to use that influence to reach the common sense of the District's youth through their music before drugs destroy their minds."[29] The magnitude of the problems faced by the District of Columbia appeared overwhelming. These efforts might seem extreme, however, in the context of the time and place, they were but meager (perhaps even symbolic) steps in combating the crack cocaine and angel dust scourge.

Significantly, these efforts to legislate control over youth and the association between go-go and violence recalls a long-standing issue: the association of black vernacular music with the lower social and economic classes, with vulgarity, with drugs and drinking, and with other negative aspects of culture in the United States. Twentieth-century examples abound. In the world of jazz, the laws that created Storyville in New Orleans in the teens helped to keep many of the nascent jazz musicians ghettoized in one section of the city. New York City was not much different; the "cabaret laws" (a melange of zoning and licensing regulations) instituted in the 1920s helped restrict the distribution of clubs throughout the city and kept some musicians from performing in New York for extended periods—notably Charlie Parker and Thelonious Monk in the 1950s, due to their drug-related confrontations with the law.

In the rural South, the Jim Crow laws placed real strictures on racial interaction, but the ingrained social customs dating back to antebellum days proved to be at least as effective by informally "legislating" the places where blacks could gather and musicians could perform. In rural Mississippi, for instance, the fife and drum band picnics (complete with homemade instruments, barbecued goat, and plenty of liquor) were held in extremely rural areas of the "Hill Country," where whites rarely ventured. Similarly, Huddie Ledbetter (aka Lead Belly), recalled the "sukey jumps" held in northeastern Texas during the first decade of the last century. "Sukey" (or "sookie") was antebellum slang for a servant or slave, and sukey jump became the term in the Ark-La-Tex for a slave dance or gathering. They were held in private homes, usually on Saturday nights (rural laborers worked at least a half-day on Saturday, taking only Sunday off), and involved gambling, drinking, and dancing to music provided by fiddles, accordions, perhaps a washboard, and that newly popular instrument, the guitar.

The music played at these and countless other black music events has historically been seen as low-class, and was viewed with a wary eye by the establishment. To most contemporary casual white observers it was just "nigger music"—unworthy of polite society. The participants, of course, reveled in the ability to celebrate their (relative) freedom and express themselves in ways pioneered by previous generations of black Americans. The idea was to blow off steam by "shaking your shimmy," "mak[ing] your backbone slip," or "rais[ing] a ruckus tonight." Hip-hoppers might call these gatherings parties; Mississippi bluesman "Mister" Freddie Spruell sang in his 1929 "Mississippi Lowdown Man," "I like low down music, I like to drink, barrelhouse, and have a really good time." One can imagine similar sentiments, though in very different language, being expressed on the streets of Harlem in 1940 or in Anacostia in the present day. Perhaps in the District, it would go something like this: "Ain't no party like an RE party, 'cause an RE party don't stop!"

The not-so-subtle legal and extra-legal curfews instituted in the late '80s did nothing but further ghettoize go-go and reinforce its complex role in D.C.'s black community. Go-go had a chance to gain national recognition with the film *Good to Go*, but for a whole host of reasons discussed in chapter 7, this did not happen. By 1990 the violence, the drugs, the actions of the city council, and the failure of the Chris Blackwell–payrolled film helped to send go-go into a tailspin. The block parties featuring go-go continued, as did a handful of the clubs in the city, but, as Max Kidd observed, "Notice how it went back where it came from. Back underground, back on the streets of Washington. Back into the hearts, back into the ghetto."[30] Even many of the stalwart clubs, including the Atlas Disco, the Paragon, and the Panorama Room, all but ceased their heavy promotion of go-go, and many of the area's larger venues—such as RFK Stadium—also shied away from the music, fearing the repercussions of hosting it.

Alona Wartofsky summarizes the effect on local musicians: "Bands don't play as frequently, and when they do it's often in smaller venues like the Safari Club. Benny Harley of Little Benny and the Masters and now of The Legends once played go-go every weekend. Now the diminutive singer performs intermittently, mostly at Top 40 clubs or cabarets. 'If they say they don't want to hear go-go, they want to hear Top 40. I play Top 40. Then I ease into some go-go.' he explains. But Harley says he doesn't bank on go-go: 'I do electronics work.'"[31] Other well-established bands (even Chuck Brown and the Soul Searchers, E.U., and Trouble Funk) did not work as often as they once had, either. All told, the fortunes of go-go had bottomed out and the reasons why were extraneous to the music itself.

The problems plaguing the go-go community were not just news in the *Washington Post,* the *Washington Times,* and the *City Paper.* New York–based writer and author Nelson George noted that after the promise of *Good to Go* and Island's Chris Blackwell's involvement with go-go, the movie flopped and became a source of disillusionment. He explained:

> The club scene [has] atrophied. According to Taylor Reed, keyboardist/percussionist/vocalist with go-go's premier band, Trouble Funk, not much is happening these days in go-go's hometown. "Redds & the Boys have broken up; Chuck Brown doesn't have a band right now, and his drummer has been working with Miles Davis. Right now, there are no good new bands on the scene. There has been a lot of trouble with handguns at some of the go-go clubs. Trouble Funk itself hasn't played D.C. in a year and a half. We'll probably play D.C. again at the end of October at the 9:30 Club, which has a half-black, half-white audience. At this point, it's the only place we'd perform there."[32]

The Committee to Save Go Go launched their anti-drug progam at precisely the time when the efforts to limit go-go were at their strongest, and its efforts received citywide support. The effect was to help rally various organizations across D.C. to help fight drugs. In a committee-issued statement, Mary McCullough, executive director of the Go Go Drug Free Project, said:

> When I contacted people and explained the purpose of the project, the response I received brought forth excitement and pledges from all sectors of the community. Triples Nightclub allowed us to transform their establishment into a studio, enabling us to record and film; *Washington Living Magazine* agreed to run a full-page ad and solicit donations; the musicians pledged to donate their share of royalties to the project; the Eugene Byrd, the Riggs National Bank, Washington Gas Light Company, the *Washington Post,* and G Street Express have given cash donations. The support that we have received thus far is deeply gratifying.[33]

The Go Go Drug Free Project not only gave the Committee to Save Go Go visibility for an important effort, it also helped to place the struggling go-go community in a better light. The committee also became involved in two other grassroots efforts. The first was the Go Go Hotline, aimed (in the days before the Internet all but eliminated the need for such a vehicle) at disseminating information about go-go bands' local gigs. It began in 1989 and was operated by a coalition of entrepreneurs under the aegis of the Malcolm X Cultural Educational Center. By calling (202) 543-GOGO, fans could listen to a recorded message that was updated weekly. The information provided was basic: who was playing, where, and when. The Go Go Hotline lasted for about a year before it fell apart due to the lack of an organized infrastructure to support the process of gathering and recording the information.

The Go Go Hotline benefited from assistance from the D.C. Commission for the Arts and Humanities, rendered almost entirely by City Folklorist Michael Licht, who offered technical assistance and advice to this project from his office at the Folk Arts Program. On allied fronts, he helped to conduct some oral histories with members of the go-go community and also guided the production of a slick and very helpful guide to go-go for neophytes, outsiders, and, when you come down to it, for white residents of the District. This fold-out flyer includes a brief history, a list of contemporary venues for go-go, and a pithy go-go glossary. The slogan also reminds people of this truth for us citizens of the District: "Washington. We live here." Amen! This good work—along with Licht's efforts to support local African American gospel groups—is the antithesis of most of the city's official response to this street-level music. It represents a pleasant change from the defensive posture usually taken by the city; rather than defend and fight, the tactic was to understand and embrace go-go. How refreshing. . . .

The D.C. Commission for the Arts and Humanities (Folk Arts Program) publication also lists the four local radio stations—WMMJ-FM 103.2, WDJY-FM 100.3, WHUR-FM 96.3, and WOL-AM 1450—that sometimes played go-go. This was the late 1980s, and go-go was still dealing with its residual popular success of five years before, as well as the controversy related to the music and violence. But the bottom line was that you could hear go-go on the radio in and around the District, albeit on a limited basis. Notably absent from the list of stations, which is still essentially accurate more than a decade later, are WPFW-FM 89.3, the D.C.-based, non-commercial Pacifica affiliate, and the local powerhouse in the African American community, WPGC-FM.

Because the formats and playlists of most commercial radio stations are driven by national sales and popularity, the position of go-go on radio in the District was already tenuous enough in the late 1980s. Go-go simply did not have enough stature outside of the metropolitan area to affect the record sales (and hence the charts) in cities like Boston, Oakland, and Dallas. Therefore, despite its undeniable local popularity, go-go was marginalized, even in its home territory. In the winter of 1990–91, Cathy Hughes, the owner of WOL, decided to take go-go off the air. A minor firestorm ensued.

Specifically, WOL cancelled the 7:00 P.M.–midnight (Monday through Friday) program of DJ Konan, which spotlighted go-go, and to a lesser degree, rap. In response, the Committee to Save Go Go essentially re-emerged, phoenix-like, as the D.C. Committee to Save Our Music, and in response to Hughes's actions this dedicated crew mounted a campaign to "Save The Go-Go Show on 1450 AM-WOL." Hughes cited "no revenues and no ratings" and a lack of product as her primary rationale (she was always—and remains—a businessperson first and foremost) for pulling go-go programming off the station in December 1990.

This 1,000-watt station, then located at the corner of 4th and H Streets NE, began airing the show in 1986, when go-go was enjoying perhaps its greatest popularity. By 1990, the violence and drugs associated with go-go, and a declining national interest in the music, helped to place go-go in a weakened position. This seems to be the real reason behind Hughes's decision. The revenues issue was questionable, given the commercials for The Wiz, Peoples Drug Store, G Street Express, Foot Locker, and other local and regional businesses that regularly aired on Konan's program. Also, the Spring 1990 Arbitron ratings are clear: Konan scored a 3.0 rating, while Hughes's own morning program scored a 2.0! As for the issue of lack of product, in the three months prior to the canceling of go-go programming on WOL, Chuck Brown and the Soul Searchers issued *Guess Who's Back, Jiggling* by Junk Yard Band came out, *Pump Blenders Live* and *Northeast Groovers Live* were jumping off record shelves, and E.U. had just put out *Funky Like a Monkey*. This incomplete list alone suggests that Hughes's assertion was simply not true. What does seem to be true is that Hughes simply did not want WOL (one of several stations in the area that she ultimately owned) associated with go-go.

In the meantime, the Committee to Save Our Music launched a petition drive and urged D.C. folk to call the station "anytime and all the time" to demand the immediate return of this homegrown music. On Monday, February 20, 1990, the committee organized a small but vocal march on WOL, which drew the media and prompted coverage in the daily papers and the weekly *City Paper,* as well as on radio and television. Ultimately, the committee's efforts to "save" go-go on WOL failed, but their point was well taken. Go-go is homegrown music that deserves support, especially from a locally owned station that caters to the black American population of D.C.

The formation of the Go Go Coalition proved to be one of the other rather brief outcomes of this action against WOL. It was a loose coalition of producers, musicians, promoters, and record company employees with an interest in go-go. The idea was to promote solidarity and a united front for the music that the members loved and which, in many instances, supported them financially. Unfortunately, the coalition, with Moe Shorter, Kemry Hughes, and Charles C. Stephenson, Jr., among its most ardent supporters, quickly fell victim to the inherently splintered nature of D.C.'s go-go community.

And so, in the first years of the twenty-first century, go-go remains a homegrown product sustained by a patchwork of street-level businesses.

Rather than legitimate compact discs, P.A. tapes and rather informally shot and produced video tapes (*N.E. Groovers: Bumpers Nite Club, Featuring Hechinger Mall Ziggy 3-18-95* is a typical release) are the staples of the D.C. go-go world. But the major record companies show no interest in the music and there is no functioning coalition and little cohesion in the community. It also remains largely unsupported by the local mass media.

Drugs and violence are lesser issues today...not only in the go-go community but on the streets as well. While the music itself is as vital and energetic as ever and the local go-go community itself is thriving, the media attention that once shone on go-go has waned. The District's government is more concerned with a new downtown convention center, a diminished number of students in the public school system, and an increasingly frail Metro system. But despite the local adoration and attention given to such other homegrown talent as Johnny Gill and Toni Braxton, go-go goes on and on and on with support from the street but not a whit from above.

Go-go still appeals to the youth (as well as those of us who used to be young) of the Washington, D.C., metropolitan region, and the interest in the music sometimes appears in unexpected places. Sometimes the interest only reinforces stereotypes about the nature of the District and its musical culture. Montgomery County is one of the wealthiest counties in the United States — a place where African Americans are a distinct minority, but which abuts both the District of Columbia and Prince George's County. A February 11, 1999, article in the Montgomery Blair High School *Silver Chips — On-Line* contains an article with the provocative title "Students Brave Violence at Go-Gos." The author, Simone Aponte, begins by writing about a hot, sweaty go-go at Sidwell Friends High School — an elite school that was attended by, among others, Chelsea Clinton. Aponte writes:

> Go-go clubs have steadily developed a reputation for violent incidents....The precautions security takes at clubs like the Black Hole, which is notorious for violent incidents, is usually for good reason. "People come up in there with guns, knives, brass knuckles, razor blades. I've been to some [go-gos] where they've confiscated so many weapons," [fellow student Britt Bowers] says.... According to devoted go-go fans, drug use and

> violence are prominent at shows.... Junior Ryan
> Tompkins, who plays drums for High Frequency...said
> that violent incidents are frequent at go-go clubs. He
> also adds that the Black Hole is generally "not some-
> where you want to be."[34]

This type of story falls in line with the attitudes displayed more than a decade earlier by Councilman Smith. It also underscores the black and white divide that continues to dominate the District of Columbia and its immediate environs. Aponte's piece also calls to mind an incident that happened in 1994 when Kip Lornell was teaching a course on "Multi-Cultural American Music" for the University of Virginia (Northern Virginia Learning Center). The course was specifically for Loudon County teachers and was held at a suburban high school located about 40 minutes from downtown D.C. The teachers were surprised to learn that Lornell actually lived in the District of Columbia, while their instructor was even more shocked to learn that nearly a quarter of the 40 students had not been to the District of Columbia for more than a decade—"too crowded," "too much traffic," or "too dangerous" were the most common explanations. "Too black," thought Lornell as he turned to scholarly and music-related matters.

5 ⦁ Entrepreneurs

I am establishing a management company....I see this as something strategic for Go-Go in general, and not just for me. Because, a lot of entertainment groups right now are coming in packs. There's strength in numbers. You look bigger and better when you come as a package, as opposed to just one. If I say, "I got Junkyard [*sic*]," that's okay. But, if I say, "I've got Junkyard, Optymistic Tribe [*sic*] and Little Benny," they're going to say, "Damn, you all are hard."...That's my new strategy going into 2000.[1]

Moe Shorter, former Junk Yard Band manager

The people involved with documenting, disseminating, and promoting go-go are mostly local residents. The overwhelming majority of them are also African Americans. These are the people who earn a living by promoting go-go events, running clubs, providing security and protection for the musicians (and clubgoers), and/or selling "gear."

The entrepreneurs who control the business side of go-go are often multitalented. The many roles played by these (mostly) men frequently overlap, especially in the realms of promoting, recording, and managing bands. Max Kidd, for example, has a long and complex history with black music in general, and go-go in particular, in Washington, D.C.—a run that stretches back to the early 1960s. Among other things, Kidd has been a record producer, a promoter of go-go acts, and a producer. The film *Good to Go* showcased Kidd, portraying him (quite rightly) as a key figure in the go-go scene. Tom Goldfogle and Becky Marcus operate Liaison Records, which is both a record company and a record distributor, but Goldfogle also serves as Chuck Brown's manager. Charlie Fenwick owns one of the most active studios in the metro area but has also managed bands as well as played in them.

MANAGERS

Maurice "Moe" Shorter is one man who wears many hats in the D.C. go-go scene. If you own the Junk Yard compact disc, *The Beginning - The End?* (Street Records 2060-2), you have heard Moe's voice; he supplies the narration that ties the CD together. But you may not know that he is also a homeboy, raised in Southeast with close ties to Barry Farms, one of the most noteworthy and often notorious public housing projects in the Anacostia section of the city. The Barry Farms sports league was operated in part by Irving Brady of Rare Essence, who sometimes had the band come in to play at the community center. Moe grew up in the '70s and stayed home to attend Howard University beginning in the late 1970s. In one way or another, Maurice Shorter has been involved with go-go his entire adult life.

It was in his college days that Shorter came to know the Junk Yard Band, which emerged from Southeast in the early 1980s. He relates how they met in 1981:

> I had been hearing about the band for about a year, but had never seen them until one day when I was coming home from work. Derrick [McCraven, the original manager] stopped me and said, "Moe, wait right here. I'll be back in five minutes. We're going to play for you." A few minutes later, he pulled up with a Safeway shopping cart carrying everything that they used to play with, and the band following right behind him. They started taking out their little boxes, folding them up, setting them out along the curb, and began playing. I was blown away.... These little guys were playing on these boxes and creating such a large sound.[2]

At the time, Shorter was a business and accounting major at Howard University, and the fit between working with go-go music and his academic work seems, at least in retrospect, like a natural one. The newly formed, self-named Junk Yard Band—which has one of go-go's best names—was being assisted by Derrick McCraven, a friend of Shorter's. McCraven's time was being stretched thin and he requested help from Shorter, who viewed the request in light of his Howard University connections: "Howard had an event called Community Day, and ... what could be more perfect than to have Junk Yard Band, a community-oriented little group, be a part of Community Day. So, I approached the Student Government with the idea. They liked it, we worked everything out in the contracts, we brought the band in to perform, and they got paid."[3] Impressed with the way Shorter worked, the youthful (they were all in junior high school or high school at the time) Junk Yard Band begged him to work with them on a regular basis. Shorter finally agreed to do it, launching his career as an entrepreneur in the music business and getting him out of the accounting business.

The tasks that fall to the manager of a go-go band are complex. Ignatius Mason, who is both a percussionist and a manager, has likened managing a band to being the head of a household—a position that calls for maximum multitasking. A band manager is part lawyer; an occasional valet; sometimes serves as a personal counselor; and must possess a strong back to help move equipment. You also have to like late hours, because go-gos rarely begin before 10:00 P.M. and often continue late into the night. In short, the job of a manger has its own rhythm and pace, but it's clearly not cookie-cutter work, not a nine-to-five gig, and not for the faint-hearted.

Mason serves as another fine example of a versatile go-go entrepreneur. He came to managing—in the mid-1990s he worked extensively with his son's go-go group, Optimystic Tribe—as an adjunct to his work as a musician and an organizer of the local African American Musicians Organization. In addition, he is the CEO of a small company with interests including event management, a record label, and providing sound for live performances. These are not roles to which Mason aspired when he was first breaking into music as a teenager in the early 1970s; he just liked popular (mostly black) music, including soul, jazz, and funk—especially Parliament-Funkadelic—and wanted to be involved with music in some capacity. Mason has accomplished this goal, mostly through mother wit and hard work.

Mason is careful to point out that while an academic background is helpful and important, real-world experience remains the only way to really learn any of these aspects of the music business. When queried by a George Washington University student about how to learn to do what he does, he was bemused but thoughtful. He suggested that taking classes in business would be useful and help to strengthen your understanding of how this complex world works (or doesn't), but that one really learns by actually getting in there and doing it firsthand. There is no substitute for experience; you need to start small and part-time—even volunteering or working as an apprentice or intern—and learn as you go.[4] That is precisely how Mason and most of the entrepreneurs of go-go have moved through this world.

If you thought that all managers of D.C. go-go bands are male, you would almost be correct. The exception to this rule is Ms. Mack, who managed Rare Essence for the first five years of their lengthy career. Her exception comes largely because of the family connection—her son Quentin was the band's drummer and most of the early members were neighborhood kids or classmates of her son. "Footz" (as Quentin was known) also named the band, by reversing the name of a popular perfume: Essence Rare. Seeing Ms. Mack as a trusted maternal figure and a well-organized human being, the band quite naturally entrusted the guidance of their early career to her.

Rare Essence began as the Young Dynamos, playing for neighborhood block parties, school dances, and kiddie cabarets at the local recreation centers. This was around 1976, when Chuck Brown was just beginning to formulate go-go. A very young James Funk was already working with Chuck Brown, quite often at the Burgundy Room in eastern Prince George's County. Chuck was, in fact, not only an early influence on Rare Essence, but he helped the young band to establish a sense of professionalism. He was the man who taught them the importance of a good sound system, the negative consequences of not being reliable and not showing up for gigs on time, and the proper ways to promote a show date. As Ms. Mack recalled, these were lessons that the band had to learn early on because "we were young in the business and really didn't know all the ins and outs and all. We were trusting the people and they were cutting, taking off what they wanted and they gave us the rest. . . . That's how things happened and you learn."[5]

And they learned how to conduct themselves in the local music business through a combination of mother wit—"The thing my grandmother told me a long time ago; she used to laugh, 'When you get your hand out of the lion's mouth, you take it out and you keep it out!'"[6]—and more experience in the real world. Along with getting advice from Chuck Brown, they learned on their own and eventually began to make their mark:

> I remember the first year that we auditioned for the city talent show. We were at the Friendship School and the different groups were auditioning with Mr. Grey in charge. So, there [was] hardly anybody in the audience and so they said Rare Essence was back there setting up.

Then somebody announced that Rare Essence is getting ready to play. The place was packed and everybody that was outside came inside. Rare Essence did their little bit and that was that, the place was empty again! Mr. Grey said "Well, I never would have believed this if I hadn't seen it myself!"[7]

By the late 1970s Rare Essence was playing on the burgeoning go-go circuit that included the skating rink at Kalorama, Green Acres, and the Crystal Underground, along with bands like Mouse Trapp, Symba, and Brute. By this time the group was semiprofessional and Ms. Mack was adamant that the members also behave and perform in a professional manner. She wanted them to follow the example of Chuck Brown, a much older and more experienced musician. This was carried out in a number of important ways, some of which were specifically relevant to a band consisting of high school–aged musicians. Ms. Mack remembered: "Early in the game I noticed that some of them didn't have clothes like some of the others. And I decided to have colors . . . red and white. And everyone had the same thing. . . . Then later on a lot of the other groups tried to copy that, you know, trying to do the uniform thing."[8]

And Ms. Mack took a close look at the finances — a notoriously contentious and difficult aspect of the go-go music business. "I did them [club owners and promoters] like they did me. I didn't do 'em dirty, but I mean I just got what I wanted. . . . They were stealing. You know they had a way of having two sheets running. . . . If you are sitting out on the outside . . . then you got some idea of what's going on."[9] Her tenacity not only assured that the band was properly compensated, she also made certain that the band paid their proper city and federal taxes. Rare Essence became one of the first bands to set up a payroll system administered by an outside company that issued paychecks on a weekly basis, tracked the group's shared expenses, and kept the members informed about all financial aspects of operating the band.

"Mean Ms. Mack," as she was sometimes known, not only insisted on an appropriate public appearance and no-nonsense financial accountability, she made certain that the band maintained a regular (usually bi-weekly) practice schedule. If you missed practice, you got a stern talking-to, and if that didn't set you straight then a monetary fine usually did. She knew that raw talent, a polished stage appearance, and a good business sense were not enough to guarantee success. Practice was critical because

Managing Jigga

The Summer of 2000

We just got back from Roanoke, Virginia. The show was going great until about 20 guys tried to jump our band's camera guy. The camera guy was filming the show and some of the people on the dance floor. A guy came up to our camera guy and asked that the light from the camera be moved, but the guy touched the camera. Well, our camera guy didn't appreciate the other guy's approach; he bucked and said "What?"

That was the beginning of the end. And it didn't stop there. Egos laced with alcohol and weed created the urge to fight. So the guy got his boys and began confronting the camera guy. They started walking towards the camera guy and, of course, our camera guy wasn't going to back down (remember ego?). So one minute my camera guy was almost beaten down, then the next minute the stage where my band was standing was bum-rushed by this crew of guys and then in the midst of it all, a pepper-spray mist and police finally calmed everything down.

Some jerk got away with the camera and the film. My adrenaline was high and so was my frustration. "Why can't we all just get along?," I'm thinking to myself. Then the club owner said, "Look, I like your band, but I was informed by someone who saw the whole incident that it was your camera guy that started the whole thing." He went on to explain that the camera guy cursed at the guy and that his filming process was not going over well with the crowd because of the bright light. I thought, "Damn!" I was looking forward to playing at this club consistently and now this. Oh well, such is life in the world of music.

The casualties were a broken sound board, missing microphone, our security guy's hip got fractured, and a broken spirit to ride home with. It was even more frustrating finding out that our camera guy was the culprit. Here we were three hours away from home promoting out new CD and the band, then this incident had to happen during the last set before the show ended. The night had been going very well. The crowd was really enjoying the band and this craziness happened. On the long ride home, I reflected and thought to myself, "Is it really worth it?" You see, this isn't the first time I've experienced violence at a live performance by my band. The last time, I actually saw someone get beat up and, needless to say, my stomach turned.

Once again, it wasn't the band's fault... it almost never is. However, I've seen so many fights now that I'm immune to the violence. I only hope each time that no one is shot or killed. I pray every time we have a show, "Please make it peaceful this time." I realize now that this is probably the silent prayer of most people who go to the go-go or see a live band's performance. Violence and go-gos seem to go hand in hand, but the violence can get out of hand if there isn't proper security or restrictions such as no drugs or alcohol (usually the hidden culprit behind all of the violence).

There are times when friends or buds of the band who get in free cause conflict because they feel this extra cockiness because they are with the band. They may expect certain band privileges that the club allows and if treated differently, some of the friends respond negatively. But not all friends have this attitude (thank goodness). The other culprit is crew or gang violence (ego). Some people use the public forum to settle beefs or disagreements.... Either way, it is disheartening to experience the violence firsthand because it almost always revolves around something small and meaningless... and almost never had anything to do with the BAND!

It's been three months since the release of our one full-length CD— May 30, 2000 (the exact release day) was a wonderful day. The weather was nice, the crowd was nice, and the band's performance was highly enhanced because of the excitement surrounding the release of Jigga's *Open Your Eyes*. This was the band's first release on a local independent label recently set up in the D.C. metro area. The label—Monarch—i sured the success of the release performance by first creating major hype with radio ads, posters, flyers, private parties for DJs to introduce them to the project, and a distribution deal with Liaison—a well-known go-go distributor. The product hit one of the major chain stores and the band performed live in the parking lot of the chain store in the area of Landover, which lies on the border of Southeast Washington, D.C., and Forest Heights, Maryland. I clearly remember the excitement and anticipation surrounding this big show. However, it was not an easy road to reach this point.

HOW I STARTED

Based on the insight from other go-go band managers and my observation of other major go-go bands, it takes the average go-go band more than six years to gain a fan base and the respect of the listening audience. These bands go through members quitting, getting fired, and the unfortunate loss of members due to violence or some other incident. Yet the strong bands maintain through it all and eventually make that one hit that gets them to the point where they have a huge fan base buying their P.A. (live show) tapes and compact discs, or at least a distributor "considering" giving the band distribution.

The average band builds a relationship with some of the major sound companies (people that supply the sound set-up for go-go shows), who in most instances are smart enough to have their own rehearsal/recording studios. They work out an agreement with the band to record and press up initial product on the band or shop the product themselves to the distributor and cut special deals with the bands and distribution companies. For example, the sound company may do sound at no cost for a band that might be doing well and arrange to recoup costs against sales—acting as an independent record label, but without all of the obligations of a record label.

When there is a hit in go-go music, it usually doesn't require a lot of work on the label's part. Most often bands can make money on P.A. tapes of live performances. In this instance they can create a master tape of a live show via the sound company and opt to reproduce the tape themselves or take the tape to one of the local stores that sells mix tapes and P.A. tapes.

The stores purchase the master from the band for a fee and reproduce and sell the tapes in their stores. The band's relationship with the store stops with the sale of the master. These live show tapes are very popular and profitable because the appeal is "I was at this show last week" or "I wasn't at the show, but this is my favorite band and I want to hear what I missed." Whatever the case, these tapes provide good publicity for the bands and are one of the ways I was introduced to Jigga (then called Jig-A-Boo, but I'll discuss the name thing later), who I now manage.

When I met Jig-A-Boo, they were a young band of guys. There was the lead talker and founder of the band—Bam; the co-founder and drummer—Larry; the other frontline rappers—Dre, Rob, and Jerry; the congo player—Spook; and keyboard players—Mark and Rasheed. Mark was in high school and the others had just graduated from high school. They were hungrily playing every show that they could get—from house parties to band battles.

A band battle is another go-go moneymaker and a good way for an unknown band to gain recognition. For example, a popular go-go club, promoter, and sometimes the bands themselves may sponsor a "Battle of the Bands" at a particular location. Sometimes the bands pay for a spot to play on the battle and sometimes the bands win cash prizes. Either way the bands compete against each other by playing for a consistent spot at the club or compete to be the opening band for a major band for a period of time. The crowd judges the winner and, of course, just like at the Apollo, the band with the most crowd support wins.

Jig-A-Boo had been performing together for three years. I'd heard of them through my kids who were going to the high school where a couple of the members attended. My daughter would bring home flyers and P.A. tapes of the band. Eventually she developed a friendship with one of the members. She mentioned that I DJed and had done some management work for artists. Mark constantly called me whenever there was a show. Most people would have given up on me because my schedule only allowed me to catch their performance once, but he was persistent.

Then, one year later, I got that phone call. "We need a manager and would like to speak with you about helping us out." I was hesitant initially because of my negative experience with the hip-hop band that I'd just managed a few months before Jig-A-Boo's phone call. The hip-hop band had broken up and, fortunately, I had been prepped for the band experience because of the first band. I thought clearly about my past mistakes and convinced myself that given the chance, I *could* pull this management thing off with Jig-A-Boo. After all, the market for a go-go band here was far better and the chances for success were greater with Jig-A-Boo because they had already created a buzz on their own. I would not have to start from scratch as I did with the hip-hop band. Little did I know what eventually was to come from managing a newly popular go-go band.

Everything started off nicely. The band was ready to go to the next level (or so they said) and I jumped in wholeheartedly, rolled up my sleeves, and got down to business. They listened to me and were more than willing to participate in the business aspect of the band. They were willing to promote their own shows; they even had a list of locations where they wanted to play. They had given me names of individuals that they wanted to do business with. They had just come off a situation where they had taken part in creating a club where they could play that, due to incidents beyond their control, was shut down. They were like sponges and were ready to listen and learn about the music business and how to do things like register their name and their music—another process that they had already begun before I came on the scene. It was too good to be true...we were on the same page in reference to how things should be run and how we envisioned the future of the band. However, there was one small glitch about which I was unaware.

THE OTHER SIDE OF THE GAME

A contract with a promoter and a record label was signed prior to my coming on board. Without the advice of an attorney (which unfortunately happens often in this business) some agreements got signed with the promoter. The band was under the impression that business with the promoter had to do with shows only. The promoter thought he had the right to pursue a recording deal and represented himself as the band's manager (another thing that can happen). Somehow a recording deal was set up between the band and this label (to this day I have not seen the original recording contract).

Two live shows were recorded during the summer of 1999 at a recreation center. The band was told that a recording got lost and that they would have to re-record in the studio. "No problem," I thought. "We'll just make this work for us." Then things got complicated. The band got impatient and pulled out of the first arrangement (that there was never any real proof they were in). They did not feel comfortable with the way things were going and wanted to hurry up and get something out in the stores while the energy surrounding the band was hype. They went into the studio with another producer (Supa Coop) and in less than a month they recorded a compete new album, *Open Your Eyes*. In turn we got a distribution deal with Liaison [Records] and were now officially on Monarch Music, Inc. The band was so well rehearsed that it only took one take per song in the studio. The rest of the energy and time went into mixing the product and pulling together the master plan on promoting the new compact disc.

I was going out of my mind because I was concerned about the master recording with the other label ("Label #1") and eventually so was Liaison Distribution and Monarch…and with good reason. A bootleg copy of the live recording was released and put into stores. I and the band were surprised and disappointed. Then again, so was the label that put out the bootleg. Of course, the compact disc was gaining some attention and a buzz about the bootleg was going on among our fans and even DJs. Label #1 wanted to meet. Bam, Larry, and I went to the meeting at Label #1's recording studio. At the meeting they justified putting out the bootleg as a way of recouping part of their investment. Apparently Label #1 was selling the CD in a misguided effort to offer the band another deal, but the guys voted to end the relationship because the label did not inform the band of their decision to put out the bootleg CD in the first place. Also, the fact that they pulled the move made the band members uncomfortable about doing more business with them.

Meanwhile, other dilemmas reared their ugly heads. The pressing company placed *Open Your Eyes* on hold because of the band's original name, Jig-A-Boo. They did not want any controversy surrounding the use of a negative term, so the name was shortened to Jigga. The band and I were also up-in-arms about the picture on the CD cover. We were concerned because our market consisted of minors and women who would not be comfortable purchasing a CD with a picture of a woman's thonged derriere on the cover. However, our investment in the project was time, not money. We were informed that Street Life's marketing concept was somewhat of an insurance policy—to help sell the product. The picture on the CD cover was an attention-getter and because we were still technically an unknown band, they felt that we needed that extra push. Even though lyrically the product was clean, the picture gave it a controversial edge that proved to work. Unfortunately, we felt a little uncomfortable about marketing the compact disc to the younger folks in elementary and middle school, so that market was overlooked to a certain degree. One of our high school promoters got reprimanded for passing out flyers with the CD cover on them, but we tried to strategize a way around the situation. Some suggested placing stickers all over the CD picture or even replacing it. I guess all I can do is fight one battle at a time.

Once the product hit the streets, other challenges embarked upon us—radio play and sales. While Jigga is doing well in surrounding areas, local sales slowed down. This can be discouraging unless you understand the way the go-go music industry works. It's all in promotions and shows. The more shows a band plays locally the better the following and sales. Also, P.A. tapes help with sales and, of course, you need live shows to release such tapes. With the school year on us, the compact disc can help breath new life into everything. Getting the word out about the band has always been workable through the school network. Anyway, that's where it all began for Jig-A-Boo. The new difference this time is that we have product in stores and this gives us the extra edge.

As for... is it worth it? Yes, it is — if you find eight guys that are positive and trying to follow their passion for music by doing something they love, it is worth the changes. Please remember that it isn't the bands or their music starting the fights. It's individuals looking to prove themselves in ways not so positive. They create the madness. That's why security is the key to the go-go shows (any live shows, for that matter). Maybe someone in security needs to tell their story; their battles are far worse than mine!

Janice Carroll
August 12, 2000

when you get down to it, the people came to hear the music; the rest was all window dressing. Because of the band's success, their expanded travel schedule, and Ms. Mack's need to take care of business at home, Rare Essence eventually moved on to another management situation. But it was she who set the band's basic values and, much to her credit, Rare Essence remains a vital band on D.C.'s go-go scene.

Charlie Fenwick is another member of the go-go community who understands the importance of practice. His Clinton, Maryland, recording studio often serves as a practice space for bands that play hip-hop, go-go, and other forms of music. Fenwick wants to groom go-go bands and then move the genre into the national arena. His site provides everything that a band needs — it's modern, clean, and has plenty of space for rehearsing as well as a state-of-the-art studio.

Fenwick also has the professional experience to carry out his dream. He's managed R&B and go-go groups — including Hot, Cold, Sweat (which he rebuilt three times over nearly a decade), Pleasure, and the Huck-A-Bucks — since the early 1980s. Starting as a bass player in 1962, he played with many types of musical groups in and around Washington, D.C. Fenwick performed on the road for approximately 20 years before turning more of his attention to managing and recording go-go bands. Now his time is devoted to making go-go happen outside of D.C. Along with the need for radio-friendly material, Fenwick believes that a grander vision, a better stage show, a more expansive sound, and some closer ties to hip-hop could help move go-go outside of D.C.

Pleasure (a group that he wanted to call Sheer Pleasure) is perhaps the most out-of-the-ordinary band that Fenwick has managed. Fenwick viewed the group as more than a novelty act; an all-female band playing go-go is a configuration that he had thought about for quite a while before putting the band together in 1985:

> I thought of . . . having a group with all girls that could play. So I started working on it, putting it together bit by bit. It was hard to find everything you need [and] when they first started off, it was like a novelty that shot out. . . . It was so crazy; I couldn't keep up with it. Being girls and being young, they kind of went to left field and I couldn't control it. It was a nightmare . . . just trying to keep them together, trying to keep guys off them, and the whole nine yards.[10]

Pleasure lasted for a couple of years and it was the most difficult managing job undertaken by Fenwick in his career.

The Huck-A-Bucks arrived on the scene in the early 1990s and they represent Fenwick's most recent and perhaps best shot at moving a group outside of D.C. and promoting them across the country. In D.C., the Malcolm X Day celebrations have been among the largest events to feature go-go bands. Fenwick was pleased to see his and other groups getting on what he stressed was a BIG stage with a BIG sound system. He viewed it as a place where the groups could e-x-p-a-n-d their musical horizons, observing: "What's the difference in playing the [cavernous] Capital Centre and playing at [the much smaller] Celebrity Hall? It should be a big difference, but it's not! And that's what E.U. and the others did. They just took the go-go and just went in a big place and just did go-go." [11]

Fenwick keeps working at his dream with dogged persistence. He has engendered this vision with the Huck-A-Bucks, though by 2000 he had not been able to break through to reach that larger market. He knows that go-go needs fresh product (hence the rehearsal space and studio) as well as distribution. To solve that problem, he has allied himself with Liaison Records, which does have the clout to get compact discs and audio tapes out to a large audience. If all of these critical factors come together, Fenwick is well positioned to see his vision fulfilled.

SECURITY PERSONNEL

The use of security personnel is not unique to musical events in Washington, D.C., of course. With its lax gun control (especially compared to other industrialized nations such as Canada and England) and millions of gun enthusiasts, the United States can be a dangerous place. The need for protection for public figures ranges across our cultural landscape. It's part of show business; movie stars from Rudolph Valentino to Julia Roberts have employed security firms to protect not only their privacy but also their physical safety. Popular musicians have had similar needs for decades. Frank Sinatra was literally mobbed by bobby-soxers in the late 1940s, and a decade later Elvis Presley's popularity escalated to the point where he, too, required security from his adoring fans. This need persisted until his death in 1977—his crew of bodyguards and other allied personnel often wore special jackets with "TCOB" (Taking Care Of Business) printed on their backs. Because musicians so often get out "among the people" for nightly, weekly, or at least regular performances, they are particularly vulnerable.

This need for protection is not just a figment of the musicians' egotistical imaginations; the violence is sometimes all too real. The infamous 1969 Rolling Stones concert at Altamont Speedway (near San Francisco), demonstrates what happens when security runs amok and overreacts: people end up dead. When John Chapman, who was admittedly obsessed, assassinated John Lennon, the world was stunned. But they should not have been surprised, for the Beatles in general and Lennon and McCartney in particular had become cult figures. More recently, at the very beginning of 2000, a man broke into the home of George Harrison, mildly wounding the former Beatle with a knife.

Such violence is not limited to the rock world. In 1995 a deranged fan shot and killed the Latina pop music singer Selena. Her sudden death shocked her millions of fans, most of whom were Hispanic (largely Mexican and Mexican American). Violence in black urban culture (especially in the hip-hop world, which has weathered the deaths of Tupac Shakur and Notorious B.I.G.) has been a major underlying topic in many discussions related to this music.

This is certainly the case for go-go in D.C. Violence has been closely associated with go-go—especially in the mid- to late 1980s, when drugs, especially crack cocaine, were helping to run and ruin the streets. The security guards that work in go-go are primarily concerned with keeping the violence on the street, out of the clubs. Clubs like the Black Hole and the Icebox usually hire off-duty police officers from the District of Columbia or Maryland to help ensure that weapons are not brought into the club and that disagreements that occur inside the club do not escalate into violence (at least, inside the club). The Ibex, formerly located on Georgia Avenue NW, was shut down in 1997 after a shooting involving a disgruntled patron and a police officer hired by the club to provide security. This makes the Ibex just one more of the victims of violence.

In addition to hiring off-duty police to help secure go-go venues, the clubs also hire private security firms. Men In Black (MIB), operated by the husband-and-wife team of Roguell and Dontriece Blue, is one of the city's premier private firms providing help in policing go-go events. Founded in the mid-1990s, MIB provides a crew that looks after and helps to coordinate security. The importance of Men In Black and their fellow organizations is underscored by a blurb that sometimes turned up on the TMOTTGoGo Web site beginning in the spring of 2000. It showed a photo of the back of a broad-shouldered man wearing an MIB T-shirt, and bore this caption: "BY THE WAY... To those bamas who want to come out & knock everybody's groove....The MEN IN BLACK Security Team will definitely be on locations!"

Although they provide security for other functions and in other situations, go-go events furnish MIB with its base income. They are important because they understand the music and the culture, and their employees know many of the people who attend go-gos. This knowledge can help to defuse potentially deadly situations. Founder of MIB Roguell Blue briefly described the role played by private security firms in the world of go-go:

> The young crowd listens to R&B, but I guess for some reason the young crowd can relate to go-go. I'd say that [at] 70 percent of go-gos they have no age limits....You're dealing with a young crowd, and with a young crowd you got some of them that [are] mature and you got some of them that's not so mature. So basically go-go has all types — the good and the bad, as far as the young crowd goes....Then you have some that are gang-related, that have beefs off the street that ha[ve] nothing to do with go-go. This crew on the street just so happen[s] to like to go see the same band and by their not crossing each other's path too often on the street, go-go is a perfect place [to meet] because they wind up in the same circle.[12]

Bodyguards sometimes accompany the bands. Both Arthur Rabbit and "Big Rosey" Littlejohn have filled this role. They are really jacks-of-all trades — often driving, making arrangements for meals, or helping to move equipment in addition to looking out for the physical safety of the musicians. Bodyguards seem to be in greater demand when bands hit the road and travel outside of the Washington, D.C., metropolitan area. Arthur Rabbit, for example, is very proud of his photo album, which contains mostly slowly fading, informal, color photographs of go-go bands he worked with in Europe in the mid- to late 1980s. Rabbit was also careful to rescue and lovingly preserve flyers and posters for some of the bands' engagements. He's particularly pleased that he helped to keep the bands safe when they were on the same bill as such notable black artists as Miles Davis and George Clinton.

Security at go-go venues has never been an easy business, but the work was probably most difficult in the late 1980s. The violence in the District of Columbia brought the city such notoriety that media from across the country made it a top story. "Big Rosey" Littlejohn provided the lead-in and closing for a front-page story written by Kevin Merida and published in the *Dallas Morning News* on April 2, 1989, with the headline: "Dealer's Choice, Law's Foe—DC drug killings fuel debate on assault weapons." The article's primary focus is on the complicated issues related to gun control, specifically the proliferation of high-powered assault rifles, but it also discusses violence and drugs as they relate to go-go, detailing Littlejohn's place in the go-go community and the streets of D(odge) C(ity):

> So gripping is the violence, so astonishing the death toll, that even "Big Rosey" Littlejohn is worried. Broad-shouldered and philosophical, the 320-pound city corrections officer works nights keeping trouble out of Washington's teen-age dance halls, known in local parlance as "go-gos." He has seen it all: Kids, too cool for words, shamelessly offer bribes to security guards to bypass a frisking and carry in their 9mm semi-automatic rifles.... Last October, Big Rosey was the bouncer at Marty's Chapter III when a 19-year-old woman was shot dead, innocently caught in the cross-fire of warring drug factions. Six months earlier, outside another go-go hall where he was working, 11 youths were sprayed with bullets and left bleeding on the pavement.
>
> At the [Breezy's] Metro Club in northeast Washington the other night, the go-go regulars were dancing and sweating to the heavy percussion and bass beat of Rare Essence.... Littlejohn spied one young man, who he claimed was one of the city's biggest drug dealers. The youth looked as if he should be in a high school lunch line. As his force of bodyguards worked the crowds, Mr. Littlejohn observed that many of the several hundred teen-agers in the club probably knew something about half the murders that have taken place in the city.... It is this kind of world that Mr. Littlejohn would like [President] Bush to take into account. "If he's going to call out the National Guard, I wish he would go on and do it, because it's time. If he waits too late, it's going to be all over. It's gotten that bad!"[13]

Although the article is a bit sensational, the topics it addresses—drugs, violence, and guns—were gripping the country in 1989. In the early years of the twenty-first century, drugs are less of an issue, but violence, particularly as it relates to the use of guns by increasingly younger people, remains a nationwide problem. The misuse of guns and the way they pervade our society were major issues in relatively few places in the late 1980s, but since the tragedy at Columbine High School (and all of the other only slightly less sensational tragedies related to gun violence that followed), the entire country seems to be embroiled in these issues. Sadly, the District of Columbia seems to have been leading the curve, and much of the rest of the country has now caught up.

Despite the changing face of violence and drugs on the streets of Washington, D.C., the essential nature of security has changed very little. Typically, security at go-gos is provided by (mostly African American) males, many of whom are off-duty police officers. Everyone who enters is "carded" to make certain that they are at least 18 years of age (D.C. finally began enforcing its "under 18" weekend restrictions in the fall of 1999). Each patron is then carefully checked for weapons or potential weapons — like a sharpened nail file — as well as drugs or alcohol. This is accomplished by looking in purses, quick body searches, and the use of hand-held metal detectors. Security officers at go-gos occasionally turn away high-profile, well-known knuckleheads. People who are known to be violent or to be heavily involved in dealing drugs are the most obvious targets, but the bouncers might also head off problems by limiting the number of people from rival posses that are known to be feuding.

In this respect, a go-go event is generally quite safe. Fistfights break out every once in a while and you can't keep out all of the drugs, but most of the venues are peaceful; the majority of the violence occurs on the streets, as it does throughout D.C. and every metropolitan area. Go-go music does not incite violence; the clubs actually help to constrain violence, but street life engenders this extra-legal activity. And there is nothing that go-go can do about this sad state of affairs.

PROMOTERS

Managing bands and keeping them (and the fans) safe are important jobs, but they would be unnecessary if there was no audience. Promotion is a crucial step in the business of go-go. It matters little if it's a regular Thursday night gig at Breezy's Metro Club, the occasional booking at Sidwell Friends High School, or a neighborhood outdoor show and pool party in Oxon Hill; in order to keep the customer satisfied, you first have to get them to come to the show.

In years gone by—when go-go was young, life was simpler, and the Internet was but a gleam in the eye of some wild-eyed Stanford undergraduates—promoters counted on flyers and posters to do the trick. You just taped up dozens of them in Southeast, Northeast, and selected sections of Northwest and your work was largely finished. This was especially true in the heady days of the early to mid-1980s, when attendance at go-gos was de rigeur for young black Washingtonians. The posters didn't have to be anything special, you simply had to state the facts and have some basic graphics with a grainy group photograph and you were good to go. Getting the information into the right hands was just about all you had to do back then.

Word of mouth is also critical in promoting go-go. The buzz on the street is more important that you could imagine: "Ju Ju won't be there tonight," "NEG are hot right now," or "More cars got broken into at the Ibex." When go-goers are figuring out where to go, these seemingly casual comments are often a deciding factor. Most of this information is relayed through informal conversation occurring in the 'hood, on the telephone, or in the corridor of local schools. But it increasingly takes place on the Internet. The Take Me Out To The Go-Go site has the most active bulletin board for discussion of this kind.

It is not always possible to tell the shills from the regular folk speaking out. The hype is real and it's there, but it's not always heartfelt; it can be motivated by commerce. The bulletin board posting styles range from well-organized, articulate, conventional English to rich, less conventional "street" language that you'd hear in many places where younger black people congregate. The talk encompasses subjects ranging from public manners to fashion, but the music (almost always go-go) is at its core. The go-go topics include "old school v. new school" bands, the veracity of promoters, the state of the music outside of the District, and various record deals.

Bands and venues, however, are perhaps the most widely discussed topics. Here are three very different examples, drawn from the TMOTTGoGo bulletin board in early 2000. The first is from "Leon" on February 18; his subject was "Junk Yard and Underground Band put on a show, yall!!"

> I didn't know that the Underground Band was tight like
> that. They had all the girls on stage; it had to be like ille-
> gal to have all those girls there. The buns on the stage

where [*sic*] the cream of the crop though, we was staring cause we couldn't believe how they was rockin!! The club was packed out, but at 1:00 it was still like 75 people outside. My man couldn't get in and he said he saw Underground lead mic, Tical, sicin' [*sic*] Southside and niggas was partyin in the parkin lot. Wink got up there wit Underground Band and took us home wit a funky old school pocket. JYB was rockin like always and Danny Boy had me sice [*sic*]. It was wild because Underground had everybody too tired to party wit JY. To all them niggas that worned [*sic*] us that Underground Band was tight, they made me a fan last night. JY is definately [*sic*] back on top!!

This note, posted by "Doc Z" on February 13 (subject: "Jig-a-boo's CD"), is witty, amusing, and more than a little tongue-in-cheek:

The debut CD by Jig-a-boo Band—Str8 Given U That—has surpassed all expectations according to their Bag of Beats Records. It's winning new fans throughout Virginia and the Carolinas and is making its way down to Atlanta. Here's a sample of what some people are saying:

"These the true Bad Boys of Go-Go"—Puff Daddy

"These boys crank so hard, I refuse to let them open for my band"—Coop

"The future of Go-Go has arrived"—Ice E Ice

"As soon as I get out of jail I'm signing these boys to my label"—Suge Knight

"When I bring my tour to D.C. I have to make sure that Jig-a-boo is not playing somewhere that night (unless they're playing with me)."—J-Zee [*sic*]

"I think Bam is soooooo cute"—Britney Spears

"These bamas make me wanna say Uhhhhhhhhhh"
— Master P

Finally, many of the notes, like this one posted by "Anonymous" on March 24 (subject: "G & P Starz in Culpepper VA"), relay the facts. This is a typical example and one that underscores that the Internet can be an effective tool for free advertising: "The G & P Starz will be in Culpepper, VA at Jamms on Friday March 31st. For those that don't know, G & P is the newest sensation in GOGO. With the worlds 1st Italian lead rapper, they are off the hook. Check em out..." Right now the G & P Starz are a very minor and new band in the world of go-go. This message on the board reads like a way to not only get out the word but to also build up the band's reputation. "Anonymous" might just be a fan, but it sounds more like a very close associate of the G & P Starz. But who knows — this band might be the next big thing, or they could be just another example of go-go wannabes. Time will tell.

The facts about shows are presented on "The Scenario," a frequently updated (whenever Webmaster Kato can find the time) feature of the TMOTTGoGo Web site. With its focus on D.C. and Prince George's County, "The Scenario" covers the vast majority of regular gigs performed by the established bands. Here's the listing for the first week of January, 2000:

SUNDAY
Backyard Band @ Juliana - 1818 New York Ave, NE
Maiesha & the Hiphuggers @ The Classics, 4591
    Allentown Rd., Camp Springs, MD
OP Tribe @ Takoma Sation
MONDAY
Do your homework
TUESDAY
Rare Essence @ Tradewinds, 5859 Allentown Way,
    Camp Springs, MD
WEDNESDAY
Chuck Brown @ The Legend Night Club
NEG @ Deno's, 2325 Bladensburg Rd., N.E.
Call 202-526-8880 for more info.
The Legends @ Takoma Station
Backyard Band @ The Icebox

THURSDAY
Backyard Band @ Deno's 2325 Bladensburg Rd., N.E.
Call 202-526-8880 for more info. (Every Thursday)
FRIDAY
Chuck Brown & Jas. Funk @ The Classics,
    4591 Allentown Rd., Camp Springs, MD
Backyard Band @ Capital City Pavilion,
    3401 Georgia Ave., N.W.
Call 202-772-0994 for more information
J-MOB @ The Icebox
SATURDAY
Rare Essence @ Byrne Manor
The Legends @ Heart & Soul Cafe
Northeast Groovers @ The Icebox

Even with the increasing importance of the Internet, old-fashioned grunt work still constitutes the majority of the work that goes into promoting go-go events. The truth is that in the early 2000s the majority of younger African Americans still do not have regular Internet access, so they find out about go-go events the old-fashioned way. Posters have always been the mainstay for advertising groups and clubs, but since the mid-1990s smaller handbills and similar "throwaways" have become important tools. These smaller posters, which are tacked up around the city (most extensively in Southeast and Northeast) are the means by which the majority of go-go heads find out about shows. And since the early 1990s, Ken Moore has been the main man advertising go-gos on the streets of Washington, D.C.

These days, Moore (aka Ice E Ice and the owner of the Icebox in Northeast D.C.) is well tied in with technology. He promotes all aspects of black business in and around the District—fashion, hip-hop music events, the Malcolm X Day Celebration—in addition to go-go. The majority of his income (about 75 percent) is generated through the promotions aspect of his business, and go-go is his bread and butter. Recently, Moore has embraced the increasingly inexpensive computer-imaging technology. He manufactures flyers, handbills, and posters in-house and commented that "the designs ... have become more elaborate and having the ability to scan whatever you want to put in the background and taking even the band pictures is great. I also have a color copier which is attached to a G3 Macintosh."[14] Moore's typical week promoting go-go includes not only running shows at the Icebox, but also designing, printing, and distributing approximately 10,000 flyers to about two dozen locations, ranging from the P.A. Palace in Forestville to a small fashion emporium in Anacostia.

Moore is a true entrepreneur with his fingers in small business ventures throughout the city. Although Ice E Ice has worked with clubs all around town, he has also done his share of running go-go shows outside of the District of Columbia. This involves more than printing and distributing handbills; in fact, it encompasses the entire range of activities. In the late 1990s, he was involved with Rare Essence, Junk Yard, and the Huck-A-Bucks. His recollections on this subject read like a travelogue from D.C. into the Carolinas:

> Well, we go through Petersburg to a club called Flavors; its more like an underground club focused more to college students....We got Richmond, the Flood Zone, which is more like an alternative club, they do rock and reggae and all of that. Let's see...a lot of venues have closed down, like in Norfolk, Hampton, Virginia Beach area over the last couple of years basically due to violence....There was a really good club down there called the Club House—we used to do that every month—and there was "Norfolk Live." Basically I think 99 percent of all of those venues have closed down, so basically our only outlet there [lately] has been universities like Norfolk State, Old Dominion, Hampton, that do a homecoming, some stuff around Christmas, some spring stuff....And in North Carolina we've been to Durham, Greensboro, Elizabeth City, Lake Gaston, Charlotte, Roanoke Rapids.[15]

It's not coincidental that all of the cities and towns Moore cites either have a significant black population or are home to an historically black college or university. For example, Petersburg, Virginia, hosts Virginia State University. Elizabeth City State University is located in eastern North Carolina, while Durham is home to North Carolina Central University. And eastern Virginia and North Carolina are like going back home for many go-go musicians—most of them have some relatives (aunts, grandparents, cousins) there. Outside of the metropolitan area of Washington, D.C., go-go probably has its strongest following in the regions Moore described.

When he's not running around, Moore oversees the venues he operates in town. In the summer of 1999, he moved his printing operation to Clinton, Maryland, but he still operates the Icebox, a go-go club located near the intersection of New York Avenue and Bladensburg Road, NE, only two blocks from the long established Breezy's Metro Club and within throwing distance of the National Arboretum. Before opening the Icebox in 1997, Moore looked around at the other clubs and analyzed what they did right and how they screwed up. He was determined to take the best aspects from all the clubs and combine them in the Icebox. One of his strategies is to run a ton of theme parties, the most successful of which requires that attendees wear pajamas. Ice E Ice told us that the attire ranges from boxer shorts to lingerie, but nothing deemed too revealing is allowed. Other themes include pool parties and the '70s. Money is the incentive for dressing up, specifically a break on the price of admission to the performance by the Northeast Groovers, Rare Essence, or whatever other band is appearing that night. The reduced price is generally between 5 dollars and 10 dollars, though occasionally the admission price is entirely waived for women.

The fact that admission fees are sometimes waived for females is an interesting phenomenon that is not limited to go-go clubs. The "Ladies Night" concept is somewhat in decline here in the early years of the new millennium, but it has been used to entice the fair gender into bars, bowling alleys, and other establishments over the years. And it works!—especially in D.C., where, as Moore points out, "there is a whole lot them coming down here that don't have no money; none . . . that's part of the realism of D.C."[16] With entrance fees in the 20-dollar range (as high as 30 dollars for special events like a Northeast Groovers reunion). Much of this money goes directly to pay the band and to other fixed expenses, while Moore and other promoters (like the operators of movie theaters) make most of their money on concessions.

The legal capacity of the Icebox is 1,200, with 10 percent slack allowed by the fire marshals. In the heyday of go-go, more than that would try to get in to hear a first-class established band. Today, a good night is one that attracts a crowd in the 800 range, especially on weekdays. On weekends the club gets busier, but it's still not bursting at the seams. Even when Moore gets a set of especially good bands together, the Icebox may be packed, but no one has to wait outside for hours. The go-go business remains profitable, but it's not as lucrative as it used to be.

P.A. TAPES

The phenomenon of P.A. tapes is not unique to go-go and Washington, D.C. Certain popular music groups (perhaps most notably the Grateful Dead and Phish) are well known for their legions of fans with tape recorders and their own extensive archives of concerts. There is a large (and not-so-underground) network of tape traders and collectors who look to one another to expand or complete their bootleg collections. The difference is that unlike almost any go-go band, both groups also have an extensive back catalogue of in-print commercially released recordings. The role of the Internet—especially with regard to MP3s, Napster, and the other related controversies—in the dissemination of music continues to evolve. It has had some impact on go-go, though relatively little in terms of actually distributing the music.

The relatively small size of the contemporary audience for go-go also sets this music apart from other pop music genres. Although it has fans worldwide, the core audience for go-go remains black and D.C.-based. Almost every other niche form of American vernacular music, including tejano, polka, and Afro-Cuban pop, has an audience that may be racially based, but is more geographically dispersed. Tejano music is no longer confined to the border of Texas and Mexico; it can be heard in the barrios of Los Angeles, Chicago, and New York City. But go-go is really born, bred, and intimately tied to Washington D.C.

All of these factors lend themselves to the widespread existence of P.A. tapes among fans of go-go. P.A. tapes are generally unauthorized recordings; essentially bootleg recordings (usually compact discs rather than tapes these days) derived from the sound mix taken directly off the P.A. soundboard at a live performance. These master tapes are then sold to one of the local entrepreneurs, who then duplicates the tapes either digitally onto a compact disc or onto an analog audio tape.

Interestingly, there are parallels between D.C.'s trade in P.A. tapes and the bootleg cassette industry for Nigerian ju ju music (the groove-driven genre that resembles go-go, which was discussed in chapter 2). Ibadan, Nigeria, (a city of 3.3 million located about 100 miles from the capital, Lagos) is the center for this activity. In outdoor markets and on street corners throughout the city, vendors sell mass-produced copies of cassettes (and to a lesser degree, compact discs) of the latest live performances. Like their P.A. counterparts, these African bootleggers cite a demand for their product as one of the primary reasons they do so well.[17]

Because these entrepreneurs operate on the fringes of the recording industry, usually deal in cash, and generally have no written contracts, the world of go-go P.A. tapes remains murky and few are willing to talk about this aspect of go-go. However, former Junk Yard Band manager Moe Shorter explains the variations on the drill:

> Some bands have a particular person to record their performance right off the board... [and] authorized by the band directly. He distributes for Rare Essence and Backyard Band... [and] you gotta go to him... There was myself who was the distributor for Junk Yard Band, exclusively, no one else. You want to take it from me, you pay me for the tape and the money from my collections went to the band's operation. Now, the person that distributes for Rare Essence and Backyard.... I don't know what percentage they give back to the band, but they do pay the band.
>   Now there are a few independent distributors who may come up on the spot, and for most bands it's an honor for someone to want to record them, so they allow people to record them and they won't look for much revenue from that. [They] sell them to the retailers, like P.A. Palace, Tape Place, Mac Attack Arcade, and so on.... The person who records Backyard and Rare Essence would sell wholesale to the stores, but he would also retail straight to the consumer.[18]

P.A. tapes are widely disseminated in the go-go community and are a source of constant controversy. The basic argument is that since national record companies have largely ignored go-go and the local labels are too underfinanced to produce compact discs on a regular basis, P.A. tapes are the best way for bands to keep product in the ears and minds of their fans. Most go-go aficionados have at least some P.A. tapes or compact discs in their collection. Sometimes it's a nostalgia item because they were at the performance or because they are avid fans and heard that a particularperformance was "smokin'" and they want to hear it, or they may be completists who want to have everything recorded by a particular band. Shorter himself has about 1,600 tapes in his personal collection; most of them are Junk Yard Band performances. He has also run into people who claim to have thousands of P.A. tapes—5,000 is the highest number we've heard!

The P.A. Palace is a widely recognized local outlet for go-go video-tapes, magazines, and compact discs. The owners have maintained as many as five locations near (but not in, for financial reasons) the District of Columbia. Go-go is their mainstay, but they do sell hip-hop material as well. On our visits to the Palace in Capital Heights, Maryland, we have seen them burning compact discs and duplicating audio tapes on the premises. Of particular interest is the log of their tape inventory at the Capital Heights location. It is a list of the scores of P.A. tapes (which go back to the late 1970s) they can supply to customers at the price of about 8 dollars for a cassette and in the 14-dollar range for a compact disc. The quality of P.A. tapes varies widely, as one would suspect, and depends on who was operating the soundboard.

Liaison Records co-owner Tom Goldfogle, in particular, is opposed to the very existence of P.A. tapes. He understands their archival value but feels that they undercut the profits and exposure a band might see from a well-produced studio recording: "The upside is exposure for the band... just the general proliferation of go-go music and exposure of go-go music and keeping the vibe alive. The whole magic of go-go is the live perform-ance and... by having it on tapes and people looking for specific nights and shows and the quick turnaround of having the recording from the night before is an incredible thing and doesn't happen in any other kind of music."[19]

But Goldfogle feels that the other side of the coin needs to be discussed:

> There are a lot of them [P.A. tapes] and the band is not getting paid. A lot of them are completely unauthorized and the downside from a commercial standpoint is when the bands do release a commercial recording, they are competing with their own sales! It's like when a new group hits—the streets a0lready hit their bootlegs two weeks before... The core audience that should want to buy it already has it on bootleg recordings or P.A. tapes, so there's no reason for them to purchase a commercial recording... months later.[20]

But it's not just the money that Goldfogle knows is not going into the pockets of the band, the record company, and the distributor of legitimate releases that bothers him. P.A. tapes also reflect the aesthetics of go-go. Goldfogle feels strongly that since bands feel their product is already "out there" on P.A. tapes and compact discs, they are less likely to come up with and hone new material. The lack of new songs does not engender more interest in go-go from outside of its stronghold. And that, Goldfogle points out, is a real problem.

While local go-go heads are happy to see the bands at the Icebox, it's a rare occasion when go-go bands perform very far outside of our nation's capital. Most people, therefore, consume go-go via analog or digital means rather than hearing the bands live. And because consumers of pop music always want something new, it's the rare bird that is interested in what the Northeast Groovers sounded like on May 5, 1996, at Deno's, or in the heat generated by Trouble Funk in the summer of '89. No...they want the latest release by Junk Yard Band or to check out Chuck Brown's most recent work. It's only the true fanatic (or go-go scholar) who wants the old stuff. As Goldfogle argues, the bands need to come up with new material in order to keep their own creative juices flowing and to keep the customers satisfied.

MAX KIDD—AN APPRECIATION

"I heard the sound and thought if I pulled all those things together and carried it nationally, even internationally, I thought I could do it."[21] It's impossible to discuss the go-go community's entrepreneurs without acknowledging Max Kidd's contributions to this musical genre. Kidd will be discussed in chapter 6—especially his work with Chris Blackwell and the Island crew as well as his documentation of some of the best old-school (late 1970s and 1980s) go-go on T.T.E.D. (Total Trust, Entertainment, and Determination or Truth, Trust, Eternal Dedication, and Determination, depending who you ask) Records. Working tirelessly, Kidd devoted much of his professional adult life to the go-go community.

These days, Max is hindered by the effects of a 1993 stroke. He doesn't move like the old Max Kidd, and you have to listen carefully to his words, but the wit, the clarity, and even flashes of the ego that drove Max in his efforts to place go-go on the world music map remain firmly in place. Max himself says "[I've] always been a champion of the cause.... You always look for me—a person doing things, helping others."[22]

Max is quick to point out that go-go (the music) evolved from go-go (the event) and that, like himself, Chuck Brown was there at the beginning.

"If you go back in time, I have been with Chuck starting in '74.... Then 'Bustin' Loose' came along. I was in L.A. on business and...[it started] to really, really roll. That [record] propelled me to do it because I had started to get the [music] worldwide."[23] Indeed, Max's vision for go-go encompassed the world. He saw what Berry Gordy had accomplished with Motown and witnessed the disco movement of the mid- to late 1970s that helped to shape popular trends throughout the Western world. With these two factors to help guide him, Max figured that he could work hard enough to make go-go a potent force in shaping contemporary music trends.

And work hard he did. In the 1980s, Max Kidd appeared to be everywhere representing go-go for the District of Columbia. He helped to promote shows at venues big and small throughout the metropolitan area as well as in Philadelphia, spreading the music of Mass Extension, Chuck Brown and the Soul Searchers, Redds and the Boys, and Trouble Funk far and wide. In the mid-1980s, if you tuned your radio to one of the local "urban music" stations (particularly WPGC), the chances are you'd hear go-go and something about Max Kidd's latest go-go exploits: a new record or a big club in New York City that wanted to book E.U.

When *Good to Go* disappointed everyone in D.C. and no one outside of the city wanted to see the movie, and when Chris Blackwell dropped out of the scene, Kidd was devastated. Not only had go-go's major commercial backer moved away from the scene in 1986, the drug culture was overwhelming greater Washington, D.C. "I could have done better but I didn't," Kidd recalled. "I went into depression after that. And I decided to smoke that damn shit [crack cocaine], and when I came out of it, I came into all the alcohol. I spent about five months getting myself somewhat together.... I tried so hard."[24] In many respects, the career of Max Kidd parallels the rise and subsequent stumbling of go-go as a form of popular black music.

But, like go-go, Max Kidd wouldn't give up and continued to fight for go-go's recognition. Without a major distribution deal, locally produced go-go records on the T.T.E.D. label could be easily obtained in D.C., but not elsewhere. Yet he continued to put out records—7-inch and 12-inch vinyl—until his total output reached about 40 releases. Most of these were done in initial runs of 2,000 and were re-pressed as the need arose. He had a falling-out with his one-time partner, Reo Edwards (which is somehow tied in with a falling-out with Trouble Funk), but that didn't stop him from promoting locally.

The first generation of go-go musicians and fans remembers the mercurial and self-assured Max Kidd working on a contract for a show at Celebrity Hall, making sure that the studio was booked for Chuck Brown's next recording date, or calling out to California to make sure that the promotion company was on top of things for Trouble Funk's upcoming trip to Los Angeles.

However, today's younger members of the go-go community are largely unfamiliar with Max Kidd and what he accomplished as a hustler, champion, and resolute entrepreneur of D.C.'s only original artistic expression. He lives quietly in Northeast, off Bladensburg Road, just shy of Eastern Avenue. The walls of his first floor are filled with photographs of him standing and smiling alongside celebrities, politicians, and musicians. His basement is a treasure-trove of master tapes, vinyl recordings, civic and business awards, audio cassettes, and—not surprisingly—more photographs.

Occasionally, "official" Washington, D.C., recognizes Max Kidd. Nearly a dozen of the photographs show Kidd with various city council members; many of them are with Marion Barry. Even the local music industry has come to place more importance on Kidd's place in the history of go-go. The Washington Area Music Association (WAMA)'s June/July 1996 Newsletter noted that "Long time D.C. Go-Go promoter, Max Kidd will be honored at the International Association of African American Music's Contributor Awards Luncheon on June 15. Kidd, who during his long career has been an artist, producer, record promoter, and distributor, will receive the Joe Medlin Award." We second that emotion!

6 • The Media

The way go-go is treated by the music industry is how black folks have been treated by the power structure. It's like you're a bastard child, we don't want you, you're not good enough to be part of it. How dare them say that! So over the next 10, 15, or 20 years I would like to see go-go reach its rightful position of prominence.[1]

Cathy Hughes, founder of Radio One, Inc.

From its inception, go-go has enjoyed an uneasy relationship with the mass media. Locally, the *Washington Post* and the *Washington City Paper* have not only devoted space to the music, but Chuck Brown and the making of the film *Good to Go,* for example, have been the subjects of upbeat, positive profiles in the *Post* by Richard Harrington and Alona Wartofsky. With the exception of pieces focused on the mid-'80s commercial interest in go-go, Wartofsky's thoughtful 1990 article "The Indestructable Beat of the District," and Ta-Nehisi Coates's fine oral history of go-go ("Dropping the Bomb") in the January 14–20, 2000, issue of the *Washington City Paper,* this weekly paper has tended to focus on record reviews and concert information. But they can't (nor should they) overlook the associations between go-go and drugs or Frank Smith's diatribes regarding his attempt to use violence at go-gos as an excuse for curfews in the late 1980s. The weekly Afrocentric papers, such as the *Washington Afro-American,* the *Capitol Spotlight,* the *Washington Informer,* and the *Advocate,* occasionally run stories as well, though usually of a less provocative nature. The *Washington Times,* on the other hand, has all but ignored this music. In short, the print media's overall coverage has been a very mixed bag.

Local commercial radio has paid scant attention to go-go, mostly ghettoizing it to short, specialized block programming—although they occasionally throw in a cut by Trouble Funk, Junk Yard, Chuck Brown, Backyard, or Rare Essence. Except for WKYS-FM's weekly two-hour "Old School Go Go" program, currently there is no regularly scheduled radio programming focused on go-go. Even Pacifica Radio's Afrocentric WPFW-FM does not devote any of its weekly schedule to this indigenous form of African American music. In the early 1990s WOL-AM made a very clear statement when the management yanked off their evening go-go show, causing a short but loud, visible, and very public outburst of protest.

Local record companies have been the only D.C.-area media that have regularly documented and disseminated go-go music. Their primary interest, of course, is not merely in capturing this music on tape, vinyl, or compact disc; they want to sell product and turn a profit. But this is where many of them display their shortcomings: they are homegrown, under-capitalized, and small companies. They generally lack the distribution essential to getting the music heard outside of metropolitan D.C. Junk Yard Band, for example, has records on several labels, including Street Records, the brainchild of Moe Shorter. But Street Records is not a "full-service" company (it assists only with recording)—it exists to get the music of Junk Yard to the folks on the streets. The sole local exception is Liaison Records, which is under Tom Goldfogle and Becky Marcus's steady hands. Liaison is not only a record label, but also adistributor that has the ability to get product not only to D.C. but throughout the mid-Atlantic States as well as certain chains of stores throughout the country. Liaison is more than a go-go operation; the company works with all types of black American popular music, including hip-hop and gospel.

The ambivalence displayed by the national and local mass media has changed somewhat with the advent of the Internet. The World Wide Web has, among other things, helped to democratize the dissemination of information. For a relatively low start-up price of several thousand dollars, one can purchase a domain name, buy the requisite computing power, and contract with an ISP (Internet Service Provider). This makes setting up a Web site much more affordable than disseminating information through almost any other form of mass media. A Web site also offers opportunities for commerce. Not surprisingly, go-go has found several notable homes on the Internet.

WWW

Lately, the Internet has provided people with an important forum for go-go. The first Web sites emerged early in 1996, but the current king of go-go sites is clearly Take Me Out To The Go-Go, owned and meticulously maintained by Kevin Hammond (aka Kato). This site (www.tmottgogo.com) includes a very lively bulletin board, a comprehensive listing of current venues and artists, photographs, record reviews, and articles, as well as an extensive list of links. Significantly, the site is subtitled "Official Gateway to a Washington, D.C. Urban Gateway Culture"—underscoring the fact that go-go is emblematic of D.C. culture and not merely a musical genre.

Kato equates the music with indigenous black culture, verbal expressions, and even the way people react to the world that immediately surrounds them. He explains that "there's a lot of people in this area who took pride, believe it or not, in [D.C.] being labeled 'the murder capital.' It's just like somebody being locked up and come out, say, 'yeah, I been locked up.'... And you can't walk up to nobody in the city, period, but especially black, who don't know something about go-go or have some kind of comment on it."[2]

TMOTTGoGo was not the first go-go Web site—that honor goes to The Go Go Page (www.amdragon.com/matt/gogo.htm), operated since January 1996 out of London, England, by Matthew Wharmby. But because Kato is first and foremost a fan, TMOTTGoGo remains the best place to find out about go-go on the Internet. Growing up in the District of Columbia, he became an adult at the same time that go-go was maturing in the mid-1980s. But Kato is also well-organized and computer savvy. When he launched TMOTTGoGo, he was "working with the Newspaper Association of America—the database department. So I was finding out about merging...and that's when I decided that I haven't got enough money to do a magazine. But I got the computer to do my job, so I'm going to go ahead and do newsletters through the e-mail.... I'd do articles on upcoming events and ask somebody to do interviews for the Internet. [That was] back in '96...."[3] In 1997 Kato took the next step. He began the Web site as an alternative to the magazine that he could not afford to print. Kato explains:

> What got me started doing the Web site was always wanting to do a magazine. Always. And I always wanted to

write a book about it, so I would always keep notes and I was keeping old articles and stuff. I think I was going to do a thing—fiction—on the story of Rare Essence. But what happened was when I discovered the Internet at work and I was becoming infatuated with Web sites, it just started as me wanting to know how to build a Web site. [Then] I decided to do it as a go-go Web site.[4]

But how could people find the site? Kato decided to fall back on some of the tricks that he learned while working at the Newspaper Association of America: "Then when I had the e-mail in there I'd add it to the database and now when I add something on the site...I also send out invitations through e-mail to check out the site. Then there are guestbooks [on other sites]...I used to sit up all night just hitting guestbooks...because you could put the link to your site on there."[5]

In the twenty-first century, TMOTTGoGo is more than a Web site, it is also an on-line and print magazine. Kato finally has the financial wherewithal to print copies of the magazine, but he reckons that more people read it on-line than actually purchase a copy. The magazine's format is the vehicle by which Kato publishes the interviews that he and his staff conduct with local musicians and others in the go-go community. The Junk Yard Band adorns the cover of the November 1999 issue, and its wide-ranging contents include: an editorial called "The Publishers Voice: Let's Get The Record Straight," a profile of a band (Junk Yard), an interview with Moe Shorter, a recollection of a defunct club "Ibex—Summer of 1995," a piece by DJ Flexx called "Clearing the Air," and a piece about public decorum, "Message to the DJs."

Visitors to the site can also access a series of contemporary and historical photographs as well as "The Scenario" (up-to-date club listings), and "You the Critic" (readers' reviews of compact discs), as well as WTGO Go-Go Radio. WTGO is an archetypal example of specialized Web broadcasting. The station's page contains an archive of weekly playlists that go back four to six weeks, in addition to a series of monthly concerts that feature older performances, often recorded live at a club. For example, in May 2000 the feature was a complete performance by NE Groovers at Deno's from October 29, 1997.

The bulletin board, also called "TMOTTGoGo Community Forum Board," receives several dozen postings daily and is fraught with many of the same problems—such as monitoring, staying "on topic," and "flaming"—that many other open forums wrestle with. Thankfully, the threads are mostly about the music and might be too specialized for anyone but the go-go heads who are frequent posters. During May 15–17, 2000, writers included Soldierette, "Big P," "Go-Go-Gear Rob," "Stan da Man," "Nann Nigguz," "Spearchucker," "21," and the memorable "Bored Ass nigga wit no job." Most of these people post regularly on the bulletin board and their subjects include the new release by an up-and-coming band ("Jig-A-Boo"), the relative merits of certain percussion instruments ("Rototoms vs. Congas"), and comments about the skills of a band consisting of well-established musicians ("Legends Suck!"). The themes are occasionally tangential and provocative—"Sex and Go Go" or "Women w/Women." Sometimes the postings are merely general-interest announcements—"Old School Reunion on 6/17" or "Whitney Houston on Arista Anniversary Show."

For some folks the bulletin board serves as more than just a means of conveying information and opinions; it provides opportunities for nostalgia as well as communication. Much like men sit around talking about sporting events and players of years ago, the bulletin board posters quite often discuss the past—the days when all go-go was old-school. One of the questions in early September 2000, "Your Best ... RE Show That You Attended" led to many responses, with more than a dozen older go-go heads weighing in:

> Can you say. . . Runion [sic] 11/24/90!!! That joint out in Va. You had Maniac, Funk, and Benny rockin the mic, and you had boogie the first 3/4 of the show, then Mickey rockin the last 1/4 with Atomic Dog and the glass house ... For an old school fan, it just doesn't get damn better than that night.
>
> *Ol' RE Fan 4Life!*

> It was around 87–88 and I was coming home X-Mas break from college (Florida A & M). I had not seen Essence in a while and one of my boys is wearing shorts to the Metro Club. We were all lifted [sic] and when we get to the door I hear them hitin the horn part from "All the Way to Heaven" and we just freaked out and partied like the old days.
>
> *Gino*

Friendly High School—They came out crankin' "Get on the Wagon," then hit "Maniac" when it was new. Second half came out crankin "Numbers;" Funk got up on stage, broke that thing down and started to hit the roll call! Whew hit to the beat everybody, back it up with Alonzo from Trouble on roto toms.

Lead Rapper

Kato also likes to keep the go-go community informed about breaking news, which is easy to do on the Internet because information enters your computer as quickly as your modem can download it. One example of this was Donnell Floyd's decision to leave Rare Essence in December 2000 in order to form a new band, 911. Floyd had intimated this move for several weeks before official announcing it on WKYS-FM's Sunday evening go-go program. Just in case you missed that December 17, 2000, broadcast, TMOTTGoGo almost instantaneously delivered it to you.

As of the spring of 2001, TMOTTGoGo is not self-supporting, although the overhead needed to keep the site on-line is minimal (the server costs Kato about 80 dollars per month). Like so many Internet entrepreneurs and community newspapers—such as the *Washington City Paper,* to which he looks for inspiration—Kevin is banking on advertising to eventually pay the freight.

But Kato is a family man and has generally supported his Internet go-go habit by taking odd jobs and temporary employment. Kato has also sold audio cassettes and compact discs, mostly of the P.A. variety. These aural documents enjoy distribution in and around the District of Columbia, but are only available by mail order to anyone living outside of the region. They also caused Kato to stop and think about the implications of selling them:

It's a catch-22. I was getting orders from Japan, from California. And when they hit me, I realized how serious this could be. I realized I'm in a position to try to help put knowledge into these musicians...about copyright, music publishing, and at the same time I'm making money off these tapes.[6]

There are other stable go-go sites on the Web. Some of the established groups, including Trouble Funk and Experience Unlimited, maintain their own sites that provide visitors with upcoming dates, record releases, and the bands' personal comings and goings. There are also fan sites — such as Funkmaster J's Go Go Links (http://funkmasterj. tripod.com/gogo.htm#Gogo) — that not only give you plenty of information and opinions but also lead you to other sites you may want to visit. A few go-go businesses also have homes on the Web; the P.A. Palace (www.papalace.com) maintains the largest site, complete with photographs, music and video downloads, and the usual links.

The Web is largely the domain of the young (mostly under 30) crew and some sites are as ephemeral as youth. Justin Jefferson has run Go-Go Central (http://members.nbci.com/gogocentral/gogo.html) since June 17, 1997. In many ways, his story is typical. Growing up in northern Virginia, Jefferson was drawn to the Web and loved go-go music, which he came into the city to experience live: "I was 17 when I went to a show at the Icebox, the Zulu Kings. And there was a show in March '97 and they had five go-go bands for one dollar — Backyard, Junk Yard, the Huck-A-Bucks . . . I got to hear all of the bands and it made me a bigger fan of go-go. And I went to a couple of block parties in the summer of '97."[7] Armed with a rudimentary knowledge of HTML programming learned in high school, Justin soon put his Web site up. In the first year and a half he got 15,000 hits. Then he got into college in northern Virginia. He has continued to maintain his site, updating it when he has time, but with school and all of his other responsibilities, he finds it difficult to do everything that he wants.

There are many other go-go Web sites that contribute to the community in various ways. Go-Go World at www.gogolive.com, for instance, often has shout-outs (some of them with a holiday message) that reinforce the importance of recognition among the go-go population. This was their greeting for Christmas 2000:

LAND OF THE GO-GO STARS
MERRY XMAS
(DC GO-GO MOBS ONLY)
REPRESENTING

THE WES'SYDE MOB - THAT DEL RAY CREW
SECTION 8 - AND THE PARK TERRACE 4600 DUKE
THE RIGGS PARK CREW
THE 13TH AND PARK
THE GLENARDEN STARS - BRIGHTSEAT ROAD CREW
THE 3RD WORLD HONEYS

GEORGIA N RITTENHOUSE
THE 24MOB ARLINGTON VA
KIMBERLY GARDENS CREW
THAT 10-80 SURSUM CORDAS
DEM 38NIGGAZ AND THE GOOD OL' HILL BOYS
T-A-Y-L-O-R (7th n Taylor)
THE BACKWOODS NIGGAZ
THE 640 BOYZ
THAT NU-TOWN CREW
RIVER TERRACE HONEYS
THE WHOLE TRINIDAD
THE WHOLE 21ST
THE EDGEWOOD LYNCH MOB
SOLO SPORTSWEAR
TOOTIE THOMAS
MADISON STREET CREW FREDERICK MD
THE WHOLE 57 CREW
THE WHOLE 9TH ST COMPOUND
THE PLAZA BOYS
CELL BLOCK 8
15TH & MONROE (THE 1-5) - THE GOOD UPTOWN
RIP LIL ANT & ROME
THE KIRK OUT HUNYZ AND THAT 17TH-N-COMPTON
THE 3D MOB - THE WHOLE 117
DA WHOLE Q.B.C. N 35-DOUBLE-O
THE WHOLE KDY
BYWATERS CREW
(1st court & Royal St. Annapolis MD)
R.I.P
KEO - NATE - CO - KK - UNCLE TOMMY
THE INSANE 44 HONEYS - THE GOOD OL 7WOODS

OVER THE AIRWAVES

For reasons that we don't fully fathom, go-go has been almost entirely ignored by electronic media in and around Washington, D.C. You would expect local television broadcasters from the major (and not-so-major) over-the-air commercial stations—NBC, WRC-TV (Ch. 4); Fox, WTTG-TV (Ch. 5); ABC, WJLA-TV (Ch. 7); CBS, WUSA-TV (Ch. 9); UPN,

WDCA-TV (Ch. 20); and WB, WBDC-TV (Ch. 50)—to overlook local black vernacular music...and they rarely disappoint. The only exceptions come in three flavors. First are the occasional shots showing a go-go band playing for a block party; these neighborhood events occasionally make the local news—for about 30 seconds. The second type of coverage occurs when go-go clubs are near the scene of street violence; then you get the brief "violence on the streets of Washington, D.C." story. Finally, when a band performs at a "pool party" that causes a scene (usually involving female nudity), this becomes quick and dirty local news.

The best example of this last type occurred in July 1994 when WJLA-TV's Del Walters hosted a short series on Channel 7's early evening and late night news about a "videotaped orgy" that promoted "a thriving underground market of filth." Walters's exposé concerned the home-grown and less-than-professional videos in which go-go bands play at local pool parties and women divest themselves of clothing. These particular videos were shot at Laurel, Maryland's Fairland Aquatics Center in May 1994 and they document behavior that can fairly be described as lewd. However, the videos show acts that are probably not profoundly different from what occurs at the "gentlemen's clubs" dotting downtown Washington, D.C., which are largely frequented by white men in business suits. Because the pool parties involved minors, public behavior, and African Americans, WJLA-TV made this top-line local news for almost a week.

Two of the local public/non-commercial stations—WETA (Ch 26) and WMPT (Ch. 22) have shown little interest in go-go. A third, WHUT (Howard University Television), on the other hand, has displayed some interest in the music over the years. This is not particularly surprising given the local popularity of go-go and its black origins (Howard is an historically black university). In 1991, the station broadcast a good hour-long documentary about go-go entitled *Straight-Up Go-Go*. Currently, however, WHUT pays little more than lip service to go-go. The station presently reserves none of its airtime for this music.

It wasn't always this way. Beginning in April 1992, the public television outlet aired a Bruce Brown–produced show featuring local soul, hip-hop, and go-go artists. *Powerhouse* aired on Channel 32 every Saturday at 7:30 P.M. with a Sunday noon reprise, quickly becoming a roaring success. Brown (under his TeleVideo & Film logo) related that it was a "show that I designed, put together to feature hip-hop, rap, and go-go. So you would have Konan sharing the stage with Chuck D....and then Chuck Brown live at the Capital Centre together with footage of Trouble Funk in

Japan."[8] Keenan "Konan" Ellerbee (host of WOL-AM's *Hip-Hop Show* until the station abandoned music for talk) served as the program's initial host, but he sometimes had other local talent, such as Little Benny, DJ Kool, and DC Scorpio fill in. After almost two years, *Powerhouse* left Channel 32 after it ran a controversial interview and piece about Sista Souljah, landing for one season each on Channel 50 and Channel 20. Go-go remained at the heart of the program and it represents the most extensive and positive television exposure ever enjoyed by go-go.

Cable access in the District of Columbia has allowed go-go a bit of airtime. *MetroWorld's Mob-TV* has been the principal outlet. It has been carried on the city's rather unadventuresome, drab, and haphazardly operated District Cablevision. And what a sporadic outfit *Mob-TV* was! Although they presented some fine footage on Channel 25, this provocatively named outfit tended to focus on the sensational, booty-shakin', and underworld (read "gangsta") aspects of go-go and the District's black culture. Their sporadic cable broadcasts tended to de-emphasize the music and the bands in favor of the "flava" of the more outlandish outdoor summer events that are typified by pool parties. Their cameras often lingered on large (often barely covered) butts and naked breasts displayed in public.

Just like some of the go-go groups that came of age in the '90s (Backyard Band, for instance), *MetroWorld's Mob-TV* style was informed by hip-hop. In every respect, MetroWorld operated in a black world, from African American speech patterns to the music to the faces that appear on the programs and those behind the camera and mixing board. Most of their programming was narrated by on-air personalities comparable to the ubiquitous VJs seen on other music-related television channels. When *Mob-TV* covered live events, the editing style clearly attempted to mimic MTV culture—lots of quick cuts interspersed with in-the-crowd shots, brief interviews, and plenty of babes sitting in the laps of young (and not so young) men. The go-go VJ also read "news" that included not only upcoming performances but also the most recent changes in band personnel and other related information.

MetroWorld's Mob-TV (the brainchild of J. Paul Blake) prided itself on its willingness and ability to go behind the scenes of go-go in a very informal fashion. For example, for their coverage of the Stop the Violence go-go event held at RFK Stadium, the camera wandered into the trailers where the bands stay before and after they perform. But the show's coverage was a bit misleading because of the emphasis on the larger outdoor events. The fact is that the small clubs provide most folks with their regular go-go fix and events at a place like RFK are very much the exception, rather than the rule.

The show itself aired on most Saturday nights for many months between 1993 and 1995 on Channel 25 in the District as well as on cable outlets that served Alexandria, Virginia, and Montgomery County, Maryland. Blake claims that it reached a total of as many as 50,000 viewers. If you lack access to District Cablevision and want to get a taste of the MetroWorld mode, you can do so by way of videotape. Like the P.A. tapes and compact discs, "homemade" videotapes are peddled locally and by mail order. They come with very plain packaging, are copied using a high-speed dubber (resulting in a poor-quality copy), and cost about 15 dollars for 120 minutes of go-go action.

The value of these tapes is severalfold. First, they permit you to view the interaction between our most invasive electronic media and D.C.'s only indigenous art form. They also help to document go-go music in a unique fashion. The other examples of go-go on film are either more highly crafted, compact documentaries or they present go-go using essentially raw footage. Finally, *Mob-TV* exemplified the entrepreneurial spirit that is a hallmark of go-go.

But even *MetroWorld's Mob-TV* did not do proper justice to one other visual aspect of go-go—the video. While commercial and public stations alike have ignored the performance videos that are largely products of the streets, they have also overlooked the shorter videos (à la MTV) that focus on a single theme or song. The go-go genre has only produced a handful of them, most notably "Ruff-It-Off" by Junk Yard and "Lock-It" and "Body Snatchers" by Rare Essence. They have never received any serious attention from any outlet: MTV, VH-1, The Box, or BET. This may be because they are either too local or too specialized. The quality of the videos is fine, but go-go videos remain a genre that constitutes a very small part of the go-go world—and an even smaller portion of the broadcast world's attention.

In 1991 an indignant Cathy Hughes berated the mass media for their lack of support for go-go. Her words, which open this chapter, are important enough to repeat:

> The way go-go is treated by the music industry is how black folks have been treated by the power structure. It's like you're a bastard child, we don't want you, you're not good enough to be part of it. How dare them say that! So

over the next 10, 15, or 20 years I would like to see go-go
reach its rightful position of prominence.

Hughes, a black woman who has built a powerful multi-station media
voice that expanded greatly in the 1990s, moved to the District of
Columbia in 1971 after graduating from Creighton University, and was
living in the city when go-go developed. By 1975 Hughes was the Vice
President and General Manager of WHUR-FM (the commercial radio station owned by Howard University), and part of her efforts went into the
development of the highly successful "Quiet Storm" nighttime format that
increased the station's advertising revenues ten-fold.

Cathy Hughes began what is now Radio One, Inc. with her 1980
acquisition of WOL-AM, which she operated under the slogan "Where
Information is Power." Her son, Alfred Liggins, serves as Radio One's
President and General Manager. It is a company with a loud and unrelenting voice in the Washington, D.C., market. In the District of
Columbia, Radio One owns two of the highest rated (by Arbitron) stations: WMMJ-FM and WKYS-FM, both of which broadcast music to a
"contemporary urban, black soul" audience. The company also owns and
operates WOL-AM, a talk station, and a gospel outlet, WYCB-AM.

In August 2000, Radio One scored a major coup when it lured Tom
Joyner (perhaps the most popular black radio personality in the United
States) away from WHUR-FM to become the morning man at WMMJ-
FM. Joyner's program, which is syndicated by ABC, reaches about seven
million listeners around the United States, but his deal with Radio One
allows him access to about one million more listeners and will include
new markets like Houston. To place this in perspective, Rush Limbaugh
reaches an audience of about 14.5 million, and Howard Stern nearly 12
million listeners weekly. By the beginning of 2001, Radio One owned 52
stations that targeted African American listeners in all of the 40 largest
black markets in the United States. Their weekly audience is estimated at
eight million listeners, some 90 percent of whom are African American.
The company enjoyed revenues of 81.7 million dollars in fiscal year
1999. In keeping with her goal to "create my world where racism and
sexism do not prevail,"[9] 94 percent of Hughes's 300 employees are
African American; interestingly, the percentage of management positions
held by women is not disclosed in any report we could locate.[10]

That Cathy Hughes is outspoken is an understatement. She very visi-
bly supported Marion Barry and led a visible and controversial 1986

boycott of the *Washington Post* that centered on its treatment of rap music and violence. An article in *BOSS Magazine* suggested that "Hughes fashioned herself into the straight-talking icon of Radio One, Inc., and in the process molded her chain of radio stations—the largest African American–owned public company in the country—into a larger version of herself: sassy, powerful, and urban. From all appearances Hughes is attaining these goals."[11]

The same article points out that "Hughes' erstwhile appeal as a black advocate is fading into the background as the company focuses more on bottom-line interests that play into a mainstream, majority financial culture."[12] Make no mistake; Radio One, Inc., is a very successful company—until the 2000 stock-market slide, its stock price consistently went up, as did its profits. Radio One is presently the eighth-largest radio network in the country and also holds the distinction of being the fastest-growing radio network. As the company grows into a more and more powerful voice, Hughes seems to be leaving D.C. behind in favor of a corporate model that is poised to become the voice for all of urban America.

The implications for D.C. radio and go-go are profound. As *the* major player in D.C.'s "urban" radio market, one would think that Hughes would be trumpeting the virtues of go-go by including a nice selection of go-go music on the playlists of the stations owned by Radio One. Yet it seems that the feelings she expressed in her outspoken and very public statements from 1991 (about go-go's treatment by "the power structure") have vanished like dust in the wind now that Hughes has become part of the structure that she so vehemently decried. The reality is that the forces driving the programming at commercial radio stations (national charts reign supreme) are antithetical to go-go's very local appeal; as a result, the inclusion of go-go on D.C.'s commercial radio stations is only given lip service.

If you tune into WPGC-FM (95.5) in the evening you will occasionally catch a contemporary go-go song by one of the long-established bands. The same is true for the other commercial FM and AM stations that serve the metropolitan area's "urban" radio listenership of approximately one million people. The many stations that marginalize go-go, including WKYS-FM (93.9) and WHUR-FM (96.3), are driven by playlists that draw from record sales and surveys that reflect trends in black popular music nationwide. There is a monumentally tiny amount of wiggle room in these playlists and go-go occasionally slides in. To give them small "props," WKYS-FM does broadcast a concise "Old School

After more than a decade of work, Sweet Cherie remains one of the premier singers on the contemporary go-go scene.

Experience Unlimited promotional picture circa 1990, while "Da Butt" rode the charts.

William "Ju Ju" House, a powerhouse drummer hard at work.

The Proper Utensils front line of singers features veterans Little Benny and James Funk.

Advertisement for *Good to Go: The Movie* (*Capital Spotlight*, July 31, 1986.)

A potential patron contemplates attending an upcoming show by Backyard Band.

"E" from the OP Tribe with his singular eye-wear on prominent display.

Dayo, lead singer for Lissen, and a crowd member share a special moment at Takoma Station, which photographer Thomas Sayers Ellis labeled "What a Look!"

Rev. Sidney Speaks takes a stand in front of one of the most important go-go venues from late 1970s.

Go-go veteran Mike Hughes, a few weeks before his sudden and unexpected death.

Go-go fans throw their hands up in the air at a performance held in the parking lot of the Holy Christian Missionary Baptist Church for All People.

Up and coming go-go fans beating their feet to hot music on a cool afternoon.

The next generation of go-go music is in the hands of BJ, the son of legendary percussionist Go-Go Mickey.

Go-Go Mickey warms up his timbales in anticipation of another afternoon at work.

Only in our nation's capital would a band's jacket feature not only the TCB moniker, but the "Bounce Beat Kings" subtitle.

What? Band brings their music to the streets of Washington D.C.

Backyard Band's "Big G," with Mayor Adrian Fenty and former Mayor Marion Barry, at a candlelight vigil for Tayon Glover, Big G's brother.

Similar informal ensembles of percussionists, which photographer Thomas Sayers Ellis aptly labeled "Bucket Family," perform throughout downtown D.C. in warm weather.

Go-Go" program on Sunday nights from 9:30–11:00 P.M. It's a pleasing mixture of P.A. tapes and commercial releases. On WPGC, go-go is sometimes heard on DJ Flexx's evening show, but this token appearance still constitutes less than one percent of the station's weekly programming. The bottom line remains: if a national act—like Toni Braxton, Chuck D., D'Angelo, or Destiny's Child—is hot, you will hear its tunes in Chicago, Shreveport, Boston, Phoenix, Fresno, and Washington, D.C. Because go-go barely makes a blip on the national charts, it is all but absent from the local airwaves.

Commercially operated radio stations are very tightly regulated, though not by the FCC. Rather, it is record sales that determine what's heard on the radio. The precise format varies from station to station, of course. WPGC-FM tends to play more rap than WKYS-FM, though both are billed as "urban hits" stations. WHUR-FM pioneered the "quiet storm" format while enjoying the "urban adult" label. WOL-AM ("black talk") now has plenty of talk and no music, so the question of their current participation in broadcasting go-go is moot.

Producer and manager Charlie Fenwick has spoken cogently on this subject. His take is that go-go's recorded selections are too long and don't lend themselves to the tightly controlled FM and AM radio markets. Fenwick feels that go-go is just not radio-friendly. He says, "it's like the vision of the [live] show . . . when you put out material. That's the way they buy it in D.C. . . . full-length tapes about 45 and 60 minutes long. . . . Puffy and all them, they do one little skit but basically we can't seem to sell [go-go musicians] around here just doing a regular 12-inch [single]."[13] No matter what the length of a particular selection, the truth is that go-go isn't happening outside of D.C., so it isn't happening on D.C.'s black-oriented commercial radio outlets.

Go-go records occasionally break through onto D.C.'s commercial radio stations at other times than on the less desirable, ghettoized time slots reserved for this music. In this regard, gospel music is treated much like go-go on pop music radio stations. Tom Goldfogle of Liaison Records remarked that "records that fit their format are going to get played in the daytime. A handful of records like 'Lock-It,' 'Go Go Rumpshaker,' and 'Bustin' Loose' that fit the bill can make it into prime-time radio. There's lots of types of specialized music that gets played in hours like go-go, which deserves more than that in this market, certainly."[14]

Because commercial radio is so segregated, it is hardly worth mentioning the D.C. stations that target the local white community. These stations tend to promote the same commercial pop music (mostly rock and, more recently, hip-hop-derived rock) that one hears everywhere in the United States. The formats also bear the same names that you'd find anywhere in the country from Peoria to Portland: "oldies" are found on WBIG-FM (100.3), "classic rock" is heard via WARW (94.7), and WRQX (107.3) sticks to the "modern adult hits" format. WHFS-FM (99.1) goes way out on a limb with their "alternative" format. But whatever derivative format these stations adopt, none of them has any room for go-go. Once again, go-go is simply too black and too local.

Support on commercial radio for go-go was not always lacking. In the early '70s, with the support of WOL's DJs, the music of proto-go-go groups such as Chuck Brown and the Soul Searchers, The Young Senators, Black Heat, and E.U. got decent airplay. Long-time area broadcaster Bobby Bennett, who has worked for WOL, WHUR, and WPFW-FM, has always been supportive of local talent, and his high standards gave go-go musicians something to strive for. In the late 1980s "Brute" Bailey, program director for the now-defunct WDJY, forged a working relationship with go-go music and its performers to help campaign against drugs and violence. Bailey wisely embraced the go-go community as soldiers in his army to combat these problems. Today, however, virtually no go-go is played on the region's commercial "urban" radio stations.

After surveying the dismal commercial radio scene, the non-commercial stations (88.1–91.9 on your FM dial) would seem to hold some promise. Wrong again. In Washington, D.C., three major non-commercial stations dominate the field. Two of them—WAMU-FM (88.5) and WETA-FM (90.9)—are part of the National Public Radio network. Both are major, flagship (meaning they contribute programming to the entire network) stations that offer the usual potpourri of news and talk shows: *All Things Considered; This American Life; A Prairie Home Companion; Wait Wait, Don't Tell Me; Morning Edition;* and *Fresh Air.* Except for *Bluegrass Overnight, Stained Glass Bluegrass,* the *Dick Spottswood Show,* and the drive-time bluegrass and country show, WAMU offers little original music programming, and their commitment to (local) black American music is virtually non-existent. WETA is no better in this regard. Most of their music programming is "classical" European art music, though on Saturday evening the station programs several hours of jazz and folk music, and on Sunday nights plays the pop music retrospective *Songs for Aging Children.* But in general, the black segment of the public seems to have been largely forgotten by public radio.

Except for Bobby Bennett's long-running (but now defunct) Saturday show, which included some old-school go-go, even the local Pacifica Station overlooks go-go. WPFW's (89.3) orientation is unabashedly towards the local black community, and it does broadcast a mixture of black-oriented musical genres. Jazz is the station's forte, but it also broadcasts Caribbean music shows. In 2000, "Jazz and much, much more" was one of their primary on-air slogans; unfortunately, go-go is not part of that "much, much more." Given WPFW's local orientation, go-go's absence from the station's weekly programming is truly surprising. It appears that go-go has never commanded much (if any) of WPFW-FM's airtime. This lack of coverage is an enigma for a black-oriented radio station that depends upon local talent for their live broadcasts and also calls itself a community station. No one at the station could offer a viable explanation. Strange things continue to happen in this world!

THE WORD

TMOTTGoGo is not the only magazine devoted to go-go. *Go Go Swings* takes into account not only the music but fashion as well. Though it is not published on-line and comes out on a less reliable schedule, *Go Go Swings* aims to reach the same audience as Kato's publication: a hip, young, black, and urban (mostly from D.C. and Prince George's County) readership who are aware of what they eat, how they look, where they work, and what music they consume.

The October 1997 issue of *Go Go Swings* typifies the magazine's style and attitude. The articles about Chuck Brown and Rare Essence's André "Whiteboy" Johnson are short and not particularly revealing. Benjy Little contributes a brief "Editor's Quote" as well as short columns about fashion ("The Wear"), letters ("Public Opinion"), and the younger set ("Children's Page"). The most interesting section is a list of hot-selling go-go releases. In the fall of 1997 this included *Straight Cranking* by RE, *Unibomber* by Backyard Band, *Roll It* by Northeast Groovers, and *Here Come the Freaks* by Junk Yard. These features are interspersed with ads for small local businesses—Planet Chocolate City on H Street NE; Rugged Wear Sports Apparel in Capital Heights and Suitland, Maryland; and Shooter's Urban Sports Apparel on Pennsylvania Avenue SE. Their willingness to advertise in *Go Go Swings* underscores not only the music's local appeal but also its entrepreneurial nature.

It is not only the music that moves go-go; it's gear, too. With go-go's youthful demographics, the importance of image is not to be underestimated. The importance of gear—clothing in particular—is reflected by local in-store marketing and in the advertisements found in local magazines devoted to go-go. *Go Go Swings* magazine bills itself as a publication "For The Young Urban Mind" that covers not only go-go but also "rap, hip-hop, R&B, jazz and entertainment." Perhaps it should be subtitled "Black Popular Music and Culture in D.C."

CEO Benjy Little, born in 1971, believes in the power and importance of go-go. He began *Go Go Swings* in 1997 to represent the city in ways that the more upscale (read white) monthly *Washingtonian* magazine can't and is not interested in doing. Little notes that "D.C. didn't have a voice, we were always on the back burner."[15] Once again, the division between D.C. and Washington rears its head. Little was exposed to go-go before he attended grade school by his uncle, Norris Little, who promoted shows at the Take-It-Easy Ranch in southern Maryland. In addition to go-go shows that lasted several days, Norris Little brought in national acts such as Roy Ayers; Earth, Wind & Fire; and the Four Tops. This business venture was quite successful until about 1979, when one of the employees, Nighthawk, absconded with all of the company's money. Benjy Little's older, trumpet-playing brother, Harold, performed with Chance Band & Show and Chuck Brown before devoting his energy and expertise to jazz.

With plenty of hard work and relatively little capital, *Go Go Swings* magazine has slowly grown. From an initial press run of 500 for the first issue, the sixth edition of the magazine has grown to 35,000 copies that are sold throughout the city and over the Internet. Little believes that his "RIP" (obituaries) and photo sections are perhaps the most turned-to sections of the magazines. Much like shout-outs at a go-go, people want to see themselves "represented" in print or from the stage, underscoring the old adage that "you've got to give the public what they want."

Publishing a small and underfunded magazine is the very definition of "scuffling." Benjy Little told us:

> I'm just trying to make this thing certified and we're going to keep going strong regardless if our advertising is not as strong, you know.... I'm trying to get everybody to understand that.... In Willie's Records, they took *The Source* magazine out because the *Swings* sells off the racks. I can't print enough magazines, you know, so I'm

trying to get everybody to understand we're a strong publication, we're a young publication and . . . everybody to
[understand] our vehicle right here the same way everybody looks at *The Source*.[16]

Washington, D.C.'s most prominent mainstream print media—the
Washington Post—displays the most ambivalent attitude towards go-go.
On one hand, this behemoth has published a score of thoughtful, intelligent, and sympathetic articles, concert reviews, or profiles about go-go,
most of them by Richard Harrington or Alona Wartofsky. But aside from
these two writers, the *Post* tends to ignore go-go . . . unless the story
involves violence, drugs, or some other scandalous behavior, such as its
reporting of the pool party videos in the summer of 1994.

Under the headline "Explicit Videos Tarnish Go-Go's Image," Louis
Aguilar and Hamil R. Harris aptly and carefully reported on go-go activity during the dog days of '94. But here is the story's hook:

At several go-go concerts in recent months, some female
fans were inspired to dance with their clothes off. Other
concertgoers videotaped them, spawning an underground
market of videos that would be rated X if they were rated
at all. . . . During the late '80s, go-go music became a
scapegoat for anxious parents and politicians looking for
a simple explanation for the drug violence that was not
uncommon at shows. . . . The number of go-go concerts
dropped dramatically, as public halls where shows took
place were hit with curfews. For a time, it seemed that
people were afraid to go out. . . . More go-gos were canceled. The recent show at De Zulu, which featured Rare
Essence along with five other bands, was originally slated
to be held at a larger venue, the Washington Coliseum.
But it was moved to De Zulu after community leaders
persuaded the Coliseum owners to cancel the gig.[17]

While this *Post* article seems rather neutral, it implies that there is
something "wrong" with the go-go scene. This time, instead of violence,
the problem is nude (or nearly nude), booty-shakin' women. Go-go, we
suppose, is simply too black and consumed by too many young people to
be taken seriously.

Except for the *Washington Times,* which avoids go-go like it was a Democratic fundraiser, the rest of Washington's print media occasionally covers the go-go scene. The *Washington Afro-American,* a black weekly, sometimes runs articles or short features on a band or an individual. The *Washington City Paper* includes a (not so comprehensive or up-to-date) listing of go-go events around town—at least they acknowledge the genre! As for the other glossy local weekly or monthly publications, such as *Washingtonian* magazine, forget it—go-go gets as much coverage a' they offer readers interested in the Italian professional volleyball league's play-offs.

RECORD COMPANIES

From the advent of the record industry in the late 1880s—in Washington, D.C., by the way—until recently, analog sound recordings were the "preservation" medium of choice for American popular music. Since the 1920s, radio has helped to promote musical genres, first in live studio per-formances and then through the playing of records over the air. Until the advent of MTV and VH-1 in the 1980s, television traditionally ran a dis-tant third. Now the digital revolution has once more altered the way we consume music. Nonetheless, records and commercial record companies have played a critical role in the dissemination of the go-go sound.

Max Kidd stands at the front of the line when it comes to document-ing go-go music. Although he did not produce the first go-go records, in 1976 Kidd founded the first record company (T.T.E.D.—"Home of the FIERCEST FUNK on Earth!") to focus on the genre. Starting out as a soul and funk label, T.T.E.D. switched its emphasis to go-go in the early 1980s. In a series of 7-inch and 12-inch singles, long-play records, and audio cassettes issued on the label, Kidd documented the scene for more than a decade, and it was during this period that go-go enjoyed its great-est local popularity and national prominence.

The multi-faceted relationship between Kidd (a native of Charleston, West Virginia, who ended up in D.C. after a military stint) and D.C.'s black popular music began in the early 1960s. His record company executive days were preceded by careers as a songwriter, singer, producer, and record promoter. Kidd saw himself (as did others) in a role similar to Berry Gordy's. He puts a finer point on the comparison by saying, "I know the music, I know the streets. It's the same thing as Kenny Gamble and Leon Huff [Philly Soul], the same thing as Al Bell [Memphis Stax], the same thing as Dick Griffy and Lonnie Simmons [Los Angeles' Solar Records.][18] These were heady times. During the early 1980s, Washington, D.C., was reminiscent of early-'60s Detroit or Seattle some 30 years later, when "grunge" rock brought flocks of national A&R men into town, resulting in the monstrous success of groups like Soundgarden, Pearl Jam, and Nirvana.

Working out of a small, crowded office on Bladensburg Road NE that he initially shared with his fledgling computer business, Kidd quickly built up a stable of artists that included many of the best go-go bands — Trouble Funk, Mass Extension, and Sluggo, among others. A keen observer of the scene, Kidd also realized the potential of newly emerging bands, such as Ayre Rayde and the Pumpblenders, viewing them as the future of go-go. Kidd exerted (or attempted to retain) control over all aspects of the bands signed to T.T.E.D. For example, he wanted to make certain they were properly represented in their negotiations with local clubs over the details regarding their bookings. He viewed himself as being near the epicenter of the go-go world and was not reticent about expressing his feelings about his place in the development and ownership of go-go: "If it ain't T.T.E.D., it ain't go-go...."[19]

The first potential big break for go-go occurred when Island Pictures owner Chris Blackwell heard "Bustin' Loose" on a New York City radio station and was intrigued by its sound, which was both familiar and unique. Fresh from his experience with reggae (as well as his even greater commercial success with the Irish pop band U2), Blackwell tracked down the source of the Brown recording and quickly discovered that D.C. was ground zero for go-go. He also very quickly learned that Max Kidd was the man to talk with in Washington, D.C., and the two forward-thinking entrepreneurs immediately hit it off.

Kidd's relationship with Chris Blackwell and Island not only resulted in the controversial film *Good to Go,* but also in a distribution deal that helped to expose go-go to a global audience. The importance of the deal was underscored by Nelson George's *Billboard* piece entitled "Go-Go Music Ready to Go Global: T.T.E.D. Label signs deal with Island; film planned" in which he wrote:

> The catalyst for this actvity is D.C.-based entrepreneur, Max Kidd, whose T.T.E.D. Records has entered into an agreement with Island for seven acts: go-go's top bands, Trouble Funk and E.U., are already signed directly to Island under a product deal with T.T.E.D.; their product

will be distributed through WEA. Five other acts will remain under the T.T.E.D. logo and will be distributed independently through 4th & B'Way Records, an independent subsidiary of Island. The latter acts are Chuck Brown & the Soul Searchers, whose "Bustin' Loose" in the late '70s on the MCA-distributed Source label was the first national go-go hit; Mass Extension; Yuggie, the only female go-go band; Redds and the Boys; and Hot, Cold, Sweat. Redds and the Boys' "Movin' & Groovin'" is the first release under the deal.[20]

The distribution deal had the desired effect. The go-go releases on 4th & B'Way/T.T.E.D. Records were now available to audiences that Kidd and the bands could have only dreamed of reaching in the past. "Movin' And Groovin'" could be heard on black urban radio stations from California to Massachusetts, though its airplay was especially strong in the mid-Atlantic states. Jack the Rapper's *Confidential Record Sheet* (an insiders' publication aimed at "black" radio station personnel) for April 17, 1985, stated: "A whole lot of action on this bad boy. Ain't no way are you gonna sit still on this baby. The groove is laid down early and the funk just oozes and oozes all over the place. If you don't dig funk before you'll dig it now. Go 'head on Brother Redds & The Boys!!!" Although "Sound of Washington, D.C." was plastered all over T.T.E.D.'s publicity material, Jake the Rapper seemed to hear the funk more than the go-go — to the point were the term is conspicuously absent from his report.

The T.T.E.D and Island Pictures alliance lasted several years. They released some very strong product during the period, especially in 1985 and 1986, when the buzz about the film was the hottest. Some of Trouble Funk's best work came out during this period and the alliance meant it was available to a worldwide audience. But some of Trouble Funk's worst recordings — for example, "Trouble Over Here, Trouble Over There" from 1987 — also came out under the Island agreement. Blackwell's clout disseminated go-go far beyond what Kidd could have accomplished without Island's assistance. The agreement also paved the way to a deal between E.U. and Virgin Records that resulted in *Livin' Large* (Virgin 91021-2) in 1989 and *Cold Kickin' It* (Virgin 91379-2) in 1990. Chuck Brown ended up on Mercury in 1987, which released one album, *Any Other Way to Go?* (Mercury 855501). On the whole, though, the potential for tapping the national — not to mention the world—market for go-go never really materialized as a result of the Kidd/Blackwell collaboration.

Most of the go-go record action has happened on small and mostly underfunded labels, and the majority of these recordings are now collector's items. Day in and year out, D.C.- or Maryland-based labels have provided local bands with a chance to record. Aside from P.A. tapes (which are fully discussed in chapter 5), all of the local bands have strived to record their music to be released either as a single or as part of an album, audio cassette, or compact disc. It is an impulse driven by the desire to not only document the band's music, but also to give the band "product" to sell and something for their fans to remember until the next show at the Black Hole or the Icebox.

Since most go-go product is locally produced and consumed, how well do commercially issued compact discs and tapes sell? According to Tom Goldfogle of Liaison Records, go-go sales represent a solid niche market in the mid-Atlantic states. A self-produced CD by a new local group might sell several thousand copies, while an established act like Trouble Funk or Rare Essence might sell in the 30,000 to 40,000 range. Compact disc sales are also greatly affected by a number of other factors, most notably airplay and in-store placement and promotion. The formula is simple: an increase in airplay on WPGC-FM means that sales of the disc will also increase.

Outside of the United States, England and Japan are go-go's strongest supporters. Outside of the mid-Atlantic, Los Angeles and New York City represent the major markets for go-go. Chuck Brown and the Soul Searchers and Trouble Funk are the best sellers outside of D.C.; Brown because of his reputation and Trouble Funk because of their extensive tours outside of the region. Rare Essence is probably the third-biggest record-seller, due once again to their touring. DJ Kool represents the best example of a man successfully melding the go-go and hip-hop worlds together. His success is both artistic and commercial, and he has helped to extend interest in go-go outside of D.C. Within the District, DJ Celo has a great following, largely because of his skills at the live mixing of go-go and hip-hop, as displayed on WPGC-FM.

Although radio airplay can greatly affect go-go sales, the importance of record stores should not be quickly dismissed. When Liaison formed in the late 1980s, building strong alliances with record stores emerged as one of their first tasks. Tom Goldfogle explains some of the details behind this process, especially as it concerns education:

We needed to ... convince the chain buyers that this was a legitimate form of music and demand real estate in the stores. Real estate in the stores is very tight and they need to turn it over a certain amount of times. ... What we basically do is then [take a new release] and talk to the buyers at the stores who are very removed from this market ... and direct them to the type of quantities that should go in a particular store and to micromarket the product.[21]

All of the go-go bands wanted to be signed by a major label and some of them succeeded. Mass Extension, one of the hottest go-go bands of the early 1980s, first recorded locally but in the mid-1980s signed with media giant MCA. Gary West (aka Go Go Black), a founding member of the band (started by his brother, Sheldon, in 1979 when they were Mackin High School students), recalled, "We were signed to MCA. ... I think that RE was signed with them ... at the same time. MCA promised that we could do our own music but make a long story short, they bojangled around and we sued to get out of our contract and got blackballed!"[22] Go Go Black's brief account is the quintessential story of every go-go band's encounter with a major record label. The basic line goes like this: the record company discovers the potentially hot sounds of go-go, they sign you to a contract, the A&R guy either tries to remold your sound or doesn't do anything for you, the relationship deteriorates, and then the band and the label part ways. This is the leitmotif of go-go and major record companies, and it is a story that is told (with only minor variations) by band after band.

Take the case of Junk Yard Band and Def Jam, which is told in the words of their then-manager Moe Shorter:

We signed with Def Jam in 1985. ... With Def Jam some things started happening and they showed a greater interest in the band than they had initially. By that I mean they wanted to include us in films. We were included in the movie *Tougher than Leather*. We had previously done a small part in a movie, *D.C. Cabs*, which featured Mr. T. ... We had a lot of conversations about what they wanted to do with us, where they wanted to take us.

Most of those conversations were with Rick Rubin, who was Russell Simmons's partner. And actually, from what I saw and was told by different people at the company, Rick was the backbone of Def Jam at that time. He was the producer and it was all about music then.... Rick had to touch every project personally that went through Def Jam Records.

It was a good and a bad thing because he had that ear for what was happening at that time. However if he didn't take to you, then you had a shortcoming and that's what happened with Junk Yard Band. Rick was busy with L.L. Cool J. He was busy with Slayer. He was busy with Slick Rick, the rapper....And it was even worse for us who were down in D.C. and all the other acts were in New York. So, it became a little harder for us to get some attention.

So we rode the wave for a while and they put out the recording, "The Word" which is the A side and "Sardines" as the B side....They just threw it out there, didn't say nothing about it and didn't promote it in anything behind it. However, I guess it was two years after it was out there, the DJs said, "Hold on, this record is good, this is a hit!" DJs picked up on it ["Sardines"], demand started growing.

Well, by this time it was 1988 and nothing has happened for us. We're thinking that it's time for us to get out of this contract 'cause we can do nothing by ourselves. So we started proceedings to get out of this contract. We were in our option year, which made it easy to get out of....We only recorded—outside of that single...maybe three other songs.[23]

Much the same thing happened with other go-go bands, including Trouble Funk, Rare Essence, and Experience Unlimited. All of the major go-go bands have endured major record company deals—none of them very financially satisfying nor artistically or commercially successful. The major labels have never really felt comfortable with go-go; they didn't really understand it and therefore held it hostage rather than letting the music stand on its own merits.

The local record labels have been the victims of bands that thrive on live performances at the expense of studio releases. Go-go is largely consumed at local and regional clubs. The groups are not oriented towards crafting short songs designed to engender radio airplay, which is part of the reason that go-go has suffered at the hands of AM and FM radio.

It's not that local record companies have not recorded and tried to promote go-go; the problem is that most of the labels are underfunded, causing major problems with distribution and promotion. Reo Edwards at Future Records has been working as a producer and small-label owner since the late 1980s. Future Records has put out plenty of product over the years and today Edwards's fortunes are most closely tied to Backyard Band. But Future Records is just one of many companies to work this territory. In the '80s, more than a score of small local labels moved into the go-go field. Most of them, such as Capitol Beat Records, Gotta Go Go, I Hear Ya!, Rhythm Attack, Sounds of the Capitol, and TWF Productions, barely caused a blip on go-go's radar screen. For the most part, these companies released only a few records which were mainly sold through D.C. mom and pop stores, at the local flea market, or by street vendors.

Since the late 1980s nearly all of the serious go-go labels have been distributed by Liaison Records. According to co-owner Tom Goldfogle: "We started off as a label in the early '80s and we started getting involved with go-go in the late '80s. [I and] my partner [Becky Marcus] were managing record stores, and go-go was just humongous and people were coming into the stores...buying a bunch of 12-inchers, and go-go was outselling anything remotely close to it."[24]

Within a year the Liaison crew had met with the corporate buyers in New York City about stocking more go-go in their stores—chains like Record World and Sam Goody. Up to this time, the go-go record business was done via COD (collect on delivery)—a cumbersome and awkward device that discouraged local chains to carry go-go. Quite simply it was so painstaking and difficult that no one wanted to do business that way. As Goldfogle observed, "A corporation that owns a thousand stores is not going to have their manager of a store pay out of the drawer for product...let alone go through anything other than the normal channels of selling music."[25]

In about 1988, Liaison found itself not only operating a small record company but also distributing local go-go product. Goldfogle recalls:

> I think it was Reo Edwards first. Not having known him
> before, [we set up] a meeting with him suggesting that we
> would like to distribute his product and try to get you

more money for your product and get you in more places. One of the problems was that [non-pop] music was being purchased at a real low price and being sold for a high price. He came on board and we took his products and [nearly] everybody else's since that day.[26]

With more than a decade of experience, Liaison remains the primary go-go distributor. A few companies try to do it alone, but almost everyone goes through Liaison because of their history and their proven ability to read and react to the marketplace.

Liaison also releases go-go compact discs; compilations that rely on licensing deals with Charlie Fenwick, Reo Edwards, Max Kidd, and other important go-go producers. The company has largely succeeded in reaching a niche audience outside of the District. Experience has shown that the core go-go audience will always look for that new Rare Essence or Northeast Groovers disc, but as Tom Goldfogle notes, "We market the compilations to people that are interested in go-go and who live outside of this market that may not buy a Backyard CD but they will buy a CD with Chuck Brown and Rare Essence and a bunch of other bands to try and expose the genre to more people."[27] Not wanting to limit themselves to the neophyte audience, Liaison has another strategy to get hardcore fans to buy the compilations: "Sometimes there'll be pieces on the compilations that are out-of-print and that can only be purchased on the compilations, or even pieces that are not available on compact disc."[28]

In 2001, go-go music—and the culture surrounding it—remains the "bastard child" that Cathy Hughes railed against so strongly a decade ago. Go-go continues to be ignored by Washington, D.C.'s media. Even the homegrown media (including the radio stations owned by Hughes's own Radio One), pays little attention to go-go—it's simply not on their radar-screen because it lacks the visibility and commercial clout of hip-hop culture based in New York or L.A. Without the consistent and diligent work of Kato, Tom Goldfogle, Bruce Brown, and a handful of other true believers, go-go's visibility would be even more limited than it is today.

7 ⟍ Go-Go on Film

You've got to remember that when *Good to Go* came out there was no *Boyz N the Hood*, there was no Spike Lee. So we *were* going to support it, you know! When Chris [Blackwell, Island Pictures mogul] came to Washington we were excited, then it was like...huh!?!?! We didn't know nothing about Hollywood politics, where somebody gotta die, we gotta have some action because we don't want to sell just the D.C. market. Nobody knows about this music but we're goin' to mix it in with this story and this action....We were...offended![1]

Bruce Brown, D.C. filmmaker

Of all of the musical genres heard in the District of Columbia—including jazz and funk—go-go is the most widely documented. There have been three important documentary films, and go-go has endured several brushes with Hollywood. The first of these resulted in *Good to Go* (1986), which was shot on location in D.C. in the summer of 1985. Both *24/7* (1998) and *D.C.—Divided City* (2001), Bruce Brown's latest feature film, are also liberally sprinkled with go-go. *Good to Go* was initially looked upon as a venture that encouraged the local go-go community into thinking that the music was finally going to gain national recognition. But the potential displayed going into the project ended up faded and somewhat tattered. The film, which came at a time when go-go was wildly popular in D.C., ended up causing one of the greatest controversies in the music's history.

STRAIGHT-UP DOCUMENTARIES

Ironically, the longest, most comprehensive, and most polished documentary film about go-go has never been shown in the District of

Columbia. Produced by Great Britain's Channel Four for a series called *Arena, Welcome to the Go-Go: Washington D.C.* has never been broadcast anywhere in the United States, nor is it available on videotape.

Shot in 1988, this 45-minute film is the usual mixture of interviews and performance footage. It features local favorites including C.J.'s Uptown Crew, Experience Unlimited, Max Kidd, and Chuck Brown. Its first-rate production values, length, and incisive commentary set it apart from other go-go documentaries. The film is also helped by some fine footage of street poet Iceberg Slim and several of his friends shot on D.C.'s downtown streets, as well as by performances by three local rappers who clearly verbalize the difference between D.C. and Washington with stark and chilling clarity (and with the Capitol smartly placed behind them!). Chuck Brown and E.U. appear in live performance scenes filmed in local clubs. The British team also filmed Experience Unlimited in the studio in a scene that emphasized Ju Ju's energetic drumming and the vibrant horn section. The footage reinforces what a strong funk-influenced band E.U. was in the late 1980s.

As the cab-driving narrator—wearing one of the brightest and most outrageous red caps on the planet—C.J. provides the glue that holds the film together. Along with WOL-AM go-go jock "Moonman," he dispenses salient and insightful commentary about go-go and Washington D.C., as well as performing in several scenes. Promoters David Rubin and Max Kidd get ample airtime to discuss their take on clubs, recording, and the importance of live performances. *Welcome to the Go-Go: Washington D.C.*'s final strength is its contextualization of go-go within the music's natural social, economic, and musical framework. With all of these positive attributes, it's a shame that virtually no one in Washington, D.C., has ever seen this film.

Another go-go documentary, *Straight-Up Go-Go*, first aired on Wednesday, March 25, 1992, on WHUR-TV, Howard University's public television station. You would think that the fact that the film was locally conceived and produced would place it at an advantage; however, this is not entirely true. The one-hour film includes interesting interview material with Ignatius Mason, Cathy Hughes, and Max Kidd, among others. It also makes some strong, appropriate connections between James Brown, funk, and go-go, addresses the influence of African music, and pays proper respect to the place and importance of the drum in go-go.

If *Straight-Up Go-Go* suffers it is because the filmmakers obviously cut corners in order to complete the film. First of all, the concert footage is taken entirely from a large outdoor event, leaving the unsuspecting viewer with the impression that go-go usually happens outdoors and in warm weather. Though this is not entirely false, it is misleading—most people experience live go-go at one of the small to medium-sized clubs found in D.C. and Prince George's County. The filmmakers could have included more footage from a more typical live show, which would have given viewers a realistic sense of what go-go is all about. A second problem is that the documentary highlights a live performance by a female go-go band, Pleasure. Since gender is always an issue in postmodern America, the fact that the film does nothing to indicate how rare all-female go-go bands have been on the go-go scene since the genre developed is also misleading.

Overall, *Straight-Up Go-Go* is very good, a remarkable effort by a group of youthful African American filmmakers. It was produced by Progressive Production. The executive producers were Shuaib M. Kedar (who also directed), Sowande Tichawonna, and Fred Brown, Jr. It is also important to note that the film represents the first effort by *local* filmmakers to tell the story of go-go. Although the producers were limited by a lack of both funding and cooperation from the go-go bands, they did make a documentary that received the attention of the city. Despite the film's problems, if WHUR-TV ever rebroadcasts *Straight-Up Go-Go,* it is well worth watching.

The shortest of the documentaries that highlight go-go, *District Music* (1993) is not just about this genre. This hour-long film is divided into four sections of roughly equal length, and go-go is just one of them. The rest of the film focuses on three other genres of black vernacular music: the Orioles represent R&B vocal groups; the Four Echoes represent gospel quartets; and the United House of Prayer Pentecostal "shout" bands close the film. The 14-minute go-go section provides viewers with a very concise and accurate introduction to the genre.

Director Susan Levitas looks at the go-go community from several perspectives, using the members of the Junk Yard Band, promoter Ken Moore, and the patrons of several clubs as representatives of the genre. She takes you inside a small club for both a Junk Yard performance and to see an informal "display" dancing contest. She also shows Moore at work, illegally tacking up go-go posters in SE—an act that could land him in the Sixth District lock-up. In this compact time period Levitas gives the viewer a clear and cogent sense of what go-go was like in D.C. in the mid-1990s. The film is accessible in another—tangible—way; *District Music* remains the only go-go documentary available for rent or purchase.

GOOD TO GO

"I can honestly say I'm proud of it. If it had come out totally negative I would've been the first to protest from the top of the Washington Monument to the top of the Empire State Building."[2] Max Kidd uttered this colorful statement about Good to Go. Some of the earliest go-go recordings were undertaken by Kidd, an important figure on the go-go scene. His T.T.E.D. Records and Films was the most active go-go company throughout the 1980s, and the height of Kidd's influence and his most public moments came about because of his participation in Good to Go and the subsequent controversies surrounding the film. The firestorm didn't really hit until the film was released and (right or wrong) Max Kidd took most of the heat because he was in town.

Like a bright, sunny April morning, the project displayed immense promise. Island Pictures, a mid-sized corporation based in England, had employed such distinguished directors as Nicholas Roeg, Peter Bogdanovich, and Bernardo Bertolucci. In 1985, just prior to *Good to Go,* Island had released two widely acclaimed films, *Choose Me,* directed by Alan Rudolph, and *A Private Function,* starring Maggie Smith and Michael Palin. Moreover, Island had just released the exhilarating music movie, *Stop Making Sense,* featuring live performances by the Talking Heads.

The initial buzz around D.C. could not have been more positive. The *Washington Post* in particular (mostly through the writings of Richard Harrington in the Style section) covered the making of *Good to Go* with great verve and enthusiasm. Harrington, an avid and well-versed observer of the go-go scene, noted that the film could lead to go-go's big leap—the breakthrough that the music needed to transcend its D.C. roots. He wrote: "When it was announced that Island Films was going to make 'Good to Go' in Washington, some people were expecting 'The Birth of the Beatles' with '80s Washington as '60s Liverpool. Others were expecting a black 'American Hot Wax' with T.T.E.D. Records' Max Kidd coming on like early rock 'n' roll DJ Alan Freed in the story of a music's struggle for respect."[3] The *Washington Afro-American* enthused in a very similar fashion, "Last year the hot sounds were rap and hip-hop. This year, it's go-go music. The new scene, out of Washington, D.C., is being discovered by the British, who are calling it 'a movement just waiting to be discovered.'"[4] As mentioned, in England, the hype was just as strong: "If the film is any good at all (and advance reports say it is very good), go-go music, after bubbling under for seven years in D.C. could finally win a national

following. There is a lot of power simmering and smoldering in this mus-
cular, extremely physical sound."[5]

In those heady days of the early summer of 1985, not only was the
film everywhere in D.C., but so was Max Kidd. He was interviewed on
television and radio as well as for the print media. The subject in the middle of 1985 was always go-go and *Good to Go*. And Max was always willing to talk...not only about the film but about go-go and the current
business of the music, but about the possibilities for the future. Some
viewed Kidd as the successor to Berry Gordy, who helped to move black
popular music in Detroit from the Motor City to an adoring audience
around the world. The buzz was that strong: Go-go was clearly destined
to be the next Motown or at least the successor to the "Sound of
Philadelphia."

Kidd and all of the other denizens of D.C.'s go-go community initially believed that the Blackwell record and film deal would help go-go to
bust out of D.C. like a five-on-zero fast break lead by Michael Jordan. It
just couldn't miss. They all knew what had happened a few years earlier,
when Chris Blackwell returned to Jamaica and became immersed in the
local music scene. *The Harder They Come* (1973) made the international
career of Jimmy Cliff, solidified the status of Bob Marley, and assisted in
heightening Grace Jones's attempts to achieve greater recognition. In
short, all of D.C. fervently believed (or at least strongly hoped) that *Good
to Go* would parallel the success of *The Harder They Come*.

Blackwell, like many others who grew up in Jamaica during the immediate post–World War II years, had his ears opened to a new world of
popular (and increasingly black) music during the late 1950s and early
1960s. Like so many others who live outside of the District of Columbia,
Blackwell first encountered go-go via a recording:

> I heard Chuck Brown's song "I Need Some Money" on the
> radio in NYC and tracked down Max Kidd and then went
> to a concert. What I saw amazed me, there were about
> seven thousand kids dancing in this auditorium, really
> going wild; in fact it was quite combustible. I had never
> heard of any of the bands playing who had drawn this huge
> crowd. I later found out the bands were Rare Essence,
> E.U., Redds and the Boys, and Trouble Funk. It reminded
> me of Lagos [Nigeria] where groove rules, but there were
> no songs really and therefore no radio potential. I thought

the best way to break this music would be to make a movie recreating my experience. This had worked for me with the Perry Henzell film "The Harder They Come" and Jamaican music.[6]

Blackwell first came to D.C. with go-go in mind in 1984 and quickly grew to appreciate the music and better understand the scene. After a bit of investigating, he also realized that Max Kidd could be his man in Washington—the insider who might be able to pull it all together. Kidd, who was 43 when all of this went down in 1985, was indeed well situated. He'd been involved with go-go since its inception and had been interested in black popular music his entire adult life. He was a record producer, a promoter, and a believer in go-go. In 1985 he had most of the important go-go bands in D.C.—most notably Chuck Brown and the Soul Searchers, Experience Unlimited, Redds and the Boys, and Sluggo—in his T.T.E.D. stable of artists. Max Kidd provided Chris Blackwell and his well-meaning crew the entrée they needed to pull off the combination film and record project.

Although most of D.C. envisioned the film as a quasi-documentary about go-go with plenty of scenes from live go-go venues included along with genuine elements of ghetto life, the crew from Island soon proved to have other ideas. Max Kidd, Chuck Brown, Big Tony Fisher (of Trouble Funk), and the other members of the community wanted the music to come first and foremost—they wanted to be true to the music and to D.C. Chris Blackwell, co-producer Doug Dilge, and their colleagues wanted more tension—a tragedy laced with violence and drugs, with go-go serving as the backdrop.

Ultimately *Good to Go* morphed into a full-blown Hollywood urban drama with a first-class soundtrack thrown in for good measure. The record deal apparently came first, closely followed by the film deal. According to a piece in the *Washington Afro-American,* "the idea for the film was conceived by Kidd as a creative venture...which could possibly take go-go from the halls of such local clubs as the Black Hole, the Panorama Room, and the Masonic Temple out to a national and international audience."[7] Kidd himself stated that "the guy that I made the record deal with at Island Records, Chris Blackwell, after we'd agreed that we could work with each other on the record end...number one was to do a movie on my business wrapped around the go-go, and also a book."[8] Things came together very quickly; in the fall of 1984—just a couple of months after they met—the deal between Kidd and Blackwell was signed and the allied projects progressed.

Go-go seemed to finally be moving forward, but it was actually simultaneously taking a few steps backwards. The undercurrents of trouble were twofold. First, the burgeoning and multi-faceted drug scene began to infiltrate the go-go scene. PCP (also called "angel dust," "love boat," and "lovely") had made devastating inroads across the country and in D.C.'s black community in particular. The bands sometimes featured drug-derived (largely anti-drug) song lyrics. The lure of dust was strong, and the bands could only deliver the message; its enforcement was out of their control.

At the same time the violence bugaboo (the perception that go-go causes violence) was only heightened by the drug scourge. The murder rate was slowly rising, and the number of gun seizures increased monthly. The streets in some sections of D.C. were becoming downright dangerous, and these trends intruded upon go-go. As Richard Harrington succinctly reported in May 1985: "The most recent show at the Washington Coliseum was canceled. The Starplex Armory won't book go-go shows. Neither will Howard University, although they did allow *Good to Go* to hold auditions there."[9]

The trouble was not limited to action on the streets. By April 8, 1985, when the filming of *Good to Go* began on the streets of Washington, D.C., the buzz was not good. The word on the street was that the music was downplayed; D.C. was being portrayed in a negative light; the script featured a rape, a corrupt cop, some gratuitous violence (especially the car chase and gun battle); and blacks were stereotyped as drugmongers. The film was not the tune-filled, fact-based film that the go-go community had hoped for, and it was beginning to look like the '70s, when blaxploitation films like *Shaft* and *Cotton Comes to Harlem* were commonplace. If only Island had aimed so high!

Doug Dilge, one of the film's two co-producers, publicly batted aside such criticisms: "We came to create a narrative that could stand on its own, not to create a docudrama about the history of go-go. We're doing a movie about a cynical and sour reporter [played by Art Garfunkel] who writes a story tying in a violent street incident with go-go."[10] In other words, we don't think that we can sell enough seats to a film featuring go-go. If we want to entice folks in Boise, Idaho, to see *Good to Go*, it has just got to be a "sexier" movie.

Blackwell made some apt comparisons between *The Harder They*

Come and *Good to Go*. Of the 1973 film, he observed that at the time, reggae was known only to a handful of aficionados (as well as the entire island of Jamaica), but *The Harder They Come* changed all of that. Blackwell felt that go-go held much the same position a decade later and that the exposure to the music could have a profound influence on go-go's ability to reach a broader audience: "The idea is that people will go to the film first and will come out having discovered the music."[11] Unfortunately, according to Blackwell, it was not a matter of the quality of the music but of the movie itself: "Perry Henzell's film is a great film and *Good to Go* is not."[12] This is true. *Good to Go* is not a disaster like *Ishtar* (it's not even close), but the film comes across as just another mundane urban drama.

Despite Blackwell's stated desire to promote the musical culture of go-go, which seemed genuine enough, it didn't work out that way. He and the creative team—most notably writer/director Blaine Novak—ended up downplaying the music in favor of action: cars flew, drug deals went down, police corruption abounded, jaded reporters saw the light, and guns were fired. Go-go's musical culture, however, became a leitmotif instead of the movie's focus. Blackwell explained it this way: "There's simply not enough strong material to break the music ahead of the film. When they made *Saturday Night Fever*, disco was enormous. You can do a film about music when the music has already happened. In this case, the music has not happened, so we need to bring people in."[13]

The music was happening in D.C., of course, but it had not really broken nationally and its reputation for being dangerous was widespread. Richard Harrington reported that Dilge arrived in Washington just after Christmas of 1984 with bodyguards at his side and apprehensions about urban ghetto life to the fore: "We'd heard it's [go-go] a bunch of kids stoned on PCP dancing around. When the music stops, fights break out. If you're white you don't go into these scenes because you're in an incredibly dangerous situation."[14] There might be some minor elements of truth to these fears, but this sounds (except for the comments with racial overtones) more like a Hells Angels convocation—"Born To Be Wild"—than the mean streets of D.C.

Protestations and explanations aside, it sounds as though Blackwell, Dilge, et al. were in search of *Fort Apache, The Bronx* meets Bob Marley in order to concoct a highly volatile mixture of street violence and niggers crazy on drugs, all highlighted by the blackest music outside of Lagos, Nigeria. They wanted something sensational and located only part of what they thought would sell to the population at large, so the drugs and violence were played up at the expense of go-go. *Good to Go* quickly became just another Hollywood vehicle and, except for the musical scenes (especially the strong Trouble Funk numbers), the locale could have been any large urban center with an extensive rundown ghetto. In other words, the film lost its D.C. specificity and therefore its essence.

Blackwell offered another explanation regarding the making of *Good to Go;* information that helps to contextualize what was going on behind the scenes:

> This project started as a "joint venture" with Jeremy Thomas, a producer I have the highest regard for. Early on during the production he managed to get the Bertolucci film *The Last Emperor* off the ground after many years. He was unable to offer [*Good to Go*] the attention that we all envisaged. *The Last Emperor* went on to win nine Oscars, including best picture.[15]

The folks behind *Good to Go* might have been busy but they were not evil-doers out to undermine go-go and Washington, D.C.—they were simply wrong-minded in their decision to turn what could have been an interesting film into a rather generic, formulaic movie. Whether it was liberal guilt or a perceived necessity, Dilge tried to make certain that the film crew was nearly two-thirds black and that the cast was approximately 90 percent African American; furthermore, most of the secondary roles went to locals. But they were hampered by a budget of one million dollars, which even by 1985 standards was low, and their vision of an "action" film didn't really get to the roots of go-go as a musical culture. Nor does it address the unique nature of the District as the "51st Colony," peopled by the disenfranchised masses. Drugs and corruption are integral to the film; Blackwell and the Island film crew were simply following that axiom of popular culture—sex and action sells.

Besides go-go itself, Max Kidd remains the only D.C.-specific thing in the film. Kidd forms the very core of the film: he works with the bands, helps to set up the gigs, and angrily confronts the Art Garfunkel (who is employed by a *Washington Post*-esque newspaper) character when he uses the "go-go equals violence" trope in a newspaper article. Blackwell realized that a Kidd-type character (an entrepreneur with his hands in every aspect of the business) was important to retain at the core of the film—"A scene like go-go couldn't exist without a character like Max to give it some focus and energy."[16] Max Kidd's fingerprints are everywhere in the film; he's not only one of its principal characters but is also credited as its "associate producer." In retrospect, Blackwell commented that "the movie might have worked if we had cast [Kidd] as himself!"[17]

What did people in and around the District have to say about *Good to Go*? The grumblings began even before the film's public release. As early as May 1985, Richard Harrington wrote: "What Washington will be getting when the film opens at the Embassy Theatre this August is a low-budget action film that takes place in and around the thriving go-go scene but makes no great effort at socio-musical accuracy."[18] Musicians and other members of the go-go community were muttering about the problems they observed as the filmmaking progressed. The basic complaints were predictable and can be summarized like this: the filmmakers and script writers don't understand go-go, the violence and drugs are aggrandized, and it's looking like another exploitation film.

One other problem emerged during the filming of *Good to Go*. Race formed the core of the controversy creating an undercurrent of uncertainty and ultimately resentment. The film's director, Blaine Novak (who is white) took over the reins in mid-stream from his then co-director, Don Letts—a black Jamaican musician and director of videos. Until June 1985, the deal was co-directorship. Suddenly Letts was out as director, which irked many of the crew members and observers. Novak, of course denied any problems: "He [Letts] never really intended to direct the film. I cast the film, I hired the crew, it was a fait accompli going in. Don Letts is a video director, used to working a day and a half at a clip...it was a very amicable separation."[19] According to Chris Blackwell, Letts was "eased out of directing the film because the writer really wanted to direct it."[20]

Others (the black participants, in particular) viewed it through a different lens—as an act of racism, just another way to keep a brother down. Vern Goff (an associate of Max Kidd who was involved with the film's production) said: "There was a blatant undercutting of Don Letts. Blaine Novak humiliated him and fashioned that film after his own distorted understanding of the go-go scene.... [He] took it and made it into something else. It's not even about go-go."[21]

Bruce Brown, filmmaker and D.C. native, talks about his own involvement with the music growing up in Anacostia, and explains how he felt about the film:

Growing up with all the guys from Ballou [High School], you know, Little Benny and everybody... we'd check out the back of the books and it never said "Douglas Junior High School," it just said "Central." We got our books second hand. We were pretty lost, and the music lent us economic freedom... pack the gym at eight dollars a head and we started becoming conscious of our economic power... with role models like Trouble Funk, Little Benny, Chuck Brown.

After seeing *Good to Go,* which Island Pictures produced... when they initially got their hands on go-go it was like, wow, this guy Chris Blackwell, he was just fascinating, talking about "We gotta do a movie, we gotta take this sound to the next level," and with Max Kidd as the associate producer... this [helped] to turn us into entrepreneurs.[22]

In light of all of these controversies, it's not surprising that Blackwell and Novak defended their final product. Blackwell reminded folks that *Good to Go* was a "music-driven film... [that] gives you a real good sense of the kind of environment in which this music was born."[23] Novak commented, "I'm a writer and a director, and this is a fictionalized version of events which I saw in Washington, D.C....What I wanted to do all along is the story of a white reporter [Art Garfunkel] who has to go down to the ghetto to find a story and who is changed by that community. The music was a vehicle to get the film made."[24]

The bottom line is that *Good to Go* was not what it could have been and what D.C. hoped it would be. Instead of being a film about the unique nature of Washington, D.C., and its important contribution to American music, it emerged as a rather faceless, generic film about street violence and drugs in urban America. The music and its true culture was submerged by the gratuitous violence, most notably the shoot-'em-up scene in an abandoned building that resulted in the destruction of several police cars and the bloody deaths of several drugdealers.

Despite the fact that the film finished shooting in June and most of the post-production was completed by the fall, *Good to Go* remained in the can for a year. The issue was Chris Blackwell's perception of timing. In the summer of 1985, he observed: "It wasn't time yet for the music to happen. I think the time, really, is *next* summer. I think we're still early for go-go to get its foot in the door. It's a street music and the street music right now is still, and has been since 1984, rap, which is stronger than ever...I wanted to wait to build what I feel is the next state of street music, which has got more melody to it. Next year is when you'll see it explode."[25] *Good to Go* detonated all right, but not in the way that Blackwell predicted.

Good to Go finally saw the light of day at the end of July 1986, and the initial reviews were mixed at best. Most critics suggested that the film missed its mark and an opportunity to present D.C.'s musical street culture in a different and more realistic light. None of the local reviewers found much to praise about the film, which enjoyed its world premiere at the Warner Theater on July 31. The *Washington Post*'s review was typical, though certainly longer and more detailed than most. Richard Harrington pointed out the problems with the plot and the music's place in the film, but he also wrote that [Novak] is "not all that competent at telling the story he's chosen, either....The photography is greenish and the sound mix makes much of the dialogue unintelligible, so that the movie's hard to follow."[26] Harrington saved his best line for last: "Garfunkel is a tad on the prissy side for a Man of Journalism—he's more like a lingerie salesman."[27]

David Brooks of the *Washington Times* reviewed the film on the day of its release and minced few words:

> The musical scenes in "Good to Go" make you want to go, go, go. But the rest of the movie says no, no, no...he has buried that fantastic music in a story that is stupid, pretentious, ponderous and more than a little racist. This movie is patronizing toward blacks. They make good music, but none are particularly admirable role models, and when a white guy enters the scene, well, they just better step aside so something can get done....They also don't seem to realize that a movie about something as black as go-go music should haveat least one black protagonist. But the musicians themselves will not be deterred. They shine even in this overcast vehicle.[28]

Other reviews of *Good to Go* were in a similar vein and the film did not do well at the box office. It was originally slated to open at 800 theaters nationwide, but ultimately opened on far fewer screens and did not last for more than a month as a first-run feature film. In the District, *Good to Go* initially enjoyed success, averaging nearly 9,000 dollars on the 11 screens showing it on opening weekend. But as the word on the streets spread, fewer patrons attended the film, and by the beginning of September 1986, *Good to Go* was history. Few in D.C.'s go-go community shed tears for its passage into video oblivion.

It is certain that the film more than recouped its one-million-plus investment, but it quickly displayed a lack of the "legs" needed for long-term financial success. Three years later it emerged on video as *Short Fuse*, starring Art Garfunkel. The video appeared as a joint Vidmark/Island Pictures release, and the description on the box describes the film as "a suspense charged, action packed, shocking look at today's urban nightmare." Zounds—doesn't that make you want to run right out to Blockbuster to rent it? This 91-minute feature film seems to still be in print, though it is not easy to find... perhaps with good reason. It also crops up a couple of times a year on late-night cable television—mostly on Showtime—under its alternate title (*Short Fuse*).

Even more than 15 years after the film's release, the mention of Island's ill-fated venture into D.C. music evokes a strong response among the community's members. The film was the subject of a discussion on TMOTTGoGo's bulletin board in early 2000, and this observation typifies the response: "'Good to Go/Short Fuse' was a terrible representation of what Go-Go was all about during that time... it could have been a hell of a lot better."[29]

"DA' BUTT"

School Daze has no direct connection with D.C. and little to do with go-go. It's Spike Lee's second feature film, and the 1988 release had a greater commercial and social impact in the marketplace—especially among blacks, than 1986's *She's Gotta Have It*. While the film did a bigger box office then Lee's first film, it was also far more controversial, presaging the issues of race that would permeate *Jungle Fever* and *Do the Right Thing*. Based on Lee's own experiences at Morehouse College in Atlanta, *School Daze* explores the pervasive issues of color and the gradations of blackness that help to shape a fraternity at an all-black college. Lee (who wrote as well as directed the film) plays Half-Pint, who is caught between the desire to find camaraderie and his wariness of the chauvinism and sexism that are also part of fraternity life.

Perhaps more significantly, Lee takes on the all-but-taboo issue of colorism in black life. "If you black, get back" refers not only to black and white relations, but to life within the black community, where light skin and "good" (straighter and less kinky) hair often accord you a higher social status than the brothers and sisters who are jet black and whose hair is nappy. Colorism forms the heart of *School Daze* and is exemplified by the tensions between the Jigaboos and the Wannabees that eventually erupt into a fight. Lee stages it as an interesting internecine battle between dark and darker black Americans seeking social and economic prestige.

Music abounds in the film, with "I Can Only Be Me," "Be Alone Tonight," and "Be One" among the featured songs. "Da' Butt," however, is the one song most closely associated with *School Daze,* and it became a sensation within the African American community, not only in the city that spawned go-go but across the United States. Lee ran into E.U. on a 1986 trip to the District for the opening of *She's Gotta Have It.* He later recalled, "Island gave a big party for the film down there and E.U. played. Them go-go bands, they can play three hours straight, non-stop, serious funk. They're bad."[30] Go-go was particularly hot at the time and E.U. was a very busy band, playing not only in the ghetto but in upscale Georgetown for a more racially mixed crowd at the 9:30 Club. "I said to myself at this party, I gotta use them in a movie. Those guys in E.U. were young and hungry, and I was happy once again to round up some talented people who haven't been given a shot.... In January [1987] four members of the group came up and cut the record with Marcus [Miller]."[31]

Lee relates that he and Miller—a talented bass player who had produced recordings for artists ranging from Luther Vandross to Miles Davis—collaborated on "Da' Butt" for the film. Miller came up with the song, and Lee, the dance: "I've always wanted to make up a dance. It's always fascinating how popular dances get started, where they come from, who makes them up."[32] When he first told Miller about his idea, his response was:

> "What kind of title is that?" I told him it was supposed to be a fun record, and if you heard it on the radio or on your stereo at home, you'd think it was recorded at a party. So the night after Marcus and the four guys from E.U. recorded the tracks, I called my friends and a couple of folks who were going to act in *School Daze.* They came down to the studio to record the party sounds. We

had a good time doing that stuff. All of us got into a debate about how we should handle this call-and-response bit where people from different states yell "We got da' butt."[33]

"Da' Butt" became closely identified with go-go, E.U., and *School Daze,* and it was a lightning rod for publicity for E.U. The song itself appears in the Splash Jam section of the film, where the students turn their gym into a beach party. Without a bathing suit and sneakers, you couldn't get into the faux beach party. Lee remembers that during the setup "before we brought the extras inside the gym, Otis Sallid was outside teaching people how to do Da' Butt." Their efforts resulted in a memorable shot where the camera moves up and over the crowd and "the frame is filled entirely with Black limbs, nothing but a sea of Black people, sweating, gyrating, to the beat y'all."[34]

Another interesting connection between Spike Lee, go-go, and Chris Blackwell needs to see the light of day. *She's Gotta Have It* came out in the fall of 1986, within three months of the release of *Good to Go.* The connection between the two releases is not simply temporal—Chris Blackwell at Island Pictures was involved with the financing of Lee's first two films (*She's Gotta Have It* and *School Daze*). Is it mere coincidence that Blackwell's flirtation with go-go, his financing of Lee's film ventures, and the "discovery" of E.U. all occurred over a period of several months?

Much like its predecessors—the Frug, the Swim, the Bump, and others—Da' Butt raged across the country in the summer of 1988. Clubs featured Da' Butt contests, radio stations played the song, and college students organized Da' Butt parties. E.U.'s bookings outside of D.C. exploded and they toured as far west as California as the song hit number 1 on the black music charts and crept as high as number 35 on the Billboard pop charts. Clearly a fad (although one with the potential to break go-go to a new audience), the Da' Butt craze lasted for a few months and E.U. milked it for all it was worth. While purists viewed it as watered-down go-go and others saw it as vulgar, it was pure gold for the band.

The song descends from a long line of booty-shakin' anthems that have been part of African American expressive culture for decades. During Reconstruction, cake-walking dances became popular, and they were followed in the early 1920s by dances such as the Shim Sham Shimmy. Blues pianists recorded songs with similar themes over the years, ranging from Sylvester Palmer's "Do It Sloppy" (1930) to Champion Jack Dupree's suggestive "Dupree Shake Dance" (1941). In the 1950s Chicago-based blues harpman Little Walter recorded an electric version of "Shake Dancer." The shake-dancing theme crossed over to mainstream American youth culture in the mid-1950s with Bill Haley's cover of "Shake, Rattle, and Roll" as part of the rock 'n' roll revolution. Hip-hop culture continues to embrace this theme in many of its videos (i.e. "Leave It On The Glass"), which have been decried as sexist, but the continuity of this trend suggests how ingrained it is in the black vernacular. In go-go, of course, we are blessed with such local classics as Pure Elegance's "One Leg Out (And Put Your Booty On The Floor)" and numerous versions of "Bounce To This."

Some purists argue that "Da' Butt" is not really go-go at all, but a watered-down version designed to appeal to the masses. Nonetheless, *School Daze* and its hit single by E.U. brought more attention to go-go than Chris Blackwell's 1986 movie flop. It was later covered by AWB (Average White Band). Even today "Da' Butt" appears, along with such other timeless classics as "Brick House" by the Commodores or Freak Nasty's "Da' Dip," on countless DJ lists and turntables as one of the most requested hip-hop or R&B numbers. It remains a staple of E.U.'s current playlist with Sugar Bear holding forth as the band's leader. After *School Daze,* Lee was not quite finished with go-go; he worked on several go-go videos, including ones for E.U., but they did not get much airplay.

BRUCE BROWN

More recently, go-go has been at the core of another movie; a feature film directed by Bruce Brown called *24/7* that was shot in the mid-1990s and released in 1998. Having grown up on the streets of far Southeast D.C. (yes, "across the river" in Anacostia), Brown knows both street life and go-go intimately, and much like real life, his film melds them together. *24/7* follows two brothers in their late twenties—Dante and Eric—over several days as they struggle with a life where they deal with poverty and crime on a daily basis. Meanwhile their mother is fearful of what might happen and works hard to keep their younger brother, Michael, out of a life of dealing crack cocaine. The film's tension is further heightened by the fact that Dante wants Michael to become one of their runners, moving money and drugs along the streets. Eric objects to this, but Dante prevails. Now their mother has three sons to worry about, one of them only 16 years old.

The brothers quickly become mid-level hustlers working the streets selling "rock" and working hard to break into the territory staked out by Raymond, who owns the action in their part of the city. All hell breaks loose when the brothers take on Raymond (inspired in part by Rayful Edmond's notorious crew, which ruled D.C.'s drug trade around the same time). First they try to move into his territory, and then they try to assassinate him as part of their high-stakes, risky move to expand their own business. The film ends on a confrontational and bloody note.

In some ways, *24/7* is what *Good to Go* wanted (and purported) to be: gritty, unrelenting, critical, and realistic. While *Good to Go* strained to bring a dramatic tension to its plot—the corrupt police detective versus the black community and the rather guileless newspaper reporter—*24/7* slides into motion with little effort. The go-go performances in *Good to Go* are pretty strong, but they are largely set pieces. Brown's use of go-go is more organic and less self-conscious. In short, *24/7* bears the mark of someone who understands go-go without having to think too long and hard about it, because the music was part of Brown's upbringing.

Brown's response to the question of why he chose to make a film about D.C., race, drugs, and go-go is not surprising:

> I guess growing up in D.C., it was always a backdrop. It was nothing going on without the sound. Except the sound wasn't the problem. It's the sound and was just situated around the sound....We had, at that time, WOL on all the time, which had Go Go Rudy...and we would always sit back, listen, and the big thing was "When is Trouble Funk goin' to the Capital Centre?" 'Cause that was like—you went to the Cap Centre and it was huge! I grew up with the guys in the bands, you know, me and Big Tony [bassist and vocalist with Trouble Funk]...we all lived in the same neighborhood and it was a sense of pride.[35]

Brown, born in 1963, attended Anacostia High School, followed by a stint at the Lemuel Penn Career Development Center, where he got a bit of training in film. He worked for a while at the Barry Farms housing project, engineered at WPFW-FM, and then washed dishes at the University of Maryland. Eventually he followed his childhood dream of working in film full-time, forming what is today called Bruce Brown Filmworks, which he operates out of an office in Lanham, Maryland. Brown's eclectic resume includes long-term contracts with Fannie Mae, films for religious organizations, and go-go videos.

In between all of his varied projects, Brown doggedly works at his feature projects. *24/7* (which was called *Streetwise* when it was released on video) earned good enough reviews to keep him going. His next full-length film project, *D.C.—Divided City* is another film about the chasm between the Washington, D.C., where people actually live and the city known to tourists worldwide. It, too, features a go-go soundtrack and was completed in the spring of 2001.

Go-go, especially newer bands like Junk Yard, forms the musical core of *24/7*. Forget the "Boris Elkis" credit for music; he may have scored the film, but the real stars are the D.C. go-go bands whose music permeates the film and helps create an ambiance that Blaine Novak strived in vain to attain. As the film's executive producer, writer, and director, Brown exercised complete control over *24/7*. There are no lame Hollywood names—like Art Garfunkel, whose performance in *Good to Go* was limp and unmoving—to help bolster the film's image. *24/7* is a D.C. product, from the scenes shot on the streets of Anacostia to the go-go soundtrack to Brown's own vision of black life in the District of Columbia.

Making *24/7* proved to be a major challenge for Brown. Money was an obvious issue; films are not inexpensive to make. Brown had to carefully watch the cash—250,000 dollars only goes so far. The film is shot in D.C., not in some Hollywood back lot built to look like Southeast. The actors are from the D.C. metro area and many go-go players—such as Big Tony Fisher and James Funk—play small roles. DJ Kool also appears as himself, while D.C. Scorpio plays the role of "Loco" in the film. *24/7* is a "small" film that eschews grand sets, computer-generated special effects, and huge crowd scenes in favor of drama and realism. All of these factors mean that the film has the quality of a documentary about it.

But Brown was also concerned about how to position his film within the pantheon of the commercial film industry. This is a major concern because any director wants people to see his or her films. Here is where Brown ran into the politics of film distribution:

> The film business is a very political thing....When I initially released this film...I had to go back to the old-boy system, which was a brick wall. It was like, "Well, who's your pimp?"...If it's not coming through Tri-Star or

New Line, then you get no screens. Not even in your own city! I still have not played this movie in D.C. yet . . . other than the Lincoln Theater, you know, one time. Then I went out to the suburbs where they gave me Rivertown and theaters out there where nobody could get to. . . . It was just a really hard thing to do and I distributed the film myself. I own the negative; I can display it to the houses; I can bypass the distributors . . . and you can come to my Web site . . . you know, you can go to the video store to pick up a copy of the movie. When I initially released the film these venues weren't there.[36]

Film distribution is a difficult game, but when Brown got his film out in D.C. it did very well. Up against such standard Hollywood fare as *McHale's Navy, Murder at 1600,* and *Anaconda* when it came out in the early spring of 1997, *24/7* held its own locally. According to Brown, it was the third-highest-grossing film out of 15 offerings at the AMC Rivertown complex (located in Prince George's County) on April 22, 1997. The problem was that Brown was hampered by a lack of money to promote the film. Without the backing of corporate America to distribute it, *24/7* (like go-go) has never gotten the attention that it deserves.

Brown's newest film, *D.C.—Divided City,* is due out just before this book goes to press, making it difficult to write much about it. A preliminary screening of the film suggests that it will be up to Brown's high standards. He is once again working with a limited budget, once again casting his eye on everyday life in the District, and once again integrating go-go into the movie. Once again the title reflects the content—our nation's capital is divided between the tourist's Washington and the D.C. where real people live, work, eat, worship, party, and die.

PERFORMANCE VIDEOS

Although they do not carry the cachet (or the intent) of a well-crafted documentary, performance videos constitute the final important facet of go-go on film. These videos sell to fans, mostly in the D.C. metropolitan area, at costs ranging from 10 to 20 dollars. For the most part, the videos are as homespun and raw as a live go-go performance by Rare Essence. Their production budgets (one wonders if this term is an oxymoron in this context) run from minuscule to non-existent. They are often shot with a single camera and have sound quality as unpolished as the camerawork. Nonetheless, go-go performance videos stand as important ethnographic work, for they capture go-go in the context in which most people experience it—live in a club or at a block party.

The opportunities to see video performances are primarily limited by your budget, for there are dozens of them available for purchase. But you have to know where to look; street vendors around D.C. carry some and a few stores around the city stock them, but the P.A. Palace carries the largest selection. Their December 2000 list breaks them down by band: Rare Essence, Backyard Band, Junk Yard Band, Northeast Groovers (NEG), and Nastygang. Their formats are straightforward; most are edited versions— usually between 90 and 120 minutes—of much longer performances. The cameras focus on both the band's performance and the crowd, so in many respects you get some sense of what it's like to be at a go-go. Watching the video of Junk Yard's performance at the Icebox on March 3, 2000, is probably the next best thing to being there. NEG have issued some of the most popular videotapes, due in large part to the notorious pool party scenes included in several of them. These tapes include scenes that involve nudity and have been described as "lewd." Because of the furor they caused in the print and electronic media in the summer of 1994, these are discussed more fully in chapter 6.

But the business behind the production, reproduction, and distribution of these videos is far less straightforward. The tapes themselves do not contain catalogue numbers, nor is it entirely clear who actually retains the rights to these performances. In these respects they are the visual parallel to P.A. tapes and occupy the murky netherworld of questionable legal ownership, royalty payments, and copyright issues. In short, nearly all go-go videos are unauthorized; they are released through casual deals where cash changes hands. Yet the sale of performance videos has never been seriously challenged though the legal system. A court case involving them would probably create such legal havoc that it would tie up someone's hands (and money) for years!

Instead, the bands have begun working within the community by informally leaning on the vendors and distributors of go-go videos. Because most of the tapes were shot informally and ended up on the streets before they were picked up, copied, and distributed, the bands can only use the force of moral and financial persuasion to help control the situation. Basically, most of the bands think that the go-go video vendors are making lots of money selling the intellectual property of the bands themselves. Some groups are now supplying multiple copies of go-go videos and asking the vendors to market them: "inventory control" would be one way to characterize this move. The bands are trying to enforce this by limiting the access of some of these same vendors to P.A. tapes; fewer audio tapes could really hurt a business built upon selling these "extra-legal" releases.

Although most go-go videos focus on a single band, the marketplace does offer about a dozen anthologies that include footage that goes back as far as 1986. If you never saw the Pumpblenders or Petworth back in the mid- to late 1980s, this is your chance. These compilations were shot at various venues, though many of them document the outdoor venues that held events that included many acts in a single day. *Block Party Summer 98,* for instance, features Maiesha & the Hip Huggers, the Legends, Optimystic Tribe, Nastygang, Inner City Groovers, and RE on a single two-hour tape. On the other hand, *Georgia Avenue Day 1991* contains one hour of Junk Yard Band, Pleasure, and Hot, Cold, Sweat.

These videotapes are invaluable if for no other reason than that they document a type of musical event that you can only attend in our nation's capital. Their very existence (as well as the sheer number of tapes) also underscores the fact that there is a market for these products. But perhaps more importantly, the videos provide another example of the "do it your-self" ethos that pervades go-go from promoting live performances to releasing sound recordings when the national companies overlook the music.

Not all of these performance videos are "down-home" and unsophis-ticated documentaries. In 1987, G Street Enterprises (mostly the brain-child of Darryll Brooks and Carol Kirkendall) released the most polished and professional video of go-go performances. *Go Go Live at the Capitol* [sic] *Centre Featuring Chuck Brown & The Soul Searchers, Rare Essence, Experience Unlimited, Little Benny & the Masters, D.C. Scorpio, Junkyard Band, Hot Cold Sweat, and Go Go Lorenzo* features tightly directed multi-camera work and a clean sound mix. It's a big and professional produc-tion in more ways than the number of acts. The Capital Centre is a huge venue (one-time home to the local professional basketball and hockey teams), but the music and the crowd more than filled it up. For once, the box's hype is not overblown: "*Go Go Live at the Capitol Centre* highlights the sound and the energy of the music that has dominated the streets of Washington D.C. for 15 years. This is go-go the way it should be seen — the rhythms drive you the way they should be heard, the call and response puts you in the front row, and its [*sic*] all done by a line-up of artists that best tells the go go story." Sadly, unlike the other videos that we've just discussed, this one is out of print and very difficult to find.

Afterword: Go-Go 2001

Kip: I see a cloudy and uncertain future for go-go as we enter the twenty-first century. Some of the bands — most notably my current favorite, Rare Essence (I'm listening to *RE 2000* a lot right now) — continue to produce creative and interesting music. Their support in D.C. provides them with steady work, but how long will they want to hang with it?

Charles: That's a good question. Matter of fact, that is the question, because I believe Rare Essence represents the best future for go-go. Unfortunately, I do not see any other band on the circuit that can represent go-go nationally or internationally. Go-go's future in D.C. may be secure, because I believe bands will always get work and be able to perform. However, the larger question is, what band can take the sound national or get a major deal? The answer is Rare Essence!

Kip: The problem with RE is that with the influence of hip-hop and rap over the last 20 years, go-go bands like Junk Yard, NEG, and Jigga are closer to the current black pop mainstream. This sound is *not* the sound of RE (good as they are) and it seems to me that if a go-go band is really going to cross over, then it will be a "younger" group. More to the point — how do you get this distinctive "regional sound" out into a larger world that is ruled by corporate America?

Charles: I see your point, but go-go bands must be able to present themselves in a manner that is consistent with national entertainment's norms. Bands must have an image and a musical direction. In addition, they must be able to record CDs that conform. Their recorded songs must have a theme, a musical hook, and be "radio-friendly." I do not see any of the current bands who fulfill all of these criteria. Another thing . . . I do agree that today's groups should be closer to emerging hip-hop and R&B artists, however, RE does fit that mold.

Kip: On the subject of "radio-friendly," what good does it do if local radio stations all but ignore go-go? Except for Go-Go Rudy on WKYS-FM and his Sunday evening show, go-go receives no regular airplay in D.C. in 2001! You can have the most highly crafted go-go record, complete with melodic and rhythmic hooks and creative lyrics, but if it receives no airplay then the sales of the compact disc featuring that song are limited. What's more, Go Go Rudy's show seems to play more selections from P.A. tapes than from contemporary (or older) commercial releases. What's with that? And don't get me started with Cathy Hughes and her (now national) radio empire. She used to be a homegirl, supporting go-go, but now that she's got a huge corporation to run—D.C.'s homegrown music is suffering because it's not regularly played on the stations that she owns. I know that I'm ranting on, but if go-go is to thrive (not only creatively) in this new millennium, we do have to be concerned with its commodification so that the music can find at least a small niche in the commercial marketplace.

Charles: You raise some very interesting points, however, I maintain that go-go musicians must structure their songs and recordings in a manner that can help as opposed to hurt. We both know how radio works. It is no different in this town than anywhere else across the nation. Radio plays what they perceive to be hits or good songs. If the recording cannot be purchased then it has little chance of being played. Therefore, distribution and marketing are very important when it comes to tunes being played on the radio.

In years gone by, local groups could work the streets. This meant that you could have your tunes played at discos and events. This rage would then translate into a tune being labeled "hot," which would force local radio to air the tune. I am not clear to what extent this is happening today.

Kip: But you know, Charles, the issues related to radio airplay are merely symptomatic of a greater underlying malaise. While the airplay is undeniably lacking, so are the venues available to bands and the commercial record releases by go-go bands. The real issue is that go-go has been reduced to a group (albeit a substantial and almost entirely African American one) core of fans that support the music in D.C. and few other places. They are passionate about go-go but most of them are in D.C. and relatively few of them are affluent. It seems to me that race *is* an issue—perhaps the major one—because as long as go-go is considered to be "D.C.'s own ghetto music," then it's never going to transcend the constrictions placed upon it by this label.

Charles: It interesting how you jumped to race as the problem with spreading go-go. I must respectfully disagree one more time. For example, one could say that rap or hip-hop would not make it until it was able to cross over. Well, you and I both know that is a bunch of crap because rap and hip-hop solidified their market, which was the black community. Point being, the go-go still has miles to go, which doesn't, at least now, mean they have to travel through the "white community." What groups must do is to broaden the appeal within their own community. I agree that the music is stuck in D.C., but that has been the problem for many years. Every once in a while a "Da' Butt" "Bustin' Loose," or "Drop The Bomb," kind of makes it out of Washington. So again, the onus is on the bands. I believe so strongly, and Little Benny alludes to this point, that bands must play music and have an image that is marketable.

Kip: Perception is at the heart of this matter. Go-go is viewed as a "black thing" conceived of by black Americans, (almost exclusively) performed by black Americans, and consumed (nearly entirely) by black Americans. A parallel can be made with radio in the metropolitan area. If you look at the demographics (in this case the Arbitron ratings) for FM stations, you will see that they also largely break down along racial lines. WPGC, for example, draws an audience that is nearly 90 percent black. On the flip side, the audience for WETA-FM is less than five percent African American. Nothing is stopping whites from listening to WPGC or blacks from tuning into WETA-FM, but they don't. I think it's largely a matter of perception: WPGC is a "black" station, while WETA-FM is thought to be a "white" station. It's not as simple as that, of course, but I'm talking about what people *think*.

Also, don't forget that it's ultimately white folks who own the major record companies and white folks (with the exception of Robert Johnson, founder of BET, who just sold out to Viacom!) who rule the television airways. And, except for Cathy Hughes—who seems to have forgotten her roots—it's white folks who rule radio's AM and FM bands. And white folks aren't ready for go-go because they don't understand it—it's simply too "black" for them. This white-manipulated power structure had to wait until funk and rap was established (read acceptable) within the black community at large that they were willing to embrace and promote it to Americans at large.

Furthermore, go-go is a "D.C. thing." Go-go is what folk from Chocolate City listen to. But why don't more folk listen to and support go-go? I agree that it might be the bands' lack of "professionalism," but unless the everyday folk of D.C. embrace go-go, it will never solidify its position among local black listeners outside the Beltway. Your final sentence actually amplifies my point—if bands "must play music and have an image that is marketable," will it still be go-go as we have known it? Think of how Island positioned Trouble Funk or what Virgin did to E.U. in the late 1980s—they pushed uninteresting funk records out of two of the best go-go bands in town. Yuck!

Charles: My answer to your final point is yes. I believe that go-go releases can contain the formula for songs without sacrificing the "go-go groove." Some examples are "Bustin' Loose," "Da' Butt," "Body Moves," and "Movin' And Groovin'." Unfortunately, the groups today are either incapable or uninterested in releasing songs like the ones mentioned. This is a huge, huge problem.

I once again would like to respond to your point on race. I agree that go-go is a Washington thing that happens to be played by black groups and to a black market. However, I submit that "white" audiences have been able to relate to go-go when exposed. The problem with markets outside of Washington, I believe, is due more to lack of exposure than race. What I mean is young folks in New York do not have an appreciation for go-go, nor do the crews in Los Angeles or Chicago for that matter. What I am saying is that go-go must be experienced in order to be fully appreciated. Even when groups have been successful and toured nationally, go-go was still misunderstood. A good example is that during the E.U. tours following the "Da' Butt" success, promoters were lost as to how to promote the group. I saw E.U. promoted as a funk group, a rap group, and so on. I cannot say that I witnessed, outside of this market, a promoter referring to E.U. as a go-go group, because it had absolutely no meaning to that specific market.

So, again, the question is back to marketing and mounting a campaign that identifies go-go as a genre. So race is not the determining factor, I believe it is the music and the image of go-go that is lacking outside of Washington, D.C. Until this situation is addressed seriously, go-go, unfortunately, will remain a force in and around Washington, D.C. (which can no longer be referred to as Chocolate City).

Kip: Of course D.C. is still C.C.! What's really changed? The city remains majority non-white (and mostly African American), we are still disenfranchised, Anacostia remains off the list of tourist's destinations, the revival of the H Street Corridor (following the '68 riots) has never happened, and the Control Board still pulls the strings behind the scenes. The millennium may have changed, but is D.C. *really* (systemically) that different than it was in '75? I don't think so!

But I do agree that go-go needs to be defined and marketed outside of D.C. in order to succeed on a financial level. But does the popular music world really need or want this music? Go-go, for the most part, sounds like hyped-off, slightly off-kilter funk, and is anyone looking for a "funk revival" anytime soon? If go-go could be marketed to the (largely white) "rave" audience then it might get somewhere. Right now ravers listen to non-stop, mostly techno-pop and I can see some crossover potential. And if it can cross over to rave, it might pull in more listeners, many of them white.

It's also white D.C. (and the suburbs) where go-go remains an enigma. Talk about marketing go-go outside of D.C. is all well and good, but many folk in the city don't know much (if anything) about go-go. And most of them are white. Except for more musically adventurous younger kids, the non-black population of go-go's home city is ignorant about the music and its culture. So... I'm not at all convinced that go-go is in the hearts, minds, and happy feet of its hometown. Now, if we can get Mayor Williams to declare go-go the "Official Musical Genre of C.C." then we might make some progress in making *all* of D.C. aware of go-go!

Charles: Declarations that spotlight go-go are just not enough to spread the "gospel." As you know, Mayor Barry declared a tribute to go-go in 1987. Also Mayor Barry did all he could to work with go-go bands in an attempt to better understand how the police were interacting with go-go establishments and fans. Again—I feel like a "dead record"—we must produce go-go songs on the level of those released in the '80s. "Movin' And Groovin'," "Da' Butt," "Drop The Bomb," "Body Moves," and so on all received good airplay on WHUR, WOL, and WDJY. Why? Because they were songs that merited airplay. The current stable of go-go bands must get back to that formula or we will only hear P.A. tapes on Sundays, I believe.

Kip: So it comes down to songwriting and a high level of performances, eh? I certainly agree that these are critical elements in defining and promoting any genre of music. But all the songs that you mention are more than 10 years old and firmly planted in the "old school" genre. To anyone 20 years old or younger (here's where the demographics are vital), it's going to sound like very old and slightly off-kilter funk. And, given the ubiquitous nature of hip-hop, who is going to take such music seriously— at least in the pop marketplace? Face it, Charles, barring some fluke, I'm afraid that go-go is going to remain as fine an example of (exceptionally) regional American music as you'll find in the twenty-first century. Unless, that is, people "discover" it in the same way that Cajun music has reached a larger audience over the past 15 years. It's not likely, but it's not outside the realm of possibility.

Charles: Unfortunately, as much as I would like to disagree, you are correct. Unless the present crop of bands and go-go musicians are able to make the transition to formulating decent songs, then the genre could be dead. When I say dead, I mean as it relates to airplay and spreading nationally. Go-go will probably be around in D.C. for many years to come. The music, with its hip-hop and rap roots, can stay popular for folks who attend the go-go.

Permit me to digress...after talking and reading Little Benny's remarks and knowing how Donnell feels, we may have a breakthrough. So let's hope that these guys pursue what they know should be done. It is one thing to have a local audience and sell P.A. tapes. That is not the end. Go-go must spread its wings to go further. I believe, with the current state of music (particularly black music), that go-go has a golden opportunity to blossom.

Epilogue: "Welcome to D.C.," 2009

Kip Lornell and Charles C. Stephenson, Jr.
November 10, 2008

In April, 2008, just as we began thinking seriously about writing a chapter to close this new edition of *The Beat!*, Jacob Ganz, the producer of *Bryant Park Project* (NPR's morning news magazine that originates from WNYC), invited Kip onto the show to discuss the recent passing of Robert Reed, keyboardist and a founding member of seminal go-go band Trouble Funk. Contrary to what you might expect, Reed was not shot outside of a go-go. He died as the result of pancreatic cancer at the age of fifty. From 8:40 to 8:54 AM on April 24, 2008, Kip spent fourteen minutes, thirty-seven seconds talking about Trouble Funk, go-go, and Mr. Reed. We think it is significant that NPR covered the story some ten days following Reed's passing, while it wasn't until May 1 that the region's most widely read daily newspaper, the *Washington Post*, printed his obituary.

In many ways the lack of attention paid to go-go by the local media suggests that the aphorism "the more things change, the more things [mostly] stay the same" sadly holds true in this context. Despite the *Washington Post*'s continued lack of understanding and respect, important changes *are* occurring in the go-go community. Most notable is the evolution of groups like Vybe, Familiar Faces, and Lissen and the emergence Mambo Sauce (a truly revolutionary group with national ambitions) as well as the maturation via the internet in disseminating and promoting go-go.

The Go-Go Community: Bad Press and Violence

Many view go-go music and culture through an apartheid prism as only for African Americans and a focal point for uncivil behavior and violence. It is troubling that this perspective continues today. Therefore the perceptions of go-go continue to skew negative. This results in go-go bearing more than its fair share of criticism and blame for what happens on Washington D.C.'s streets and in its nonwhite neighborhoods.

These decades-long associations reemerged as part of the city's extended and determined attempt to shut down Club U over the winter of 2004–05. Using rhetoric wearily similar to that voiced by D.C. council member Frank Smith some eighteen years before, Cmdr. Larry D. McCoy of the 3rd Police District told the D.C. Alcoholic Beverage Control Board that "It's this go-go. If you have a black-tie event, you don't have any problem. But if you bring go-go in, you're going to have problems" (*Washington Post* February 20, 2005, page C1).

Ultimately, Club U lost this battle and was forced to lose its go-go flava. It wasn't the only club to shut down due to its booking of live go-go acts. On June 4, 2008, the *Washington City Paper* published Amanada Hess's cogent article "The G Word: What D.C. Won't Call Its Own Music," about liquor licenses and the performance of go-go at specific venues. Ms. Hess's article makes it abundantly clear that Alcoholic Beverage Regulation Agency [ABRA] officials want to further disconnect go-go venues from the almost entirely African American community that supports these live performances of the music. Several other clubs—most notably Club Rio (aka Deno's, nee Breeze's Metro Club) and Capitol Hill's Heart & Soul Café—have closed in light of the ABRA's interest in keeping violence off D.C.'s streets and live go-go music from its stages.

Such negative public associations are somewhat mitigated by the work of Peaceaholics, an African American group formed in 2004 and dedicated to promoting peace and harmony within Washington, D.C. Harry Jaffee wrote the following piece:

> You might recognize Anwan Glover's face from HBO's hit crime show *The Wire*, where he plays drug enforcer Slim Charles. Glover, known as Big G, grew up in D.C.'s gun culture. He's been shot nine times; his younger brother was shot and killed last year. "I was fascinated by guns at a young age," says Glover. "I took my brother's gun from him when I was thirteen. I just liked to fiddle around with it after school."
>
> Off-screen, Big G has joined Peaceaholics, a D.C. nonprofit dedicated to making peace on the streets. He goes into schools and housing projects to preach against gun violence. A few months ago, his younger brother was killed by gunfire. One day Glover was hanging out on a street corner in D.C.'s Columbia Heights when he heard shots. "I found myself on the ground," he says. It was the first of some nine occasions, by his count, on which he took a bullet. At thirty-five, he's been arrested multiple times for gun possession.
>
> On June 26, 2008, the Supreme Court issued a 5-4 ruling striking down the District's highly restrictive laws related to the ownership of handguns. The effects of the decision are currently unknowable as District lawmakers scramble to shape new laws that will conform with the ruling, a task that will take many months, if not years. Most certainly, however, there

will be more guns on the streets of Washington, D.C., which we believe cannot have a positive effect on violence in our nation's capital.

"There are more guns on the streets than ever before," he says. "If they lift that ban, it will be even more horrible." That's Big G's forecast if residents can get licenses to carry guns. The current challenge to D.C.'s ban law seeks to permit guns be legal only in the home. "I would love to have one at home to protect my wife," says Big G. "Then again, there might be a kid in the home who's fascinated by guns like I was. You would have to find a way to keep them safe. This is a tough debate." (http://www.thejustusleague.com/lawn/index.php?showtopic=41215).

Formed in 2006 the Go-Go Coalition, a musician's trade association with broad membership, has successfully fought the closing of Prince George's clubs that employ go-go bands. The coalition represents the interests of go-go musicians to various boards and commissions throughout the metropolitan area. Because the coalition includes so many members on its board and serves so many different constituencies, calling a quorum is difficult, which leads to difficulties on agreeing to the best course of action for the groups. Any such coalition also faces issues related to leadership and vision in addition to carrying out its mission, which their website states includes preservation, promotion, and advocacy (gogocoalition.org).

Not surprisingly, the Go-Go Coalition sometimes partners with Peaceaholics on mutual issues, including a Behind the Beat Go-Go Conference! held on May 30, 2007 at the Community of Hope Church inside Iverson Mall: "This event was designed to help facilitate discussions about how Go-Go can be a tool to help address community issues, including but not limited to violence prevention and positive media campaigns to help reach young people. The conference also addressed ways in which the Go-Go community should help ensure public safety at venues through self regulation and the development of creative strategies. Also, there was dialogue about ways in which the Go-Go Community can help expand their market and develop a structure for Go-Go music to be able to function as a viable member of the music industry" (gogocoalition.org).

On April 4, 2007 (page B4) the *Washington Post* published an article by Avis Thomas-Lester about the decision of Prince George's county executive Jack Johnson to close clubs under a law passed to address establishments that pose "an imminent danger to the public" in the wake of eleven homicides in eleven days in the county. The article bore the headline "Protesters Offer to Be Part of Solution, Go-Go Community Criticizes Closing of Night Spots but Suggests Ways to Stem Violence." It reported that on April 4, 2007, a hundred members of the Go Go Coalition and Peaceaholics, "representing musicians, sound engineers, and club owners and operators marched in Upper Marlboro from the Show Place Arena to the County Administration Building about a mile away to deliver a message to Johnson (D) and his administration: Let us be part of the solution to the violence that has recently plagued the county." This coverage allowed some of the musicians to promote their strongly held contention that very few direct relationships exist between go-go and violence.

Go-Go Pioneers Pass On: R.I.P.

Robert Reed was not the only member of the go-go community to pass away since 2001. The May 2005 suicide of pioneering go-go promoter David Rubin also shrouded the community in sadness. Rubin, who died on May 9 in Cecil County, Maryland, at the age of forty-two, opened one of the District's first hip-hop clubs in 1984. His IAG Theater Group also arranged for stage shows by African American troupes that appeared in both local and national venues. But, perhaps most importantly, Rubin was involved with promoting go-go for nearly twenty years.

Sarah Godfrey's heartfelt obituary of Rubin in the May 27, 2005, *Washington City Paper* offered these observations:

> By all accounts, he will be fondly remembered as the coolest white man to ever set foot in a go-go. "I call him D.C.'s Kid Rock," says Darryll Brooks, co-owner of the promotions company CD Entertainment. "He was all about it." . . .
>
> The New York native became consumed by the music while studying at George Washington University and working with its campus radio station, WRGW. One of his missions was to create hybrid shows that would bring different sorts of music fans to one venue. He created a concert series that paired Dischord Records artists with early go-go superstars, and he is credited with being one of the first promoters to book go-go bands for area private-school dances. . . .

Although Rubin was always enthusiastic and ambitious, Brooks didn't realize Rubin was a force to be reckoned with until learning that he'd successfully charmed the no-nonsense matriarch of Rare Essence. "Annie Mack, mother of James Funk, manager of Rare Essence, told me, 'Dave Rubin's over here eating crabs.' I fell out laughing," Brooks says, recalling a conversation with Annie Thomas, or "Ms. Mack," who passed away in 2003. "I said, 'This boy is serious—this boy is eating crabs at Annie Mack's house.' He's either trying to be in the game or he is in the game. He wasn't just playing the outside." . . .

"He would go anywhere—he was so dedicated," says [one-time spouse Alona] Wartofsky. "He used to have this beat-up old white Firebird, and he and I used to drive around— we'd start late to avoid the police—and hang up those Globe posters. . . . He'd drive all over the city putting those up, in the craziest neighborhoods. Everybody knew him, and everybody gave him respect."

November of 2007 marked the death of Philip Harris, who grew up in Southeast Washington, D.C., graduated from Ballou High School, and was the original trumpet player for E.U. Under the influences of jazz masters Miles Davis, Lee Morgan, Freddie Hubbard, and long-time Chuck Brown trumpet stalwart Donald Tillery, Philip played with a flair that added a touch of funk to the early E.U. grooves. Along with Oscar Smith (saxophone), and Kenneth Tracey (trumpet), Harris provided E.U.'s audiences with ingenious and danceable music and found an increasing passion for jazz that increasingly informed his playing with bands after E.U. In the months prior to his death, Philip had developed a jazz education and appreciation website and died while editing it.

In June 2008, long-time advocate for go-go and local promoter Peter Edward Hale Dean died. Peter Dean, as he was affectionately called by all who knew him, was indeed a unique soul who loved the music business. As president of the Student Government Association at Strayer College in the early 1980s, he used his position to book campus entertainment, which would always include go-go acts. Dean also served as the road manager for E.U. during their "Da Butt" tour.

Vern Goff, president of Emerald City Communications, wrote in Peter's tribute the following:

In a multi-faceted career, Peter Dean was well known as a man of great drive, strong will, humor, boisterous personality, imagination, and great vision. He worked passionately and tirelessly on the many projects he undertook to ensure results. Dean cofounded the Comedy Connection in Prince Georges County, Maryland—a pioneering effort and platform for numerous comics who eventually achieved national fame. Peter's other business ventures included: a record label, promoter, marketer, road manager, auto detailing, providing transportation for D.C. senior citizens, a limousine service, a transportation/bus company, and the list goes on. From the time he gave birth to his vision, he promoted various artists which included E.U. Up to the week before he entered his final rest, Dean was always busy wheeling and dealing—always looking for the next act, show, or idea to promote, always doing what he LOVED. Peter will truly be missed by all of the many people he touched.

Keyboardist Michael Hughes lost his life much too early when he died in October 2008. Mike was respected by all and was a musical genius, a description that was unanimous throughout the go-go community. He began his musical career playing with several bands prior to joining E.U. in the late 1970s. Once Mike joined E.U., his talents helped to propel the group to the greatness that it has enjoyed for many years.

In the early eighties, Mike left E.U. and with former E.U. band members Cleveland Battle and Girard Butler formed the group Vaughn Mason's Crew, which recorded the hit single "Bounce, Rock, Skate, Roll." This single lead them to tour nationally and internationally, opening for such stars as the Bar-Kays, Rick James, and Prince. Mike later founded AM/FM, which also toured nationally, and recorded the top-selling hit "You Are the One."

Although Mike was known as a keyboard player, his musical talents extended to playing the drums, bass, and lead guitar. He was also an accomplished audio sound engineer, operating Renegade Studios—an important resource for many local musicians during the 1990s. Because he understood go-go music, his studio became a favorite for go-go acts. Mike operated the sound board for Trouble Funk when they performed at the 9:30 Club during the Ben's Chilli Bowl 50th Year Anniversary Concert in September 2008. An active member in the Beulah Baptist Church, he worked there on Sundays as the audio engineer. At the time of his death Mike was working as the audio engineer with go-go legends James Funk and Roy Battle on a new gospel go-go release.

Local Props: Print and Electronic Media

The *Washington Post*, in particular, generally continues to report only negative stories on go-go. The *Washington City Paper* sometimes covers go-go events, mainly live performances and the occasional compact disc release. The city's other daily, the *Washington Times* (owned by Rev. Sun Young Moon) doesn't even seem to know that go-go exists.

The latest information about D.C.'s go-go scene can be found on the internet, which is particularly helpful for timely news about concerts, changes in band personnel, and the newest in P.A. tapes. In 2008 the old-style "Globe" posters have been replaced by full-color hand circulars and increasingly by electronic mailing lists and other web-based vehicles. In addition to group web pages, most notably those maintained for Chuck Brown (www.windmeupchuck. com) and the myspace.com pages devoted to Experience Unlimited and Mambo Sauce, most folks turn to Kato's "Take Me Out to the Go-Go" website. Most go-go fans, (the authors included), have TMOTTGoGo.com bookmarked.

TMOTTGoGo.com continues to thrive under the careful and caring leadership of Kato Hammond, who has expanded go-go's web presence by continually updating and revising his site several times a week. Clearly the best and most up-to-date source for information about go-go, the site includes a community forum board, where the talk is often spirited and highly opinionated. In addition, Kato maintains the most comprehensive and current list of clubs which feature go-go on almost any night of the week. If you want to know when Mambo Sauce is hosting its video release party, where Chuck Brown is playing over the weekend, which band is playing at the Tradewinds on Saturday night, or where to hear a gospel go-go band, then you will probably check Hammond's site. Within the last year Kato has added "TMOTTGoGo TV," which features a variety of streaming videos.

The modest but notable expansion of go-go on D.C.'s commercial radio stations, especially WKYS-FM (one of the leading "urban" stations in D.C.) on its hour-long Sunday night go-go show hosted by Big G, has brought more go-go music to an appreciative local audience. With the expansion of internet radio broadcasting, it's now possible to hear go-go over the computer anywhere in the world. The streaming broadcasts of WPGC-FM, WKYS-FM, and TMOT-TGoGo.com 24/7 provide opportunities for go-go fans who live outside the region to hear what's going on in D.C.

In 2006 WKYS-FM initiated the Go-Go Awards, an annual autumn celebration of the music held at Constitution Hall. The first show, broadly promoted by the station, included such grand statements as "Go-Go music has been and will be the pulse of the city, so to show respect and pay homage to the members of the go-go community we are throwing the first ever 93.9 WKYS DC Go-Go Awards." In late November 2008 this awards show, now adhering to more rigorous standards and greatly improved from its beta version, is slated to celebrate its third anniversary.

But, according to *Washington City Paper* writer Jessica Gould, before enlisting the help of local experts the station initially stumbled forward in a somewhat disjointed fashion:

> Bobbie Westmoreland, a writer for *Take Me Out to the Go-Go* magazine, suggests the radio station might need a go-go refresher course. When WKYS-FM first posted its nominations, she says, "there were a lot of categories that were, one, wrong, and, two, it's not clear what period they're covering." For example, she says, the nominations included the Huck-a-Bucks, who have "been broken up for a while," as well as venues that are now extinct mixed in with those that are still operating. Meanwhile, Westmoreland complains, some of the most "legendary" hot spots such as Ibex and Metro Club, also known as Deno's, were left out altogether. "It's kind of confusing, because everything is so mixed up," she says. (http://www.washingtoncitypaper.com/tell/2006/tell1027.html)

Go-Go as Serious Business: Your Tax Dollars at Work and Electioneering

The D.C. Commission on the Arts and Humanities sponsored The Business of Go-Go, a symposium held at the District of Columbia Historical Society on September 24, 2008. Moderated by Kip Lornell, the panelists included TMOTGoGo.com magnate Kato Hammond, entertainment lawyer John Mercer, former Junkyard manager and president of the Go-Go Coalition Moe Shorter, and William "Malachai" Johns, the manager of Mambo Sauce. The ninety-minute symposium, the brainchild of Dene Mitchell, who is working on a go-go documentary, focused on these questions:

MANAGEMENT
1. What's needed to move Go-Go beyond D.C. or should it?
2. What are record company responsibilities and the importance of management companies in expanding go-go's audience base?

3. Indeed does/should this include a grander vision, better stage shows, more expensive sound, and closer ties to hip-hop to help go-go move out of the greater D.C. area?
4. What about the importance of song writing in spreading go-go?

MEDIA
1. Why have local radio and the print media generally ignored go-go, except when violence erupts at clubs?
2. Describe the P.A. tape distribution. Is it the best way for bands to keep product in the ears and minds of their fans?
3. How important is airplay and will more airplay increase sales?
4. What about the importance of local independent record companies in recording and selling go-go material?
5. Will any stations besides WPGC-FM and WKYS-FM even play go-go?
6. Does internet airplay have any impact on breaking go-go songs and bands?

MAXX KIDD
Considering his place in go-go in the 1970s and 1980s, Maxx Kidd straddles the line between management and media. What's the importance of Kidd in these roles and discuss what he did for the business and the music?

Viewing go-go as a business (underpinned by the twin themes of professionalism and management) proved to be the evening's most lively and heavily discussed topic. John Mercer, who was closely involved with the intellectual rights of the 1985 film *Good to Go*, particularly emphasized the importance of understanding how the music publishing business works. He addressed the issues of royalties and song writing credits as important revenue streams by stressing that the music business is much more complicated and multidimensional (and potentially lucrative) than the income produced through live performances.

Mercer's observations were echoed and amplified by Malachai, who indicated that the changing nature of the business demanded a clearer understanding of not only its legal complexities but also how recording and distributing go-go has undergone a sea change over the past few years. Recordings of go-go, like other forms of American vernacular music, are increasingly disseminated via downloads, which means diminishing sales from compact discs and more cash coming via i-Tunes. Malachai also emphasized the importance of the Mambo Sauce myspace.com page as the principal means of reaching fans with news about the band, upcoming live performances, and links to other, related videos and downloads.

Kato further emphasized the role that the internet now plays in go-go. Not only does his TMOTTGoGo.com site announce upcoming live performances; it also includes a bulletin board and an ever-changing array of images, many of them provided by Thomas Sayers Ellis. This denizen of go-go on the internet looks at the digital realm as the music's salvation. Why, he argued, do you need AM or FM (or satellite, for that matter) radio when you can hear the latest go-go joints or old school performances over the internet? Kato's ever-expanding (though sadly not very lucrative) internet empire also includes live radio shows and video updates in addition to its fore-mentioned attributes.

Moe Shorter had less to say about the internet than about issues related to management and his years with Junkyard Band. He also commented at great length about the critical role that Maxx Kidd played in promoting go-go in the 1980s. Shorter, who now works full-time as a budget analyst for the District of Columbia Public Schools, remains tied to the scene through his involvement with the Go-Go Coalition and as a member of the D.C. Commission on the Arts and Humanities.

The fall of 2008, pivotal in the United States because of the historic election of Barack Obama as president, also demonstrated the maturation and involve-ment of the Go-Go Coalition in D.C.'s local election. The Go-Go Coalition con-ducted voter registration drives and get-out-the-vote efforts during the election season, which helped solidify its political status in the city. Prior to the election, the Go-Go Coalition in coordination with Returning Citizens United sponsored a Voting Commitment Rally (Vote Now or Cry Later) on Monday, October 27, 2008, at the Covenant Baptist Church in Southeast Washington, D.C. The event was attended by approximately two hundred citizens and six out of the seven at-large city council candidates, each of whom addressed the issues of both organizations. The Returning Citizens United represents the interests of the formerly incarcerated, whose concerns were addressed by the candidates.

At this forum the Go-Go Coalition presented several issues of importance to the industry, most notably its stance that local politicians stop the slander and defamation of go-go and a proposed agreement to meet with the coalition within thirty days after the election. Each candidate addressed the concerns and the majority of them were in agreement. Though it might not seem so important to a non-Washingtonian, this important step could begin a process by which the

Go-Go Coalition works in concert with city leaders to address issues that affect the entire city.

Media Recognition Outside the Beltway: The Rock Hall, *Vibe*, and Hollywood

On February 16, 2002, the Rock and Roll Hall of Fame, located in Cleveland, Ohio, sponsored a symposium about the music and business of go-go, in which Kip Lornell and Charles Stephenson both participated as panelists. This half-day program, not surprisingly, attracted a mostly local crowd. Along with a handful of other Washingtonians one musical group, UnCalled 4 Band (UCB), represented go-go in Cleveland.

Vibe magazine ran a nicely written piece on go-go, "Bang the Drum," complete with a fine set of black-and-white photographs, in November 2001. Although the author, Jeff Chang, lives in California, he understands black American popular music and wrote one of the most insightful and balanced books on the cultural history of hip-hop—*Can't Stop, Won't Stop: A History of the Hip-Hop Generation* (St. Martin's Press, 2005). His piece largely focuses on Backyard Band and its charismatic lead talker and spiritual leader Ralph Anwar Glover: aka G, Ghengis, or Big G. Chang's focus on Backyard makes sense because the group was probably the most youth-oriented, streetwise, hip-hop influenced go-go band in 2001.

The importance of go-go culture infuses other recent artistic efforts emanating from the city. Anyone growing up black in the District in the 1990s, as Lindsey Christian did, knows about go-go culture. A graduate of the Duke Ellington School of the Arts (2001) and MIT (2005), Christian appeared at Kip Lornell's "Musical Cultures of Black Americans" class at The George Washington University on September 18, 2008, to talk about *Jazz in the Diamond District*, a film that she co-wrote, produced, and directed, and which finished postproduction in the spring of 2008. The film premiered in New York City the week before her GWU appearance and the film is scheduled for release on DVD by the summer of 2009.

According to a preproduction piece about the film, it is a

> drama that chronicles the summer of a D.C. native, Jasmine
> "Jazz" Morgan, who joins a go-go band in hopes of becoming
> a singing sensation. . . . When Jazz (Monique Cameron) loses
> her mother to a long-time battle with lung cancer, she can
> only focus on one thing—becoming a famous singer. Ignor-
> ing the wishes of her father, Blair Morgan (Clifton Powell), a

strict doctor who prefers that she return to college, Jazz rebel-liously spends the summer entrenched in the hypersexualized, drug-influenced D.C. music scene, dragging along her naive younger sister, Leah (Erica Chamblee). The film was shot on location in the often-overlooked residential neighborhoods of Washington, D.C., where the thump of go-go music reverber-ates in the streets and where the volatile energy that spawned the nickname "Murder Capitol" in the '90s still lingers in the air. (http://www.jazzinthediamonddistrict.com/)

When answering a student question about the film and growing up in the District, Ms. Christian recalled, "I grew up listening to go-go music. It is a regular part of urban radio programming in D.C. and I also attended go-gos, whether they were at clubs like The Palace or The Icebox or at schools like Sidwell Friends or Cardoza [High School]. We all had P.A. tapes of our favorite bands, and it just became a part of our musical upbringing—like rock or hip-hop or R&B." With such close ties to the District and go-go, and that old adage "write about what you know" ringing in her head, it's hardly surprising that Lindsey Christian's first dramatic feature-length film focuses on go-go and the culture surrounding it.

In November 2008 another film with the go-go flava, *Toe to Toe*, entered postproduction. Go-Go's use in *Toe to Toe* represents another contemporary example of how the music represents the District and African American culture like no other cultural marker. One of the scenes consists of a go-go performance, filmed at the CFE in Maryland, by Backyard Band in which it's impossible to miss the onstage charisma of Big G. The other scene, which was filmed at Bullis School (a private school located just outside the Beltway in Potomac, Maryland), features Rashid AKA "Sand Nig" (who mixes go-go with Middle Eastern) performing at a talent show alongside the Beat Ya Feet Kings.

According to film-maker Emily Abt:

Back in the early '90s, I spent a life-defining summer in Washington, D.C., as an intern investigator for the Public De-fender Service. That summer provided me with the inspira-tion to create *Toe to Toe*—my first narrative feature, set in Washington, D.C., and also introduced me to go-go music. My boyfriend at the time, a Maryland native who went by the name of "Spoon," showed me videos of go-go concerts he had attended. I was put off by some of the rowdy crew behavior

I saw and images of bikini-clad women humping the stage, but something about that beat and the energy of those videos got me intrigued. And I loved the call and response aspect of the live performances that amped-up the crowd and kept them coming back for more. As I made my daily trek to Southeast from the Maryland suburbs where I was staying with family, go-go became my summer soundtrack. I learned a few go-go dance moves too, perhaps to the irritation of sisters at the clubs who would glare at my skinny, blonde self as I cheerfully bounced my shoulders to the beat. Years later, when the script for *Toe to Toe* began to take shape, I knew that the intense and unique go-go culture in D.C. *had* to be a part of the film.

Thanks to the wonderful assistance of *Toe to Toe*'s associate producer "Six," a well-known promoter in the D.C. area, I've been given incredible access to the go-go scene in D.C. Six made sure that before we cast our go-go group, I got to see a wide variety of super talented bands. I met and watched some of the greats perform: Mambo Sauce, TCB, Backyard Band, etc. We ended up casting Backyard (and their incredibly charismatic frontman Anwan Glover AKA Big G) for our go-go scene in the film, but we are also using tracks from TCB, DJ Flexx and other independent go-go drummers as part of our film's score. Many other D.C.-based talents including Tabi Bonney, Wale, Sheba, The Kid, Haziq, Thievery Corporation, select artists from D.C.-based labels Dischord Records and 18th Street Lounge Music are also featured. The film also includes the incredible dancing of the Beat Ya Feet Kings whose work, and manager Diallo Sumbry, I have great admiration for.

Everyone in the go-go world who I've had the pleasure of being introduced to has greeted me with open arms and without the skepticism that I thought an out-of-town white girl might warrant. This may be in part due to my associate producer Six being so well regarded within the go-go scene, but I also feel it was because folks like the idea of being part of a project that will hopefully give go-go some long overdue national exposure. Among some critics, go-go is deemed as a trouble-making music form with a penchant for inciting violence. For those who love it, like me, go-go is a thriving music form with a beat and fan base that just won't quit. (Emily Abt, via e-mail, November 7, 2008)

In regards to go-go and the electronic media, perhaps most intriguingly (though not go-go specific) is the YouTube.com phenomenon. Since its February 2005 launch by three former PayPal employees as a means to share videos that fall below an X or an R-rating, YouTube.com has radically increased the number and variety of videos available on the internet. In November 2006, Google acquired YouTube.com, a move that only furthered its popularity, and today viewers can see an astonishing array of moving images that range from Fred Astaire dancing to lessons on speaking French to home movies of baby's first step. Music has emerged as a YouTube staple and go-go is among its seemingly innumerable musical genres.

Simply typing "go-go" into the search engine will yield these videos, but entering a more specific query for "Junkyard Band" or "Da Butt" or "Chuck Brown" produces better results. Of the scores of go-go clips available, some are poorly shot, all-but-unlistenable, unedited performance footage, while others feature high-quality, professionally shot promotional videos. We'd love to suggest particularly strong go-go performances on YouTube.com, but since the urls are forever changing, searching on the site is the smartest course of action.

Musicians and Bands: The Old School Revisited and Ben's Chili Bowl

Thankfully many of go-go's best known and longest-running bands continue to perform. Chuck Brown remains the most well-known go-go musician, and he's finally receiving local and national accolades and recognition. Chuck Brown's September 2001 birthday tribute included the production of an in-depth DVD (*Put Your Hands Up*—Raw Venture, 2002) that includes the best concert footage ever shot of go-go as well as a brief documentary film *From the Belly of the Drum*. Brown has gained even greater local recognition since 2004 through his appearances on local television commercials as the spokesperson for the *Washington Post* and the D.C. Lottery, some of which were shot at the Hard Rock Café in downtown D.C.

After being nominated by Kip Lornell in 2002, Brown was awarded a prestigious National Endowment for the Arts National Heritage Fellowship award in the fall of 2005. (http://www.nea.gov/honors/heritage/). In addition to a $20,000 cash award, the winners assemble in the District each September to attend a series of luncheons, press conferences, and meetings that culminate with a public display of their talents at the NEA Heritage Awards.

Having played for newly elected Mayor Adrian Fenty's thirty-seventh birthday party on December 7, 2007, Brown continued a tradition as the black mu-

25

sical artist of choice for mayors of Washington, D.C. It is a tradition that first blossomed when Marion Barry was mayor during the 1980s. Brown sometimes performs with such nationally known musicians as Carlos Santana. However, much of his work continues to be at major local public events. Recent typical performances include the Safeway 16th Annual National Capital Barbecue Battle that took place June 21–22, 2008, in downtown D.C. and the Kennedy Center Millennium Stage on September 13, 2008. Brown also continues to play local African American–oriented clubs, such as the Icon in Waldorf, Maryland, where he performs several times a month. During the summer of 2008 he also played dates in New York City as part of Lincoln Center's Mid Summer Night Swing Series and in Detroit.

In 2004 Experience Unlimited (E.U.) was elected to the Washington Area Music Association (WAMA) Hall of Fame in the same class as "Mama" Cass Elliot and Foster "Ken" Mackenzie III (Root Boy Slim). E.U. joined fellow go-go stalwart, Chuck Brown, who was elected in 1991. In announcing the election, WAMA described E.U. as "one of D.C.'s original go-go bands, a seminal group that helped define, refine, and combine the musical components of the genre, which originated here." (http://www.crosstownarts.com/wama/hof_2004.html)

In addition to Chuck Brown, such classic go-go groups as Rare Essence, Junkyard Band, Backyard Band, along with Sugar Bear and E.U., continue to perform at new venues around metropolitan Washington, D.C., including clubs located along the revitalized U Street section of Shaw near Howard University. But because it's a vital, energized, and evolving genre, new and reconstituted go-go bands are always emerging and revitalizing the sound. Newly formed, important bands such as Lissen, Suttle Thoughts, Uncalled 4 Band (UCB), Vybe, and Familiar Faces have all come onto the scene in the twenty-first century.

Founded in 2001 Familiar Faces illustrates this trend as well as any group. Donnell Floyd (vocals and saxophone—Rare Essence and 9/11), Derek Paige (vocals and trumpet), and Eric "Bojack" Butler (percussion—Rare Essence) were among its founding members, each of whom was looking for a new way to express themselves in the world of go-go music. By November 2008 the group has gone through several key personnel changes but all three of its founders remain with the current thirteen-piece ensemble.

Familiar Faces typically plays several nights a week and contains all the essential elements of the original go-go configurations; most notably a rhythm section comprised of two guitarists, a bass, and drums works very hard to keep the groove in "the pocket." The intense, versatile vocals supplied by Frank "Scooby" Marshall, Marquis Melvin, and Damila, who all can sing with the best of them, provide a nice foil to the go-go beat. Such expressive singing is not a trait normally associated with go-go, but it's critical in opening up the music to larger (non-D.C.) audiences.

Aside from all things political, the National Mall, and the Smithsonian Institution, Washington, D.C., is perhaps best known for its NFL team (the 'Skins), go-go music, mambo sauce for its wings, and Ben's Chili Bowl. How appropriate, then, that Ben's Chili Bowl weekend celebration of its fifty years in business culminated with go-go performance featuring Mambo Sauce, Trouble Funk, and E.U. held at the 9:30 Club on August 24, 2008. This special weekend show also underscored the fact that the 9:30 Club has promoted go-go groups for twenty-eight years. This is significant given the fact that the club features all types of popular music, including many national acts. Although the weekend began with a star-studded show featuring Bill Crosby, Roberta Flack, and local music performer Safe Infinity at the Lincoln Theater—located next door to Ben's Chili Bowl on U Street—it closed with go-go.

Ben's anniversary go-go show turned out to be a reunion, both because of the range of groups featured and go-go luminaries who adorned the audience. The day was particularly special for Mike Hughes, formerly of E.U., Rare Essence, and AM/FM, who worked as the audio engineer for Trouble Funk. Mike, who passed away less than two months later, was a member of the house band at the Apollo Theater in New York City. He strongly believed that once performers play go-go they can never truly divorce themselves from the music; a credo that Mike himself lived by.

Back in the day, Trouble Funk was known for its huge sound. Thankfully, they still have it! Although their hearts were heavy, because it was Trouble's first big performance without Robert "Dyke" Reed, the founder and heart and soul of the group, they did justice to the memory of Dyke, who would have been proud in how they represented his legacy.

Big Tony, the leader of Trouble Funk, displayed his ultra-funky bass playing and his gigantic vocals as both a singer and lead talker throughout their set. The group indeed "Pumped It Up" as they tapped into the old time go-go energy and had the folks working their bodies with the go-go beat. The Trouble Funk horns lifted the energy level of the entire house. Horns add color and a rhythmic drive to the music and are essential to old-school go-go music, as Trouble Funk flawlessly demonstrated.

Trouble's set at the 9:30 Club was reminiscent of sets once heard at old go-go venues such as the Howard Theater, D.C. Coliseum, Club LeBaron, and the Panorama Room. The accents of the horns helped the band to deliver excitement to the audience. On their hit "Let's Get Small," the entire club joined in by displaying their hands with the broad gesture that is associated with the song.

As the band continued to rock, Tony announced a surprise guest, and out came Chuck Brown, who took the mike as the crowd commanded, "Wind me up, Chuck." Fronting Trouble Funk, Chuck fell into the groove of "Feel Like Moving That Body." Trouble ended the set by "Dropping the Bomb" on all the crews, from Southeast, Northeast, Northwest, to the White House, (which you can only do at a go-go in Washington, D.C.).

Next to take the stage was Sugar Bear and E.U., which kicked off the set with a song by Rianna, "Over Now" with the go-go groove that featured the vocals of Myra Griffin to add a touch of the old E.U. to the band. The high energy of E.U. was evident as Sugar Bear met the challenge presented by Trouble Funk, that certainly brought back memories of past performances. With Sugar Bear still at the helm, the 2008 version of E.U.—consisting of Mike Smith, drums; Tony Cofthars, lead guitar; Ivan Goff, keyboards; and Derrick Smith, percussion—performed an old favorite "Sexy Lady" that had the audience waving their hands and having a great time in rocking to the go-go beat.

E.U. then demonstrated why they remain popular after several decades when Tino Jackson sauntered onto the stage. He led them in a go-go version of the Funkadelic's "Cosmic Slop," which caught the audience by complete surprise. Tino played with emotion and talent that matches the best guitarist in the country, and his solo pierced the crowd, letting them know that the "Mother Ship" had arrived with E.U. in total command.

Following "Cosmic Slop," Sugar Bear was joined by Little Benny, formerly of Rare Essence, Little Benny and the Masters, and Chuck Brown and the Soul Searches, who led the band in an old E.U. crowd participation song the "E.U. Freeze" during which the audience stops in place every time the band stops playing. The "E.U. Freeze" has been around for more than two decades, remaining in their repertoire because of its audience participation, which is central to all go-go music.

It was evident during E.U.'s performance that Sugar Bear can still command the attention of an audience. Even after nearly twenty years their closing song, "Da Butt," still elicits screams, shouts, hand waving, and butt shaking from the audience. Sugar Bear invited members of the audience on stage to show off their dancing prowess and illicit moves prowess that predictably work them into a frenzy. Sugar Bear and E.U. displayed the best elements of go-go and showed why after playing for thirty years, they remain one of D.C.'s best bands.

The Newer Faces of Go-Go: Familiar Faces, Vybe, WHAT? Band, et al.

Go-Go appears to be at yet another crossroads. It's an indisputable truth that the music continues to enjoy enthusiastic support from the local African American community, thousands of whom also purchase P.A compact discs, listen to go-go on-line, and attend live performances. Trouble Funk, Familiar Faces, Lissen, Vybe, UCB, or Backyard Band are among the bands that can be heard on any given night of the week at venues such as Mirrors Lounge and Restaurant in downtown D.C., the Icon Entertainment Complex in Waldorf, Maryland, or Takoma Station (Takoma, D.C.). And go-go is mixed into the daily play lists of the city's two preeminent "urban" radio stations, WPGC-FM and WKYS-FM.

The underlying issue is that go-go continues to be confined by the Beltway, by marketing, and by race. Unless you are African American and have strong ties to the Washington, D.C. metropolitan region or you have an uncommonly inquiring ear and a strong interest in wide range of contemporary black popular music, then the chance that you have heard go-go is close to zero. These three facts undermine the possibilities for national reach in the future.

"Sweet" Cherie Mitchell, Chuck Brown's current keyboard player, underscored the national significance and respect that go-go music has generated throughout the country. Cherie, a graduate of both the Duke Ellington School of the Arts and Howard University, has go-go experience with Sugar Bear and E.U. as well as national artists including Pieces of a Dream, Chic, Stephanie Mills, and Howard Hewitt. She knows that musicians can make a living in Washington, D.C. playing only go-go, a luxury not available to musicians who reside in other cities. Noting that national musicians respect what go-go musicians have created in Washington, D.C., Cherie added that local musicians can therefore afford to be more musically creative and innovative than many of their peers around the United States. This freedom of expression, the soul of go-go musicians, is definitely a positive.

Cherie further believes that females are not only integral to go-go, but also responsible for the music's continued local success. Going back to Maiesha [Rashad] and the Hip Huggers in the late 1990s, which would eventually include Sugar Bear and Ju Ju, the band's appeal skyrocketed when they added a go-go flavor to their music. More go-go bands began adding female vocalists in the early 2000s; a change that also cut down misogynist lyrics. At present, many of the top go-go bands feature females as vocalists or musicians. Females in the go-go bands make business sense given the fact that females constitute the majority of the music's patrons.

In November of 2008 Cherie debuted the female group "Be'laDona," which promises to make a splash on both the go-go and R&B music scenes in Washington, D.C. The group consists of several local top-flight female musicians: Candra Rutledge, bass; Karis Hill, congas; Shannon Brown, drums; Sharli McQueen, vocals; Deanna Hawkins, keyboards; Genny "Jam" Konechnick, guitar; and the leader herself on keyboards. The focus of Be'laDona is in performing heart-felt R&B with a go-go feel emanating from its rhythmic pocket. Through the years there have been several unsuccessful attempts to duplicate the success of Pleasure Band, a very popular female go-go group from the mid-1980. Be'laDona's emphasis on connecting with the audience by playing challenging music, having fun, and extending the boundaries of go-go may fill this void.

Stanley Cooper, lead guitarist, has an impressive résumé that includes playing with jazz and pop musicians such as Marcus Johnson and Roy Ayers. Stanley echoes Cherie's assertion regarding the level of respect afforded Washington, D.C., go-go artists. He also believes that many national groups seek out D.C. musicians because of the feeling they bring to every musical performance. They uniquely demonstrate a special ability to reach out and touch audiences.

The respect that go-go musicians have generated nationally is important to understand the future potential of Washington's home-bred music. For many years notable national artists have added slices and pieces of go-go vamps and percussion breaks to their songs. Most recently The Roots, along with Chrisette Michele, provided perhaps the best examples of national artists inserting go-go elements in their songs.

The essence (pun intended) of Vybe, another recently formed go-go band, is to have fun. Many patrons on the go-go circuit believe that Vybe offers a time-tested style of go-go that has been around for nearly three decades. An admitted and unabashed Chuck Brown disciple, founder and lead singer Derek Holmes underscores that Vybe's purpose is to ensure that the people have fun. Vybe, as its name projects, eschews rehearsals and takes pleasure in playing cover tunes that are transformed by the insistent and compelling go-go beat. Catch a Vybe performance and it's hard to tell who is having the most fun: the band or the audience, which is the way many fans think it should be.

Lissen offers another facet of the current go-go scene. Founded in 2006 by Michael Thompson (a man who takes his music very seriously), Lissen was established with one ear on go-go and another on classic funk-driven R&B groups along the lines of Earth, Wind and Fire and Mint Condition. A listen to Lissen's summer 2008 compact disc, *Can You Hear Us Now*, which was recorded on Marcus Johnson's Three Keys label, reveals more R&B elements than go-go as well as professional musicianship and strong vocals that are on par with established, nationally recognized groups. This aesthetic is explained by Thompson's quest to establish Lissen as a serious group of D.C.-bred musicians that happen to play go-go music.

With its high energy, crowd-pleasing performances WHAT? Band represents another side of contemporary go-go that has rejuvenated the go-go circuit. Not a "grown and sexy" group, this band generally attracts a very enthusiastic younger audience. WHAT? Band has gained the respect of many go-go musicians who appreciate their youthful following and the straight ahead form of go-go that they perform.

Gospel go-go continues to be a small but important musical niche for local black Christians. Several go-go musicians, including Roy Battle, a member of the seminal go-go group Hot Cold Sweat, who is now the musical director for Beulah Baptist Church, have turned their attention to serving God. Battle observed that several musicians have approached him over the years because they know he is a Christian as well as a musician. He said that many are looking for ways to turn their lives around and to serve the Lord. The late Michael Hughes, who worked with Roy as the audio engineer for Beulah Baptist Church, provides another good example.

As a result of his ongoing interest in go-go, Battle decided to do a gospel music project. James Funk of Rare Essence and Proper Utensils fame, joined with Roy to produce a go-go CD, which was released in November 2008. The CD features other notable go-go musicians such as Go-Go Mickey, Sweet Cherie, Shorty Garris, and Michael Hughes. Roy believes the project will help convert others to the service of the Lord as part of his calling to "take it to the streets" in an effort to expand gospel music's impact. He stated, "Of course the beat is important, but the lyrics are more important. People will be able to enjoy the go-go beat, but will also hear the word of the Lord" (Charles Stephenson in conversation with Battle on October 20, 2008).

Jazz pianist and former local radio personality, Marcus Johnson incorporates the pocket beat in his repertoire during jazz sets at local upscale clubs and hotel lobby bars. The Marcus Johnson Project, which consists of many of D.C.'s accomplished jazz musicians, can be heard weekly at the Holiday Inn located several blocks from the nation's Congressional and federal building. Their loyal audience primarily consists of federal and Congressional workers looking to get their groove on, reduce stress, and add years to their lives.

Although Marcus was raised on go-go music as an original member of Ayre Ryde in the 1980s, he made his musical mark playing jazz. Johnson is currently working on a go-go/jazz project that will certainly turn ears and attention to

Washington, D.C. Because Marcus is nationally renowned for his success as a jazz musician, his reexploration of go-go will not go unnoticed.

Stanley Cooper, who also grew up playing go-go, is the brain trust behind the group 76 Degrees West (the longitude of Washington, D.C.), which recently produced the single, "School Boy Crush." This remake of the Average White Band smash hit has a smooth jazz appeal and is played with a beat in the pocket. The song features the deft sax playing of "Pieces of a Dream" member Eddie Bacus along with the soul-stirring guitar of Stanley Cooper.

In response to the ever-growing problems associated with the performing and dissemination of go-go music, some bands have redefined themselves. Go-go bands have always wanted their music to grow feet that would lead to national exposure. Many believe the constant association with crime and violence has hampered the ability to extend go-go's popularity beyond the Beltway. So a small but increasing number of bands now underplay or entirely reject the go-go tag and describe their music as "grown and sexy" (a mature brand of go-go), "pocket music" (definitely straight-up go-go) or R&B. This rebranding has several rationales. One is the need to respond to local government authorities and law enforcement officials who persist in their knee jerk and blanket prosecution of go-go as a negative force in the community. The go-go industry resents the continued association with crime and violence and as a result decided that by not calling their music go-go, they may get a pass.

Some bands, such as Vybe, OP Tribe, and Mambo Sauce, wanting to break from the past and forge out new musical territories, find go-go too confining a marketing tool. Although these groups clearly understand that they stand on the shoulders of Chuck Brown, Rare Essence, and E.U., they want to open new musical avenues built upon their go-go foundation. Thus the "pocket beat" and "grown and sexy" are used to describe and market the inevitable hybrid forms of go-go that will no doubt continue to emanate from D.C.

Some groups believe that rebranding only improves their ability for success nationally. It is no secret that few sound recordings have successfully captured the essence of go-go, further distancing this music from more prominent record companies with national clout. Contemporary go-go groups such as Mambo Sauce, Lissen, and Uncalled 4 Band have each experimented with different approaches to enhance the music.

Go Go's Great Black Hope?: Mambo Sauce

This rebranding/refocusing/regrooving has resulted in the greatest amount of recognition for go-go outside of D.C. in many years, arguably since Spike Lee showcased "Da Butt" in *Schooldaze*. Mambo Sauce provides perhaps the best case study of a go-go band pushing outside of D.C. and towards a broader demographic with a new marketing strategy. Their music has found a wider audience (both inside and way outside of the Beltway) by way of electronic media exposure on VH1-Soul and BET. And, like so many bands since 2003, they have carved their presence on the web at www.myspace.com/mambosauce. Their myspace.com page remains *the* source for all things Mambo Sauce including upcoming events, downloads, and a blog.

Mambo Sauce is largely the product of William "Malachai" Johns and his partner Treehouse, who co-managed the band until mid-October 2008 when Johns split from the band. Because of Malachai's strong and longstanding ties to the local music scene Mambo Sauce consists of seven musicians (one lead talker, one first-class vocalist, a drummer, a timbale player, a guitarist, a bassist, and a keyboardist) with whom he had already worked and others that he knew. Some members of Mambo Sauce previously performed with other local go-go bands—most notably Northeast Groovers and Uncalled 4 Band. As of October 2008 the group consisted of Alfred "Black Boo" Duncan, lead vocals; Yendy Brown, lead vocals; Jermaine "Lil Pep" Cole, percussion; Barrington "Barry" Talbert, drums; Andrew "Drew" White, lead guitar; Christian "Lil' Chris" Wright, keyboard; and Khari Pratt, bass (http://www.redcrecords.com/artists/mambo_sauce.htm).

According to their regularly updated website

> There are three things that you can only get in Washington D.C., The President, Go-Go Music, and Mambo Sauce. This electrifying group takes their name from the mystery sauce popular at Chinese/Soul Food carry-outs throughout D.C. Comprised of seven of D.C. and Go-Go music's most prominent musicians, the band has created a new form of music called "Pocket" that effectively blends D.C. Go-Go percussion with well crafted songs, explosive raps, and sultry melodies. Mambo Sauce and their label Red C Records intend to use this formula to infiltrate the national music market with the D.C. Go-Go sound.

Establishing Mambo Sauce took many months and it wasn't until their single "Miracles" came out and got strong local buzz that the group gained serious local attention. In the summer of 2007 they released "Welcome to DC," which immediately gained local airplay and became the "official intro song" for the NBA Washington Wizard's team. Early in 2008 "Welcome to DC" appeared on the Billboard Hip-Hop/R&B charts, the first go-go ensemble to do so in nearly twenty years.

Listening to Mambo Sauce live in August 2008, Kip gained a better sense of how Mambo Sauce might accomplish this goal. On August 1, when they appeared as the closing act of a community-based Battle of the Bands at a community center in Arlington, Virginia, several factors rang true for Kip:

1) They have a wide mix of musical influences, all of which were propelled by a wicked groove and their ability to hit a conventional old school go-go pocket.

2) They have a strong sense of go-go's musical and cultural heritage, mostly through their frequent—often subtle—references to Backyard Band and Chuck Brown.

3) Most of the non–African American audience left when Mambo Sauce hit the stage for their hour-long set.

4) There was the strong interaction between the audience and the band. By the end of the set the majority of the audience (numbering about a hundred at that point) was on stage bouncing/dancing/moving.

Charles took his fourteen-year-old daughter Zora to a go-go performance by Mambo Sauce on August 9 at Jammin' Java, a suburban club near Tyson's Corner in Vienna, Virginia. Admittedly this is not your traditional go-go venue. It is an all-age's club that relies on the patronage of white suburban youth. The location in itself scores a victory for go-go, because it shows how the music has broadened its racial and geographical reach since 2001.

On this evening Mambo Sauce showed why they are in the vanguard of delivering the go-go sound internationally. The band took to the stage playing a rock rendition of the "Star-Spangled Banner," which featured the excellent guitar playing of Andrew "Drew" White. Drew was fantastic as he played with precision and feel unexpected in a go-go guitarist. His playing was definitely reminiscent of a version of the song that Tino Jackson once played for E.U. during the 9:30 Club gigs that preceded their 1988 connection to Spike Lee, which ultimately lead to go-go reaching new heights. After the introduction, Mambo Sauce began to take the audience on a pure go-go ride that enabled the band to display their musicianship. During the show the lead talker and vocalist "Black Boo" asked the audience for a moment of silence in honor of Bernie Mac, who had recently passed. Well, the audience for the most part ignored his plea, and the band continued to play. However, when the band finished their next song Black Boo took the mike and said to the audience, "I am serious this time, you will honor Bernie Mac with a moment of silence." The audience complied and

Importance of Management & Direction of Go-Go

I think that the importance of band management takes a backseat to the importance of vision. It's hard to steer the ship correctly if you don't know where you're going. I don't think most Go-Go artists start with the end in mind. They just want to play music and make money doing it. The role of the manager is to set the course (the vision) and make sure the band adheres to it (management) and hope the rest of the world takes to it. Of course this is assuming the manager comes along at the inception of the band, which is all that I've had experience with.

I was inspired to start Red C Records and subsequently Red 1 Management and Mambo Sauce when, through a confluence of events, I was living in Los Angeles. The first was that I was going out to see these live "Neo-Soul" bands in L.A. and I thought to myself that they couldn't hold a candle to the energy of a Go-Go band, but still had some of the same elements. They sounded like the "Grown and Sexy" bands of DC, except they were playing their own tunes and to my dismay, they never dropped it in a pocket!

During this time, I applied for an assistant position in the promotions department at Def Jam. I interviewed with the head of West Coast Promotions Motti Shulman (Lyor Cohen's brother) over lunch. I didn't get the job, but he noticed Northeast Groovers on my resume and flipped his wig because Shulman loves Go-Go. The rest of the time that I was in L.A. before I came back to MD/DC in 2005 to start the company and band, I was giving him Go-Go CD's from Backyard to SOULO, the band I had just left in order to move to Vegas and then L.A.

I had left SOULO because I was frustrated with playing cover songs, when the band had so much potential to write its own hits (members went on to write music for Jennifer Lopez, Mya, Keyshia Cole, Ludacris, T.I., etc.). My friend and the manager and Rototom player of SOULO Dig Dug (of Northeast Groovers fame) and I had many a heated argument about this. His position at the time was that the band needed to play whatever kept us hot in the city, and I wanted to break Go-Go on a national scale and thought SOULO could do it. When Dig Dug, who was my biggest critic about my idea of taking Go-Go to the national stage, called and told me that he finally understood and agreed with what I was talking about, that gave me the inspiration I needed. Knowing that bands in the entertainment capital of the world couldn't hang with the bands from my area, that a middle-aged, Jewish white guy from L.A. loved Go-Go and my biggest critic was now my biggest supporter, I was on my way.

My experience as a Go-Go musician impacted my vision for Mambo Sauce in many ways. However, the most important thing was that I knew the frustration of dedicating yourself to an instrument, mastering it, but then being looked down on by others in the "industry" because the music that you love and chose to play is looked at as second-class by the rest of the world. This attitude set me on my mission to change the way people look at Go-Go music. To hopefully show it in a light where it receives the same kind of respect as any other form of popular music.

I think that Go-Go has suffered from stagnation over the years partially because of the lack of visionaries. The genre has been content to stay within the confines of the Beltway due to a resistance (intentional or not) to learn and follow the rules like the song structure of popular music that shape the larger popular music industry. All of contemporary popular music from country to hip-hop is structured on a variation of the a, b, c (verse, bridge, chorus) format. Go-Go is a very loosely structured, improvisational music, which is part of the reason for its tremendous success in the live arena. Additionally, the lack of original material in Go-Go not only diminishes its credibility as a viable art form to many outsiders, but also severely cripples its potential for financial reward as the lion's share of revenue in the music business is generated through publishing.

Due to Go-Go's previous inability to "edit" the music on recordings to versions that would be palatable to those not familiar with the music form and only hearing the recorded version, very few Go-Go recordings have had much success. I believe this is largely due to the fact that Go-Go musicians take the opposite approach to recording and performing than that of the larger popular music industry. Go-Go bands try to recreate in the studio what they perform on stage rather than simply expanding upon what they wrote in the studio.

On the business side, Go-Go has traditionally only focused on performance income as their only source of revenue, while the larger music industry understands that in order to be successful, an artist and the team behind the artist need to capitalize on multiple revenue streams such as recorded music, publishing, licensing, film synchronization, merchandising, touring, etc. The resistance is not a result of a strong anti-establishment sentiment, but simply a lack of knowledge and a lack of strong leaders that have the fortitude to do the hard work and make the hard decisions such as "Do we stay home and play for $2000 or do we lose money to play in NY and gain fans?"

My opinion is that "the beat" is what makes Go-Go . . . Go-Go. For all of those who say that it's about the crowd interaction or not stopping in between songs, or that you have to have a lead talker, etc.—I ask them to remember the first thing they said when they heard, "It's Love" by Jill Scott or "One Thing" by Amerie. Anyone who knows Go-Go said, "Hey, that's Go-Go." The only thing Go-Go about those songs was its insistent, D.C.-inspired beat.

If I have anything to do with it, Go-Go will maintain its authenticity while dominating the world. There will still be bands here playing 7 nights a week here in D.C. I don't think that has to cease in order for there to be bands playing 7 nights a week in different markets as well."

William "Malachai" Johns

the silence was deafening. This moment was important because it displayed the group's presence and their command of mutual respect from their audience.

During their set the group demonstrated an important performance practice that sets them apart from other go-go-style bands—they stop between songs. This is a major distinction, because the music is known for keeping the beat going between tunes. Mambo Sauce stops, gets applause, the talker interacts with the audience, and then they go on to the next song. This group has proven that bands do not have to resort to misogynist and negative lyrics in order to be popular. Young people are hungry for lyrics that speak to the real world; Mambo Sauce provides a pleasant and popular alternative.

About a month later on a Sunday evening Charles and his family were relaxing at home when the phone rang with a recorded message encouraging him to look at *MTV Jams* at 10:00 PM for its premiere of Mambo Sauce's music video, "Welcome to DC." This phone message was significant: The band's management has partnered with post-digital technology to promote Mambo Sauce, a fact that underscores why Mambo Sauce represents a new era in go-go music.

Locally it has been almost impossible to recognize and truly understand the benefits that the go-go industry brings to Washington, D.C. New Orleans, known for its role as the birthplace of jazz and, later, for funky R&B, has worked very hard to create an industry and infrastructure to support its home-bred music. Similarly Memphis has long traded on its stature as the home of soul (Stax Records) and rockabilly (Sun Records and Elvis Presley) D.C., on the other hand, although recognized by national musicians, still does not command the respect of the music industry. D.C. musicians, even with a chapter of National Academy of Recording Arts and Sciences, Inc (NARAS, an organization best known for the Grammys) in Washington, D.C., struggle for national attention from music industry leaders.

Our Concluding Thoughts: Early November 2008

After seven months of carefully revisiting the current go-go scene and thinking about how it's changed over the past seven years, what do we foresee for go-go in the near and long term? After about thirty-five years and three generations who have performed or consumed go-go, it's clear that go-go remains culturally and musically important among black Americans living in or near Washington, D.C. The local scene grows more interesting as it becomes more complex during the music's maturation.

The music has been around long enough to establish the time-honored category of "old school go-go," which includes such pioneer groups as Trouble

Funk, E.U., and Proper Utensils. These groups tend to be funkier and offer a broad array of dance music rooted in go-go but touched with elements of R&B. Because all of them have been around for many years Rare Essence, Backyard, NE Groovers, and Junkyard Band are locally categorized as "leaders of the old school," a brand that is more often tinged with hip-hop. Today some groups with a more mature following, such as Chuck Brown, Lissen, Shuttle Thoughts, and Familiar Faces often embrace more varied play lists that include smooth jazz and more sophisticated R&B in addition to go-go. The label "grown and sexy" has been attached to this music since 2007.

On a more recent note, the "bounce circuit" or "acronym" bands—exemplified by TCB—tend to be groups with younger members that attract a larger, more energetic, and youthful audiences. The "new generation" bands are lead by Mambo Sauce, which has forged new territory by not starting out in the typical go-go venues and with a larger vision that will certainly expand. In short, it's a very strong local musical and cultural institution, and we can state categorically that go-go is not going away anytime in the foreseeable future and will only continue to create hybrids.

CD and downloadable tunes will continue to be offered by go-go groups. In November 2008 both Chuck Brown and Rare Essence are in the process of recording new material. Tom Goldfogle, manager and producer for Chuck Brown, believes the newest package of tunes may surpass anything that Chuck Brown has done previously. This is very good news for go-go fans, both in D.C. and around the country and underscores the use of digital media in spreading the music.

And the genre continues to spread, albeit rarely in the national spotlight. It is universally understood that "the beat," which is centered on the drums and congas, contains the heart of go-go. Increasingly, go-go's distinctive clave-based rhythmic pattern has begun to transcend the usual limits of D.C.'s Beltway.

It's equally clear, however, that go-go continues to struggle for recognition outside of its racial comfort zone and geographical home and that most bands play to their core local audience. Unfortunately Washington D.C. is rarely recognized as a vibrant diverse musical city, not to mention a place where go-go now permeates through many genres of contemporary African American music forms. Even with groups such as Mambo Sauce working hard to break out of the typical go-go mold, the chances that they will achieve unbridled regional, national, or even international success with their brand of "pocket" music remains murky. While pulling hard for go-go to make a splash across the world, we remain confident that go-go will represent for the District for many years to come.

Appendices

The following terms, excerpted from T.T.E.D. Records's soon-to-be-published *Guide to GO-GO* (circa 1986), are exclusive to the go-go scene, and in a larger sense, to inner-city living. They represent a means of communicating through slang or go-go English the simplest, most unadorned interpretations of feelings, emotions, and impressions.

Break Camp   To leave; to go.

Bumpin'   It's bad; it's super-dooper; it's terrific. Used interchangeably with *hittin'* and *holdin'*.

Bamma   Someone whose dress (or action) is outdated but isn't aware of it; someone from the country (rural area) who has not adjusted to city life.

Bust You Out   To put someone down; humiliate them.

Bustin' Loose   Originated by Chuck Brown, et al.; letting it all hang out; letting your hair down; acting crazy, having big fun; getting/breaking out; getting away.

Crackin'   Moving on someone to get to know them better; to put them down or play the dozens.

Drop the Bomb   Originated by Trouble Funk; the point in a song where the go-go crowd is pumped up and the band drops its heaviest and funkiest sound, i.e., bass line, percussion; synthesizer; depending on the context, can also refer to the moment when someone drops critically good or bad news on you.

E.U. Freeze   Originated by Experience Unlimited (E.U.); means a split-second pause in go-go music when the crowd strikes and freezes different poses.

Freak   Stepping out; going wild and doing it to death. "A party over here, a party over there"; to be freaky.

Freak Body   At the go-go, the freak bodies are the ladies who get the most attention, who dance the best, who have the best figures and wear the sexiest and most current go-go fashions. Also refers to hard-edged ladies who are the easiest for men to approach and pick up.

Good to Go   The ultimate approval; when something is hot and ready for action.

Go-Go (music)   Popular term used to describe the bottom, hard-core end of the music market; full bodied-funk that leads with the bass drums, heavy percussion, cowbells and congas with tasty timbales and strong, brassy horns. A non-stop continuous form of dance music where there are no breaks between songs; sound is based on African rhythms with street/inner-city life interpretation.

Go-Go (scene)   To go for it; functions where go-go music is performed live; generally a traveling party moving from high school to recreation and community centers, skating rinks or any dance hall where go-go bands can perform and young adults [are?] admitted; where there is a call and response involvement between the band and the crowd making the party happen.

Holla At Me   Call me; talk to me; come to see me.

Home Boy/Home Girl   Someone you're totally familiar with; someone originally from your neighborhood, school or hometown.

Hittin' and Holdin'   Anything that is right or perfect, i.e., if a song or an appearance is really together it's hittin' and holdin'.

Love Boat   The nickname for P.C.P., an addictive chemical compound known universally as Angel Dust. Love Boat has ruined the lives of some youths. It takes users on a false voyage into moods of anger, [and] extreme hallucination. Go-go bands have waged a major war against indulgence of Love Boat through the lyrics of their songs.

Let's Get Small   Let's get down.

Movin' and Groovin'   Originated by Redds & the Boys; means having a good time; everything is A-OK; moving in a positive direction; hanging loose.

Mug   Your face; your facial features; your attitude according to your facial expression.

No Ins or Outs   Unique to go-gos where after admission patrons cannot leave or re-enter without paying [an] additional fee.

Numb to the Max   Totally overwhelmed by go-go music or heavy partying; full blast.

Pumpin'   Jammin'; when go-go bands elevate music to maximum sensation.

Pump   When a person is down and you/band try to motivate them, i.e., "pump me up."

Raw   Go-go at its best. A natural inner-city funk sound.

Sucker   A loser; someone who comes to the go-go alone looking for some action but never gets it . . . always leaves alone.

Sure You're Right/Sure You're Right   When you're telling the truth and no one believes you; spoken with sarcasm.

Safe/That's Safe   Something that's alright; that's outstanding; i.e., "that safe."

Say What!   When you're totally undecided still, yet deciding during the course of a discussion or rap.

Syce' It On Up   Ab-libbing go-go music; vocal or instrumental changes created on the spot, spontaneously.

Take It To The Bridge   Going to the change in the song.

Thrown Down   Get down; party all night; Go-go bands that pump all night.

Y'all   You all; all of you.

Yo'   Hello; hi; hold on; wait a minute.

What's Up Like That?   What's happening?; where are the happenings tonight; what's going on?

"Work" That Body   "Work" is the final four letter word. It means to labor, to party. It defines funk at its best . . . sweat, dance, and the toil of a hard night's play at the go-go. Work that body to death.

D.C.'S GO-GO BANDS

The following is an alphabetical listing of all of the go-go bands that we (with some help from Moe Shorter) have been able to identify during the course of our research. It is based on a compilation published by the Folk Arts Program of the D.C. Commission on the Arts and Humanities in 1991 as part of a brochure entitled *D.C. Go Go: what's the time?* In addition to the obvious names, such as Experience Unlimited (E.U.) and Rare Essence (RE), our list encompasses some of the proto-go-go groups (like Mouse Trapp) as well as some of the more ephemeral groups—such as Secret Code Crew—who made only a small mark on the scene. Most of them are/were groups that worked in clubs, but a few—such as T.T.E.D. Allstars—were studio aggregations:

Absolute Chaos

The Aggression

All-N-1

A.M.-F.M.

And The Echoes

Ayre Rayde

Backyard Band

Big Tony & T.F. Crew

Black Heat

Brute

Busey Brothers

Central Goove

Chuck Brown and the Soul Searchers

C.J.'s Uptown Crew

Class Band

Cold Sweat

Crosstown Express

Cummings Electric Sound

D.C. All Stars

D.C. Scorpio

Deep Cover

Distance

Double Agent Rock

Epitome

Experience Unlmited

Familiar Faces

Fate's Destiny

Go-Go Lorenzo

Groove Masters

High Fidelity

High Performance

Hot, Cold, Sweat

Huck-A-Bucks

Intimate Groove

Jaguars

Jig-A-Boo (aka Jigga)

Junk Yard Band

Keisha

Keystone

King of Hearts

Klyxx

Leadhead

The Legends

Little Benny and the Masters

Luv

Mass Extension

Master Groovers

Matadors

Maiesha & the Hip Huggers

Mouse Trapp

Nastygang

New Dimension

Nine One One (911)

95th Congress

Northeast Groovers

Northwest Youngins

Occupation Band

Obsession

Omega

100 Years Time

Optimystic Tribe

P.C. Groovers

Peacemakers

Petworth

Physical Wonders

Pleasure

Precise

Proper Utensils

Prophecy

Publicity Band

Pumpbenders

Pure Elegence

Quality Band

Raw Groove

Rare Essence

Raw Image

Reality Band

Redds and the Boys

Regency Band

Remote Control

Scacy & the Sound Service

Secret Code Crew

Shadows

Shady Groove

Skibone

Sluggo

Southeast Sounds

Special Request

Stinky Dink

Sweat

Superior Funk

Superior Groovers

Suttle Thoughts

Symba

T.T.E.D. Allstars

Ten Feet Under

Third Dimension

Three Stones from the Sun

Tom Slick and Wikee G

Total Control

Total Recall

Touch of Essence

Trouble Funk

Ultimate Groove

Uncalled 4 Band

Under Pressure Band

Uptown Young 'uns

Wild Bunch

Wild & Wonderful

X-Clusive Band

X/O Band

Young Experience

Young Groovers

Young Naturals

Young Senators

INTERVIEWS

In addition to individual taped interviews from which most of the book's quotes are taken, we have included quotes from two other sources. The "Go Go Roundtable" took place at the Capital Pavilion on Georgia Avenue on December 13, 1999. We put together this forum to informally discuss quite a few issues of interest to the go-go community, and the score of participants spoke freely and at length. The "Go Go Conference" refers to "Gimme That Beat: 25 Years of Go Go on the Streets of Washington, D.C." a day-long conference held at The Martin Luther King Jr. Memorial Library with the generous support of the Humanities Council of Washington, D.C. These taped interviews will be donated to the MLK branch of the District of Columbia Public Library, where (along with other material used to write this book) they are to be placed in the Washingtoniana Collection.

INTERVIEWEE	INTERVIEWER	DATE
Bill Barlow	Go Go Conference	4/15/00
Chris Blackwell	Kip Lornell, via e-mail	9/20/00
Dontriece Blue	Go Go Roundtable	12/13/99
Roguell Blue	Go Go Roundtable	12/13/99
Bruce Brown	Go Go Conference	4/15/00
Bruce Brown	Kip Lornell	8/4/00
Chuck Brown	Go Go Conference	4/15/00
Joseph Carter (aka Weaze)	Go Go Roundtable	12/13/99
Terance Cooper	Go Go Roundtable	12/13/99
Rene Dickerson (aka Soldierette)	Kip Lornell	11/3/99
Jimi Dougans	Charles Stephenson	1/3/01
Gregory Elliot (aka Sugar Bear)	Charles Stephenson	11/5/00
Charlie Fenwick	Kip Lornell and Charles Stephenson	3/10/98
Leora Fenwick	Go Go Roundtable	12/13/99
Donnell Floyd	Kip Lornell and Charles Stephenson	10/28/98
James Ford	Go Go Roundtable	12/13/99

INTERVIEWEE	INTERVIEWER	DATE
James Funk	Kip Lornell and Charles Stephenson)	10/28/98
Tom Goldfogle	Go Go Conference	4/15/00
Tom Goldfogle	Kip Lornell	8/1/00
Kevin Hammond (aka Kato)	Kip Lornell and Chris Flores	2/17/99
Kevin Hammond (aka Kato)	Go Go Roundtable	12/13/99
Kemry Hughes	Go Go Roundtable	12/13/99
Kemry Hughes	Go Go Conference	4/15/00
Benny Harley	Kip Lornell	1/22/99
Justin Jefferson	Kip Lornell	10/29/98
André Johnson	Kip Lornell and Charles Stephenson	10/28/98
Max Kidd	Kip Lornell and Charles Stephenson	10/7/00
Benjy Little	Go Go Roundtable	12/13/99
Rosevelt Littlejohn (aka Big Rosey)	Go Go Roundtable	12/13/99
Andre Lucas	Charles Stephenson	10/11/00
Ms. Annie Mack	Kip Lornell and Charles Stephenson	10/6/98
Ignatius Mason	Go Go Roundtable	12/13/99
Ken Moore (aka Ice E Ice)	Kip Lornell and Charles Stephenson	3/31/98
Warren "Scooter" Magruder	Kip Lornell	4/3/98
Norm Nixon	Go Go Roundtable	12/13/99
Arthur Kay Rabbit	Go Go Roundtable	12/13/99
Maurice ("Moe") Shorter	Kip Lornell	3/17/98
Darien Towns (aka "Funky D")	Kip Lornell	11/3/99

Notes

CHAPTER 1: THE ROOTS AND EMERGENCE OF GO-GO

1. Wilson & Alroy's Record Reviews, www.warr.org/trouble.html.
2. Jay Bruder, "R & B in Washington, D.C.: The TNT Tribble Story," *Blues & Rhythm,* no. 45 (July 1989): 5.
3. Ta-Nehisi Coates, "Dropping The Bomb: An Oral History of Go-Go," *Washington City Paper* 20, no.2, 14–20 January 2000, 21.
4. Ibid.
5. Ricky Vincent, *Funk: The Music, the People, and the Rhythm of the One* (New York: St. Martin's Press, 1996), 5.
6. James Funk Interview, 28 October 1998.
7. Coates, 21.
8. Ibid.
8. Take Me Out To The Go-Go Web site(www.tmottgogogo.com), 1 December 1999.
10. Coates, 21.
11. Ibid., 22.
12. Billy Ray Edwards interview by Jackie Peters, 4 October 1989. [Where?]
13. Coates, 22.
14. Ibid., 24.
15. Carl Jones interview on 29 March 1987, quoted in John Rice and Christopher Cooper, "It Don't Mean a Thing If It Ain't Got That Go Go Swing—The Go Go Phenomena and Its Relation to Traditional African Music" (Undergraduate honors thesis, Yale University, 1987), 6.
16. Coates, 24.
17. Ibid., 26.
18. Ibid.
19. Billboard Spotlight Reviews, www.billboard.com.
20. Coates, 26.
21. Ibid.
22. Henry Rollins, liner notes for *Trouble Funk Live* (Infinite Zero Records), 1998.
23. Mark Jenkins and Mark Anderson, *The Dance of Days: The Early History of the Washington, D.C. Punk Scene* (New York: Soft Skull Press, 2001).
24. Jeff Zeldman, "Go Go," *Washington Weekly,* 18 June 1984, 34.
25. Ibid.
26. Ibid.
27. Ibid.
28. Richard Harrington, "Go-Go: A Musical Phenomenon Bonding a Community," *Washington Post,* 19 May 1985, Style Section, 1.
29. Coates, 27.
30. Ibid.
31. Ibid.
32. Harrington, Style Section, 1.
33. Coates, 27.

34. Coates, 31.
35. Ibid.
36. Charlie Fenwick interview, 10 March 1998.

CHAPTER 2: GOING TO A GO-GO

1. Jay Strongman, liner notes for Chuck Brown's *Live '87* (Future Records), 1987.
2. Glenn Hinson, *Fire in My Bones* (Philadelphia: University of Pennsylvania Press, 2000), chapter entitled "Sing Till The Power of the Lord Comes Down," 1–25.
3. To hear this music (and for more information about shout bands), please consult *Saints' Paradise: Trombone Shout Bands from the United House of Prayer,* (Smithsonian Folkways SFW CD 40117), 1999.
4. Tom Goldfogle interview, 1 August 2000.
5. Murray Forman, "'Represent': race, space, and place in rap music," *Popular Music* 19, no. 1, (January 2000): 65–90.
6. Chris Waterman, *Ju Ju: A Social History and Ethnography of an African Popular Music* (Chicago: University of Chicago Press, 1990), 166.
7. Ibid.
8. Waterman, 182.
9. Waterman, 175.
10. Waterman, 187.
11. Jeff Zeldman, "Go-Go," *Washington Weekly,* 18 June 1984, 33.
12. Kevin Hammond, "Hey Maniac: Lawrence West," *TMOTTGoGo Magazine,* Summer 2000, 5.
13. Ibid.

CHAPTER 3: BAND PROFILES

1. Jimi Dougans interview, 3 January 2001.
2. Ibid.
3. "An Interview with Chuck Brown" *Get Busy Magazine,* Fall 1988, 12.
4. Ibid.
5. Ibid.
6. Richard O'Connor, "A Conversation with the Godfather: Chuck Brown—The Creator of Go-Go," *TMOTTOGoGo Magazine,* Winter 2000, 4.
7. *Get Busy Magazine,* 13.
8. Ibid.
9. Ibid., 14.
10. O'Connor, 5.
11. Ibid.
12. Mark Fisher, ". . . And Chuck Brown Made it Go-Go," *Washington Post,* 14 August 1994, section G, page 12.
13. *Get Busy Magazine,* 14.
14. Benny Harley interview, 22 January 1999.
15. Ta-Nehisi Coates, "Dropping the Bomb: An Oral History of Go-Go," *Washington City Paper* 20, no.2, 14–20 January 2000, 22.
16. *Get Busy Magazine,* 14.
17. Gregory Elliot interview, 5 November 2000.

18. Ms. Annie Mack interview, 6 October 1998.
19. James Funk interview, 28 October 1998.
20. André Johnson interview, 28 October 1998.
21. Coates, 20.
22. Gregory Elliot interview, 5 November 2000.
23. Ibid.
24. Ibid.
25. Ibid.
26. Tom Terrell, "Go-Go Guide," *Rock America Magazine,* June 1985, 45.
27. Elliot interview.
28. Ibid.
29. Ibid.
30. Ibid.
31. Ibid.
32. Ibid.
33. Ibid.
34. Ibid.
35. Ibid.
36. Ibid.
37. Ibid.
38. Ibid.

CHAPTER 4: COMMUNITIES

1. James Avery, quoted in "Go-Going in Style: Getting Small with Trouble Funk" by Bill Bentley, *LA Weekly,* 29 November 1985, 67.
2. Theophus A. Brooks and Bridget T. Miller, *Shadows Behind the U.S. Capitol* (self published, 1998), 24–25.
3. Ibid., 53–55.
4. All Around Honies Web site, www.geocities.com/Paris/Arc/8173/about.html.
5. Tricia Rose, *Black Noise: Rap Music and Black Culture in Contemporary America* (Middletown, CT: Wesleyan University Press, 1994), 6.
6. Quoted in Rose, 47.
7. Charlie Fenwick interview, 10 March 1998.
8. Kevin Hammond, "Michelle 'Sweet Shell' Peterson: From Pleasure to Precise to Praise," Take Me Out To The Go-Go Web site, www.tmottgogo.com/peterson.html
9. Ibid.
10. Ibid.
11. René Dickerson interview, 3 November 1999.
12. Ibid.
13. Ibid.
14. Ibid.
15. Benny Harley interview, 22 January 1999.
16. Ibid.
17. Alona Wartofsky, "The Indestructible Beat of the District," *Washington City Paper,* 22 June 1990, 17.

18. Ibid.
19. Ibid.
20. Ibid.
21. Ta-Nehisi Coates, *Washington City Paper* 20, no. 2, 14 January 2000, 29.
22. Wartofsky, 20.
23. Ibid., 20.
24. Ibid., 17.
25. From the Testimony of the ACLU of the National Capital Area before the District of Columbia Committee on Cosumer and Regulatory Affairs, 24 June 1987.
26. From the Statement of Charles C. Stephenson, Jr. on Bill 7-220, District of Columbia Public Hall Regulation, June 1987.
27. From the "Request for Funding Of An Anti-Drug Record and Video Go Go Drug Free Project" submitted to the D.C. City Council, 23 June 1986.
28. Ibid.
29. RAP press release, August 1986.
30. Wartofsky, 16.
31. Ibid.
32. Nelson George, "D.C. Go-Go Fizzles, But Trouble Funk Survives," *Billboard,* 3 October 1987, 23.
33. "Mayor Marion Barry and the Mayor's Youth Leadership Institute Join Go Go Drug Free Project in Speaking Out Against Drug Abuse," undated (probably summer 1987) press release from the Committee to Save Go-Go.
34. Simone Aponte, "Students Brave Violence at Go-Gos," Montgomery Blair High School *Silver Chips—On-Line,* 11 February 1999, 10.

CHAPTER 5: ENTREPRENEURS

1. "'Moe' Shorter—Ode To A Manager," Take Me Out To The Go-Go Web site, www.tmottgogo.com/moeart.html, November 1999, 3.
2. Ibid.
3. Maurice Shorter interview, 17 March 1998.
4. Ignatius Mason addressed some of these issues at Kip Lornell's George Washington University class, "Musical Cultures of Black Americans," on 29 February 2000.
5. Ms. Annie Mack interview, 6 October 1998.
6. Ibid.
7. Ibid.
8. Ibid.
9. Ibid.
10. Charlie Fenwick interview, 10 March 1998.
11. Ibid.
12. Roguell Blue, Go-Go Roundtable, 12 December 1999.
13. Kevin Merida, "Dealer's Choice, Law's Foe—DC drug killings fuel debate on assault weapons," *Dallas Morning News,* 2 April 1989.
14. Ken Moore interview, 31 March 1998.
15. Ibid.

16. Ibid.
17. Christopher Waterman, *Ju Ju: A Social History and Ethnography of an African Popular Music* (Chicago: University of Chicago Press, 1990), 151–52.
18. Maurice Shorter interview, 17 March 1998.
19. Tom Goldfogle interview, 1 August 2000.
20. Ibid.
21. Max Kidd interview, 7 October 2000.
22. Ibid.
23. Ibid.
24. Ibid.

CHAPTER 6: THE MEDIA

1. Cathy Hughes, from the 1991 documentary film *Straight-Up Go-Go.*
2. Kevin Hammond interview, 17 February 1999.
3. Ibid.
4. Ibid.
5. Ibid.
6. Ibid.
7. Justin Jefferson interview, 29 October 1998.
8. Bruce Brown interview, 4 August 2000.
9. www.computer-daze.com/RadioOne/CathyHughes
10. Bloomberg/Women.com 30 Index, www.womenswire.com/30index/bios/-30roia.html.
11. "Money of Color: Radio One," *BOSS Magazine* Web site, www.boss-magazine.com/Streetwatch.html.
12. Ibid.
13. Charlie Fenwick interview, 10 March 1998.
14. Tom Goldfogle interview, 1 August 2000.
15. Benjy Little, Go Go Roundtable, 13 December 1999.
16. Ibid.
17. Louis Aguilar and Hamil R. Harris, *Washington Post,* 27 August 1994, sec. C, 1.
18. Richard Harrington, "Go-Go: A Musical Phenomenon Bonding a Community," *Washington Post,* 19 May 1985, Style section, 2.
19. Ibid.
20. Nelson George, "Go-Go Music Ready to Go Global," *Billboard,* 9 March 1985, 65.
21. Goldfogle interview, 1 August 2000.
22. Mass Extension/Gary West interview, www.members.aol.com.ngang123/mass.html.
23. Maurice Shorter interview, 17 March 1998.
24. Goldfogle interview, 1 August 2000.
25. Ibid.
26. Ibid.
27. Ibid.
28. Ibid.

CHAPTER 7: GO-GO ON FILM

1. Bruce Brown interview, 4 August 2000.
2. Kim McCullough, "Go-Go Kidd Speaks Out On 'Good to Go,'" *Capitol Spotlight,* 14 August 1986, 17.
3. Richard Harrington, "Getting Go-Go on Film," *Washington Post,* 20 May 1985, sec. C, p. 4.
4. "Hey, Hey, Hey! Drop The Bomb—It's Party Time: They are Making a Movie about D.C.'s Go-Go," *Washington Afro-American,* 23 April 1985, 13.
5. Richard Grabel, "Crackin' That Go-Go Gadget," *Melody Maker,* May 1985, 66.
6. Chris Blackwell e-mail interview, 10 September 2000.
7. Roland R. Hanna, "Conversation with Go-Go Guru Max Kidd," *Washington Afro-American,* 18 May 1985, 1.
8. Ibid.
9. Harrington, "Getting Go-Go on Film," sec. C, 4.
10. Ibid.
11. Blackwell interview.
12. Ibid.
13. Harrington, "Getting Go-Go on Film," sec. C, 4.
14. Ibid.
15. Blackwell interview.
16. Ibid.
17. Ibid.
18. Harrington, "Getting Go-Go on Film," sec. C, 4.
19. Ibid.
20. Blackwell interview.
21. Richard Harrington, "Go-Go Controversy," *Washington Post,* 1 August 1986, sec. D, 8.
22. Bruce Brown interview.
23. Harrington, "Go-Go Controversy," sec. D, 8.
24. Ibid.
25. Harrington, "Getting Go-Go on Film," sec. C, 4.
26. Richard Harrington, "On the Beat," *The Washington Post,* 6 August 1986, sec. D, 7.
27. Ibid.
28. David Brooks, "'Good to Go': Out of Tune with Blacks," *Washington Times,* 31 July 1986, sec. B, 1–2.
29. Take Me Out To The Go-Go Web site (www.tmottgogo.com), Community Forum, 31 January, 2000.
30. Spike Lee and Lisa Jones, *Uplift the Race: The Construction of School Daze.* (New York: Simon & Schuster, 1988), 130.
31. Ibid.
32. Ibid.
33. Ibid.
34. Ibid.
35. Bruce Brown interview.
36. Ibid.

Audiography

Compiling an audiography (also called a discography) for this book underscores the problems of documenting sound recordings in the twenty-first century. Prior to the close of World War II, such work was relatively easy. The majority of sound recordings were made by a handful of commercial record companies, most notably RCA and Columbia or one of their subsidiaries. This changed after the war, with the proliferation of small record companies inspired by an entrepreneurial spirit and the availability of the magnetic tape recorder. In the present day we face an ever-increasing maze of small record labels, which presents the discographer with an almost overwhelming task.

Go-go music is a unique case because the genre is so localized. Nearly all go-go recordings have been made in Washington, D.C., or Prince George's County. The time-frame is limited, too; go-go has only been around since the mid-1970s. These two factors help, but it's still a nightmare. In the 1980s, the following companies alone issued a variety of 7-inch and 12-inch vinyl recordings of go-go: Big City, Capital City, Capitol Beat Records, CD Enterprise, Creative Funk Records, D.E.T.T., Flash, Full House, Future, Galaxy Unlimited, Go-Bin, Gotta Go Go, Hi Hut, I Hear Ya!, Jam, Jam Rose, Kapitol Sity Wrecords, Kolossal, ND/Goff Records, Raw Venture, Resolution, Rhythm Attack, Sound Music Company, Sounds of the Capitol, Street Records, Studio Records, Teddy Bear, The Bush Records, T.T.E.D., TWF Productions, Washington Hit Makers. (Source: Washington D.C. GoGo Labels— http://laurent.thiebaut.free.fr/bmc/labels/gogocatalogue.htm)

Fully documenting these releases—even basic information such as recording date, location, personnel, instrumentation, and vocals—is all but impossible. Many of the sessions were done in small or private recording studios that did not keep logs. Quite often these studios or companies are no longer in business. Nor did the bands—many of which no longer exist—themselves retain such information.

Because they are so ephemeral, we do not address P.A. tapes in this audiography. Instead, we have limited the audiography to two sections. The first section is a highly selective list of classic go-go recordings that help to define the genre. They are difficult to find—many are long out of print—but they merit inclusion in this book. The second list consists of go-go recordings available on compact disc as of spring 2001. Anyone wishing to sample go-go might be interested in the CD compiled by Liaison Records to accompany this book.

Finding go-go discs outside of the metropolitan Washington, D.C., area is difficult. Some of the bands have Web sites — Rare Essence: www.rareessence.com; Trouble Funk: www.troublefunk.com; JunkYard: http://blackplanet.members/JunkYardBand — and you can purchase their product directly from them. But as we write this in January 2001, the best source for go-go material over the Internet is the P.A. Palace. This long-established business has a Web site (www.papalace.com) and is perhaps the most comprehensive source for ordering commercial go-go releases as well as P.A. tapes.

A few final words about go-go and the Internet. Two sites are always worth checking. The first is Kato's www.tmottgogo.com, not only for the latest word on go-go and for the bulletin board, but to check out the links. The other important site is maintained by Jordan Rich (http://funkmas-terj.tripod.com/gogo.htm). Rich keeps the most comprehensive set of go-go links, which are broken into the following categories: "Articles, General, & Online Clubs," "Labels, Vendors, and Venues," "Bands," "Go-Go Fan Homepages," "Go Go CDs," and "Go Go Radio." He also maintains the site with great regularity. Funkmaster J is also working on a complete discography of commercial albums, and while it's not comprehensive, it is by far the best information out there. Our own discography owes a tip of the hat to Mr. Rich and his work.

A SCORE—MORE OR LESS—OF CLASSIC GO-GO RECORDINGS

BACKYARD BAND

- "Skillet"

CHUCK BROWN AND THE SOUL SEARCHERS

- "Bustin' Loose"
- "We Need Money"
- "It Don't Mean A Thing (If It Don't Have The Go-Go Swing)"

EXPERIENCE UNLIMITED

- "Rock Your Butt"
- "E.U. Freeze"
- "Shake It Like A White Girl"
- "Da' Butt"

HUCK-A-BUCKS

- "Chronic Breakdown"

JUNK YARD BAND

- "The Word"
- "Sardines"
- "Ruff-It-Off"

LITTLE BENNY AND THE MASTERS

- "Cat In The Hat"
- "We Came To Boogie"

MASS EXTENSION

- "Happy Feet"

NORTHEAST GROOVERS

- "Bounce To This"

PURE ELEGANCE

- "One Leg Up"

RARE ESSENCE

- "Body Moves"
- "Body Snatchers"
- "Overnight Scenario"

REDDS AND THE BOYS

- "Movin' And Groovin'"

TROUBLE FUNK

- "Drop The Bomb"
- "Let's Get Small"
- "Hit 'Em Wit Da Super Grit"

GO-GO COMPACT DISCS (IN PRINT AS OF SPRING 2001)

BAND	TITLE	LABEL/RELEASE NUMBER
All-N-One	Duckin' the Reeper	SBC 719-2 0
Backyard Band	We Like It Raw	Future 1019-2
Backyard Band	Hood Related	Future 1025-2
Backyard Band	Skillet	Future 1027-2
Chuck Brown	Greatest Hits	RV 007-2/9
Chuck Brown	Go Go Swings Live	Future 007-2
Chuck Brown	This is a Journey	RV 004-2
Chuck Brown	Hahman	RV 005-2
Chuck Brown	The Spirit of Christmas	RV 008-2
Huck-A-Bucks	3rd Mo. YR 2000	Listen Up 1728-2
Huck-A-Bucks	Chronic Breakdown	SBC 711-2
Huck-A-Bucks	Huck-A-Bucks Live!	SBC 714-2
Huck-A-Bucks	You Betta' Move Somethin'	SBC 1720-2
Jigga	Open Your Eyes	Monarch 5001-2
Junk Yard Band	Y'all Don't Understand	Future 2002-2
Junk Yard Band	The Beginning/The End	Street 2060-2
Junk Yard Band	Don't Sleep on Us	Street 2020-2
Junk Yard Band	Creepin' Thru the Hood	Street 2030-2
Junk Yard Band	Reunion '95	Street 2040-2
Junk Yard Band	Go Hard	Street 2050-2
Little Benny	Live at the Cafe	Hoop-Tee 4000-2
Maiesha & the Hip Huggers	Whatz Up!	Trivia 1681-2
Northeast Groovers	Straight from the Basement	Future 1016-2
Northeast Groovers	Jams	Future 1017-2
Northeast Groovers	Northeast Coming	LU 1724-2
Northeast Groovers	Northeast on Fire	Future 2001-2
Optimystic Tribe	The Awakening	LU 1723-2

BAND	TITLE	LABEL/RELEASE NUMBER
Pure Elegance	Keep Ya Movin'	Future 1021-2
Rare Essence	Live PA #2	Rare One 3002-2
Rare Essence	RE2000	Rare One 2001-2
Rare Essence	We Go On and On	Rare One 2000-2
Rare Essence	So What You Want?	Rare One 850-2
Rare Essence	Get Your Freak On	Rare One 315-2
Rare Essence	The Essence of Rare Essence	Rare One 320-2
Rare Essence	Live!	Rare One 612-2
Rare Essence	Body Snatchers	Rare One 900-2
Trouble Funk	All the Way Live	Swollen 7100
Uncalled 4 Band	We Got Next	Bag 084-2
Various Artists	Live at Wilmer's Park	Future/ST 1014-2
Various Artists	Go Go! D.C.'s Best	Listen Up 1730-2
Various Artists	Gimmie Dat Beat/Vol. 2	Liaison 1227-2
Various Artists	Always in the Pocket/Vol. 3	Liaison 1228-2
Various Artists	Can We Do It Again/Vol. 4	Liaison 1229-2

Selected Bibliography

BOOKS

Brooks, Theophus A. and Bridget T. Miller, *Shadows Behind the U.S. Capitol.* Self published, 1998.

Hinson, Glenn. *Fire in My Bones.* Philadelphia: University of Pennsylvania Press, 2000.

Rose, Tricia. *Black Noise: Rap Music and Black Culture in Contemporary America.* Middletown, CT: Wesleyan University Press, 1994.

Vincent, Ricky. *Funk: The Music, the People, and the Rhythm of the One.* New York: St. Martin's Press, 1996.

Waterman, Chris. *Ju Ju: A Social History and Ethnography of an African Popular Music.* Chicago: University of Chicago Press, 1990.

ARTICLES

Aguilar, Louis and Hamil R. Harris. "Explicit Videos Tarnish Go-Go's Image." *Washington Post,* 27 August 1994, sec. C, 1.

Aponte, Simone. "Students Brave Violence at Go-Gos." Montgomery Blair High School *Silver Chips—On-Line,* 11 February 1999, 10.

Bentley, Bill. "Go-Going in Style: Getting Small with Trouble Funk." *LA Weekly,* 29 November 1985, 67.

Brooks, David. "'Good to Go': Out of Tune with Blacks." *Washington Times,* 31 July 1986, sec. B, 1–2.

Bruder, Jay. "R & B in Washington, D.C.: The TNT Tribble Story." *Blues & Rhythm,* no. 45 (July 1989): 5

Coates, Ta-Nehisi. "Dropping The Bomb: An Oral History of Go-Go." *Washington City Paper,* 14–20 January 2000, 21.

Fisher, Mark. "...And Chuck Brown Made it Go-Go." *Washington Post,* 14 August 1994, sec. G, 12.

Forman, Murray. "'Represent': race, space, and place in rap music." *Popular Music* 19, no. 1, (January 2000): 65–90.

George, Nelson. "D.C. Go-Go Fizzles, But Trouble Funk Survives." *Billboard,* 3 October 1987, 23.

———, "Go-Go Music Ready to Go Global," *Billboard,* 9 March 1985, 65.

Grabel, Richard. "Crackin' That Go-Go Gadget." *Melody Maker,* May 1985, 66.

Hammond, Kevin."Hey Maniac: Lawrence West." *TMOTTGoGo Magazine,* Summer 2000, 5.

Hanna, Roland R. "Conversation with Go-Go Guru Max Kidd." *Washington Afro-American,* 18 May 1985, 1.

Harrington, Richard. "Go-Go: A Musical Phenomenon Bonding a Community." *Washington Post,* 19 May 1985, Style Section, 1.

———. "Go-Go Controversy." *Washington Post,* 1 August 1986, sec. D, 8.

———. "On the Beat," *The Washington Post,* 6 August 1986, sec. D, 7.

"Hey, Hey, Hey! Drop The Bomb—It's Party Time: They are Making a Movie about D.C.'s Go-Go." *Washington Afro-American,* 23 April 1985, 13.

Merida, Kevin. "Dealer's Choice, Law's Foe—DC drug killings fuel debate on assault weapons." *Dallas Morning News,* 2 April 1989.

O'Connor, Richard. "A Conversation with the Godfather: Chuck Brown—The Creator of Go-Go." *TMOTTOGoGo Magazine,* Winter 2000, 4.

Terrell, Tom. "Go-Go Guide." *Rock America Magazine.* June 1985, 45.

Wartofsky, Alona. "The Indestructible Beat of the District." *Washington City Paper,* 22 June 1990, 17.

Index